T0330069

The Dynamics of Technical Innovation

The Dynamics of Technical Innovation

The Evolution and Development of Information Technology

Geert Duysters

Department of International Business Studies
University of Limburg, The Netherlands

Edward Elgar
Cheltenham, UK • Northampton, MA, USA

Published by
Edward Elgar Publishing Limited
Glensanda House, Montpellier Parade
Cheltenham
Glos GL50 1UA
UK

Edward Elgar Publishing, Inc.
136 West Street, Suite 202
Northampton, MA 01060
USA

Reprinted 2002

British Library Cataloguing in Publication Data
Duysters, Geert
   Dynamics of Technical Innovation:
   Evolution and Development of Information
   Technology
   I. Title
   338.064

Library of Congress Cataloguing in Publication Data
Duysters, Geert, 1966–
   The dynamics of technical innovation: the evolution
and development of information technology / Geert Duysters.
   Includes bibliographical references and index.
   1. Information technology. 2. Technological innovations— Economic
aspects. I. Title
   HC79.I55D89   1996   95–39636
   338.4'7004—dc20   CIP

ISBN 1 85898 400 9

Printed and bound in Great Britain by
Bookcraft, Bath

Contents

Tables

Figures

1. Introduction

Ever since Thorstein Veblen (1898: 374) proposed his famous question 'Why is Economics not an Evolutionary Science' theorists have been trying to incorporate biological concepts into economics. The introduction of evolutionary analogies into economics through the early work of influential scholars such as Marshall (1948), Schumpeter (1942) and Alchian (1950), however, did not lead to a fundamental change in economic thinking. Evolutionary ideas turned out to have only a modest impact on mainstream economic theory and did not challenge the position of the traditional neo-classical school of thought as the dominant paradigm in economic theory. Clark and Juma (1991) put forward three main factors which accounted for the observation that economic theory tends to neglect evolutionary concepts. 'first, the limited knowledge on evolutionary and human behaviour opened the way to arguments by analogy; such arguments are often fallacious. Second, social change was not obviously gradual, and therefore the theory was not particularly consistent with the observations of social historians (especially of the Marxists). Third, the rules of the hard sciences (especially Newtonian physics) combined with the Cartesian philosophy of nature as automata and the Baconian appeal to empirical rigour, had become the legitimate view of reality. And economics readily adopted this mechanical world-view' (Clark and Juma, 1991: 45). In spite of this widespread aversion against evolutionary ideas in mainstream economic theory, the 1970s showed a steady growing interest in evolutionary perspectives. This was due particularly to the difficulties of the dominant neo-classical paradigm in dealing with the growing complexity and radical changing nature of our society. In particular, the growing impact of technology was difficult to grasp in the traditional frameworks. This led a number of economists to search for alternative approaches that were better equipped to deal with patterns of change and instability. Their search soon turned to the biological sciences, which featured a promising and already well-developed framework for the analysis of dynamic change. Since Darwin published his 'The Origin of Species', biological theorists have been involved in the study of longitudinal

1

time-bound phenomena. The long tradition of evolutionary thought in biological sciences paved the way for economists to go beyond the static notions of neo-classical theories and enabled them to construct an inherent dynamic framework.

The search for alternative scientific paradigms in biology led to two distinct but closely related new frameworks. The first framework was sparked by the seminal work of Winter (1964, 1971, 1975), Nelson and Winter (1982) and Dosi (1984, 1988) and would eventually lead to the creation of a school of thought based on evolutionary economic theories. The second framework, thriving on work by Stinchcombe (1965), Hannan and Freeman (1977, 1984, 1989), Aldrich (1979) and Carroll (1987, 1988), constituted another school of thought which would soon be known as the organizational ecology school. As in biological theory, evolutionary and ecological approaches address different questions. Evolutionary theories are primarily concerned with the ability of species (or economic actors) to adapt to changing environments, whereas ecological theories tend to focus on the relative importance of specific species (or organizational forms) under different environmental conditions. We might say, therefore, that evolutionary and ecological theories study the same process from a complementary point of view. Although many theorists would argue that these theoretical perspectives are still in their infancy, the growing number of publications, the establishment of a journal dedicated to evolutionary economics (*Journal of Evolutionary Economics*) and the publication of seminal books on evolutionary economics by Nelson and Winter (1982) and on organizational ecology by Hannan and Freeman (1989) can be seen as indicators of a rapid maturation of biology-inspired approaches to economics and organizational theory.

In this book I will demonstrate that the use of dynamic insights which were originally developed in biology can improve our current understanding of the evolution of complex industrial systems over time. My commitment to non-conventional biology-inspired approaches does not imply that I completely ignore the important theoretical contributions made by neo-classical theorists. I, however, think that although the neo-classical framework can be extremely well suited to deal with complex theoretical problems, it is often less well suited to deal with dynamic patterns of change and instability. Although more recent neo-classical models incorporate imperfect information and uncertainty and are much more dynamic than the earlier models, Krepps (1990) has argued that incorporating all kinds of costs such as adjustment costs and search costs in a neo-classical framework seems to be an awesome undertaking and is likely to be impossible. Instead of rewriting traditional economic theory I will therefore follow the lead of more dynamic heterodox theories that are particularly developed to study longitudinal time-bound phenomena.

This study departs from a long tradition in economic theory which studied the development of market structures, technological development and company strategies as separate entities. It tries to provide an alternative to the traditional Structure-Conduct-Performance (SCP) approach which, for a long time, has dominated industrial organization theory and industrial economics.[1] In my contribution technological development is not regarded as an exogenous variable, but is seen as an endogenous factor that is not only influenced by the existing market structure but also by the innovative actions of particular categories of companies. Following Schumpeter's notion of 'creative destruction' I will argue that technological changes are able to destroy existing industry structures and create new ones. My main argument is that the evolution of complex industrial systems is shaped by the interplay of industrial structures, company strategies and technological developments. Therefore, in order to understand the complex dynamics of industrial systems it is necessary to analyse not only the development of market structures, but we also need a thorough understanding of the nature of technological change and the role that is played by various organizational forms over time. Central to my approach is the model of natural selection. The natural selection model was addressed by Darwin and Wallace in 1858 and is based on the principle of the 'survival of the fittest' (Winter, 1964). The model argues that species which are best adapted to a specific environment survive, while other less well-adapted species die. In this study I will argue that firms better equipped to meet environmental changes than others may grow successfully, while other less successful firms decline. However, unlike orthodox theories, competitive forces are not supposed to establish a static equilibrium in which successful firms achieve their optimal size, and unsuccessful firms disappear (Nelson and Winter, 1982; Hagedoorn, 1984). My contribution proposes a more dynamic analysis in which technological changes, market structures and firm strategies constitute a dynamic interactive system.

My adherence to biology-inspired theories does not imply that I accept the complete models presented in these theories. Neither do I plea for the gratuitous reproduction of biological models into economics and business studies. As in biology, ecological and evolutionary models can be used to describe different phenomena. Evolutionary economic theories concentrate on incremental changes over time whereas ecological theorists tend to focus on the evolution of organizations of a particular type: i.e. take a population-level view. Although both frameworks generate an adequate description of the dynamics at each level, they do not provide us with a method for integrating the distinct levels analytically (Levinthal, 1990). In this book I will argue that if I want to describe the full dynamics of organizations and market structures, it is necessary to integrate the two distinct levels of analysis into one all-encompassing framework. Describing the dynamics of industrial systems itself is, however, not sufficient. In order to understand these dynamics we need a thorough understanding of the underlying mechanisms which induce these systems to change. I will argue that in high-technology industries the main engine for change is technological progress. We therefore need a thorough understanding of the nature of these technological changes. As suggested by Rosenberg (1982), opening up the 'black box' of technology is considered to be the first step in a process which leads to a better understanding of the complex dynamics of industrial systems. For a detailed understanding of the nature of technological change I will build on the elaborated framework developed by evolutionary economists. For the study of the evolution of market structures and the importance of particular organizational types under various environmental circumstances I will take on a more ecological-inspired perspective. The integration of both theoretical perspectives enables us to cope with the interaction between the previously separate entities. Our approach is, however, not only biologically inspired. Although ecological and evolutionary approaches form the basis of my framework I take on a more eclectic approach, combining evolutionary concepts with ideas from strategic management, organization theory, industrial economics, new institutionalism and international business studies.

From an empirical perspective it is necessary to create a better understanding of the evolution of industry structures, the strategies undertaken by various categories of companies, the broad patterns of technological evolution, the internationalization tendencies that characterize today's markets and the networks of cooperating companies. The core of my empirical study will focus on the historical development of three major sectors of the information technology (IT) industry: i.e. computers, telecommunications and semiconductors. I decided to study the information technology industry because this industry can be referred to as one of the most dynamic industries of all times. Both market and technological evolution have been very rapid and competition has always been very intense. The second reason to study IT sectors is that the underlying technology bases of these sectors have undergone strong patterns of change. Technological paradigms in this industry are strongly interacting and are likely to converge in the near future. We will try to find out whether these dramatic changes in the underlying technology base bring about important implications for both market structures and for the strategies of the companies involved. The information technology sector is also a field which is characterized by global competition among a large number of multinational corporations. This allows us to study market development and company behaviour in an international setting. A further advantage of studying the IT sector is the relative abundance of reliable corporate and technological indicators which allows us to analyse the structural and behavioural aspects of the major producers in more detail. It might be clear that most of the specific features of the information technology industry are very difficult to deal with in traditional economic frameworks. It can therefore be seen as a major challenge to deal with these complex dynamics in an alternative framework.

1.1. PLAN OF THE BOOK

In the second chapter of this book we will develop an integrated evolutionary framework for the analysis of complex industrial systems over time. Our framework proposes the integration of dynamic biology-inspired theories of technical and economic change. We will argue that the use of such a framework considerably improves our current understanding of the evolution of complex industrial system and that it allows us to study dynamic phenomena from a longitudinal time-bound perspective. In this chapter we will first describe the two basic approaches that are fundamental to our integrated framework: evolutionary economics and ecological organization theories. Then we will come up with a number of hypotheses that can be derived from our integrated theoretical perspective. The hypotheses as formulated in the second chapter will be empirically evaluated in the following three chapters. In these chapters we will study the evolution of three different industrial systems over a long period of time. The three systems have in common that they are part of the information technology industry, but they are characterized by very diverse features.

Chapter 3 studies the development of one of the most dynamic industry sectors of all times: the international computer industry. In this chapter we will examine the history of market structural and technological changes in the computer industry from its initiation up to recent developments in the market. The international computer industry has traditionally been characterized by intense competition among a relatively small number of large international companies. At present the industry is undergoing a period of major consolidation and reorganization. We will end the chapter with a critical evaluation of the hypotheses that are put forward in the second chapter. We will then consider how well the assumed pattern of evolution of industrial systems fits the evolution of the computer industry.

Chapter 4 deals with the development of a previously strongly regulated sector: the telecommunications industry. This sector is particulary interesting because it has traditionally been dominated by so-called 'national champions' but is now challenged by new firms that are eager to grasp the opportunities that emerge as a result of both technological as well as institutional changes. After we describe the historical evolution of the telecommunications industry we will evaluate the predictions of our integrated framework under the specific conditions of the (regulated) telecommunications industry.

Chapter 5 describes the evolution of the semiconductor industry. This industry is especially important as a generator of technological progress in other IT fields. In contrast to other IT sectors, competition in the semiconductor industry has been dominated by relatively small, technology-oriented companies. Technological progress in this sector has always been extremely fast and forces of 'creative destruction' have brought about significant market structural changes.

Because the three IT sectors are marked by structural, institutional and technological differences, it is very interesting to examine the effectiveness of our integrated framework under such very diverse industrial settings. Although there are major differences between these sectors they share one very important feature: i.e. technological progress in each sector is increasingly dependent on progress in the other sectors. It will be argued that the basic design parameters that form the core of the relevant technological regimes have become increasingly similar and that the underlying technology bases are likely to converge in the near future. Chapter 6 is therefore concerned with an analysis of the effects of this process of technological convergence. The basic argument is that the convergence of technological paradigms of the three previously separate markets may lead to a significant shift in the boundaries of the markets and technologies involved. The major aim of the chapter is to examine whether the so-called convergence of information and communications technologies has led to a growing similarity of the firms that are active in the different industry sectors. Empirical testing of the convergence hypothesis will be based on patent data and on patterns of intercompany strategic alliance behaviour.

Chapter 7 is concerned with a detailed empirical analysis of cooperative behaviour within the IT industry. In this chapter we will argue that the strategic value of alliances can be assessed only if one pays attention to the structure of the total network in which a firm is embedded. We will show that with few exceptions agreements are generally studied from a dyadic or firm-level perspective. Such a perspective seems, however, simply inadequate to study industry sectors where virtually all companies are linked to each other. The chapter will start with a general theoretical introduction on the use of strategic alliances and proceeds with the identification of historical trends in strategic technology alliances and the analysis of the developments of the basic networks over time. The structure of the networks in each IT sector and the positions of the major actors in these networks are analysed by means of a statistical technique which is known as network analysis. Network analysis enables us to examine the overall network and at the same time provides us with an examination of the role and importance of the individual players in the network.

In Chapter 8 we discuss one of the most noticeable phenomena that characterizes the present-day information technology industry, namely internationalization. We will make use of recent data in order to assess the importance of the internationalization of innovative activities during the 1980s. In this chapter we will also pay attention to the importance of national backgrounds of companies in relation to their corporate strategies. We address the question of whether large firms are gradually losing their national characteristics and becoming truly globalized companies. An empirical analysis is performed in order to understand whether firms, operating in such a dynamic and globalized sector as the international information technology industry, can still be identified in terms of their country of origin, given their structural, technological and strategic characteristics.

Chapter 9 is concerned with an evaluation of the results of our empirical studies and with an appraisal of the usefulness of our integrated biology-inspired approach. We will start with a summary of the findings of the first five chapters. We will consider how the predictions of our integrated framework have been evaluated under the diverse conditions that characterize the various industry sectors. The second part of the chapter is concerned with the results of our empirical analyses of the three major forces that have marked the development of the IT sector over the past decade: i.e. technological convergence, cooperation and globalization. Finally we will present some suggestions for future research.

NOTE

1. The first to propose the Structure-Conduct-Performance (SCP) approach was Edward Mason in the 1930s (see e.g. Mason, 1939). His work described a one-directional relationship between structure, conduct and performance.

2. Theoretical Framework

In order to obtain a better understanding of evolutionary economics and organizational ecology we will start with a brief introduction to these theories. We then proceed with a critical evaluation of both theories and an explanation of how they fit into our integrated framework. This is followed by the discussion of a number of hypotheses that are to be tested in the next three chapters.

2.1. EVOLUTIONARY ECONOMICS

2.1.1. Evolutionary Economic Theory

Evolutionary economic theory emerged as a reaction to orthodox theories that were being criticized as lacking 'descriptive realism in the characterization of behaviour and events', and which were not equipped to deal with uncertainty and change in advanced theoretical work and many applied contexts (Nelson and Winter, 1982: 33). Textbook neo-classical theories have been widely heralded for their mathematical and logical structure. These features provided textbook neo-classical theory with an inherent logical structure, but at the same time removed it far from reality. Textbook neo-classical theories have been criticized on many different grounds but the larger part of these criticisms is related to three major issues, i.e. the simplistic characterization of the firm and the use of information, the static underpinnings of these theories and the awkward treatment of technological change.[1] These 'weaknesses' of so-called 'orthodox' theories led Nelson and Winter (1982: 33) to use an analogy stating that 'orthodoxy builds a rococo logical palace on loose empirical sand'. Others used the term 'economics of Nirvana' to refer to the, in their perception, unrealistic notions of the orthodox neo-classical economists (Kay, 1986).[2]

In textbook neo-classical theory, firms are seen as homogenous units which act completely rationally. All information which is necessary to maximize profits is readily and freely available, i.e. there is perfect information. Evolutionary theorists try to create more realistic models of the role and behaviour of firms in their economic environment. Largely influenced by Herbert Simon's (1955, 1959) concept of bounded rationality, they argue that economic actors cannot conceive all the possible alternatives in our complex and continuously changing world (Winter, 1964, 1971, 1975; Nelson and Winter, 1982). Incomplete information ensures that firms are merely satisficing rather than maximizing profits. The concept of profit satisficing or 'striving for profit' implies that if existing strategies work well firms do not feel the need to change their strategy. Our preoccupation with the uncertainty and dynamics of turbulent high-technology industries makes the distinction between profit maximizing and profit satisficing very important. According to Nelson and Winter (1982: 1) 'In a sufficient calm and repetitive decision context, the distinction between striving for profit and profit maximization may be of little moment, but in a context of substantial change it matters a great deal'.

In the textbook neo-classical framework profit-maximizing behaviour of firms was assumed to establish a static equilibrium.[3] Evolutionary theorists try to replace these static notions with an inherently dynamic framework. In such a framework the analysis of static states is replaced by the analysis of change over a long period of time. In analogy to biological evolutionary theories, the evolutionary economic model is based on the assumption that change is gradual and cumulative. In an evolutionary framework, economic and organizational changes are primarily due to the interaction of three fundamental forces: variation, selection and retention (Campbell, 1969; Aldrich and Pfeffer, 1976; Aldrich, 1979).

Variation refers to the differences among organizations with respect to their organizational structures and strategies. Deliberate strategic choices account for most of the planned variation whereas unplanned variation occurs through strategic mistakes or as a result of incomplete information. Asymmetry between organizations is subsequently reinforced by the cumulativeness, tacitness, and partial appropriability of knowledge (Dosi, 1988). In contrast to the textbook neo-classical notion of knowledge as a public good, evolutionary theorists argue that knowledge is often very difficult to transfer (see Nelson and Winter, 1982; Freeman, 1982; Dosi and Orsenigo, 1988). Such is especially the case for what Polanyi (1958) called 'tacit knowledge'. Tacit knowledge refers to knowledge which cannot be transferred in codified form. Firm-specific tacit knowledge is often accumulated within a firm by processes of learning-by-doing and learning-by-using (Arrow, 1962b; Rosenberg, 1982). The accumulated tacit knowledge in combination with the more general available public knowledge comprises the knowledge base of a company and determines the asymmetric character of organizations. Variation among organizations is essential for the successful operation of selection mechanisms.

In an evolutionary economic framework the term *selection* is used to describe the economic equivalent of the natural selection process as put forward by Darwin and Wallace. The concept of natural selection is based on the principle of 'the survival of the fittest' (Winter, 1964) and argues that species that are best adapted to a specific environment survive, while other less well-adapted species die. Inspired by this conception of natural selection, Alchian (1950) stressed the importance of selection among firms on the basis of their ability to make profits. He asserted that 'those who realize positive profits are the survivors; those who suffer losses disappear' (Alchian, 1950: 213). This idea is in accordance with the notion of Schumpeterian competition, in which asymmetries between organizations may lead to a process of 'creative destruction'. Firms better equipped than others to meet environmental changes may grow, while other less successful firms decline. However, unlike in orthodox theories, competitive forces do not establish a static equilibrium in which successful firms achieve their optimal size, and unsuccessful firms disappear (Nelson and Winter, 1982; Hagedoorn, 1984). Instead, the industry is in a constant disequilibrium moving from one state to the other. Variation and selection are, however, not sufficient to bring about changes in the economic system. Selection takes place only if there are firms that are not able to achieve an optimal 'fit' with their environment. Thus, in order to make selection effective there have to be some sort of retention mechanisms in the system.

The main sources of *retention* in an evolutionary framework are brought about by so-called organizational routines. Evolutionary theorists have argued that apart from a stochastic element in the choice of decisions and their outcomes, most of the behaviour of firms is relatively predictable and repetitive. Nelson and Winter (1982) described such patterns of behaviour as routines. Routines can be compared to biological genes because they govern a firm's behaviour and are inheritable in the sense that future behaviour is largely based on today's characteristics (Nelson and Winter, 1982). Evolutionary theorists assert that firms grow by the replication of successful routines.[4] The continued reliance on basic routines, however, severely reduces the speed of adaptation of organizations. Because adaptation to new environments is generally low in relation to the speed of change, adaptation is often not possible and selection is likely to take place.[5] Dosi (1983, 1984) enriched Nelson and Winter's model by introducing the Lamarckian-inspired concept of 'mutation generating mechanisms'. In a Lamarckian approach not only Darwinian ex-post selection takes place, but also feedback effects are taken into account.

2.1.2. Technological Change as an Evolutionary Process

One of the areas in which the evolutionary approach has been rather successful is the study of technological change. From a textbook neo-classical point of view technological progress is often described as merely a shift along the production function. Technological change is often considered to be an exogenous variable and the nature of technological change remains a 'black box' (Rosenberg, 1982).[6] In an attempt to open up this 'back box', evolutionary economic theory studies technological change as an endogenous time-bound process. Evolutionary economic theorists believe that technological innovations are the outcome of deliberately planned research and that technological progress is considered to be an incremental cumulative process that follows consistent technological paths and that is evaluated by its 'selection' environment.[7] Technological paths or trajectories are often shaped by selection or focusing mechanisms which guide technological progress in certain directions. In evolutionary theory these focusing mechanisms are often referred to as technological paradigms. In analogy with Kuhn's definition of a scientific paradigm and inspired by Rosenberg's (1976) 'focusing devices', Dosi (1988) has defined a technological paradigm as 'a "pattern" of solution of selected techno-economic problems based on highly selected principles derived from the natural sciences, jointly with specific rules aimed to acquire new knowledge and safeguarding it, whenever possible against rapid diffusion to the competitors' (Dosi, 1988: 1127). The establishment of a new paradigm entails a 'communis opinio' about the nature of the solutions of 'selected techno-economic problems' (Dosi, 1988). In such a framework, the direction of technological progress is more or less irreversible. Although irreversibility is generally associated with acquired system-scale economies or prior investments in education and equipment (David, 1985) often the focusing capabilities of the prevailing technological paradigm are much more important, in the sense that while technological progress is locked-in a specific path, previous technologies are disregarded and eventually 'forgotten' (Cantwell, 1990). However, unlike biological evolution, technical evolution can in some instances be characterized by partial reversibility to previous technologies (De Bresson, 1987). None the less, reverting to previously abandoned technologies is often very difficult and seems to be very rare in practice. Technological paradigms often evolve from a conception of vague ideas into very strong paradigms which blindfold technicians from pursuing other more uncertain directions. Within those technological paradigms progress develops along relatively straight paths which are referred to as technological trajectories (Dosi, 1983). Although this may seem to be a handicap for rapid technological progress it turns out to be an essential condition for the development of a certain technology. Path dependency makes the research process cumulative and facilitates the rapid expansion of the boundaries of a technology.

The emergence of a new paradigm gives way to a series of technological innovations and experiments. If specific experiments accumulate a critical mass of consensus then a technological regime may be constituted (Nelson and Winter, 1982). A technological regime can be seen as a specific technical system which operates within the boundaries of a paradigm. Technological regimes are often physically embodied in so-called basic designs[8] which arise if there is consensus about a specific product or process which stands out above other products or processes. A basic design establishes a foundation on which other developments can be based and often serves as a kind of 'technological guidepost' (Sahal, 1981), which steers the direction of future improvements in technology.

Although technological paradigms and technological regimes may be very strong for a considerable period of time, technologies do not follow the same technological path for ever. Kuhn (1970: 64) argued that 'novelty emerges only with difficulty, manifested by resistance, against a background provided by expectation'. Thus, a change of regime may arise whenever there are diminishing returns in improving the basic characteristics over time or when other technological developments give way to a change of the basic characteristics of a design. Change can, however, also be induced when there are significant changes in the nature of the selection environment, which favour other technological alternatives.

14   *The Dynamics of Technical Innovation*

2.2. ORGANIZATIONAL ECOLOGY

Originating from a different discipline (sociology), but also inspired by theories of biological evolution, a new approach to organizational theory was introduced in the mid-1970s: the organizational ecology approach. Whereas evolutionary theorists are primarily opposed to the assumptions of orthodox neo-classical theorists, ecological organizational theories can be seen as a reaction to contemporary organizational theories which stress the flexibility and adaptability of organizations in response to their changing environments. Whereas a large part of the organizational and strategic management literature views organizations as rapid flexible adapters, organizational ecologists argue that most of the variation in organizations comes about through the creation of new organizational types and the demise of old ones and is only for a small part influenced by adaptive behaviour of organizations. Whereas organizational and strategic management theory has focused on adaptive change within organizations, organizational ecologists emphasize the importance of inertial forces that prevent organizations from achieving the required adaption. It is claimed that in a rapidly changing environment it is doubtful whether firms are capable of changing their forms fast enough to deal effectively with a new environmental state. Ecologists refer to this relatively slow process of adaption as 'relative inertia': i.e. relative in comparison to environmental changes. Sometimes changes in the environment are so radical that adaption to these changes is not possible. Hannan and Freeman (1977: 957) have used the analogy 'failing churches do not become retail stores nor do firms transform themselves into churches' to characterize the difficulties that organizations face when they try to adapt to radical changes. From an ecological perspective, inertia arises from both internal as well as from external pressures (Hannan and Freeman, 1977). Internal pressures comprise: (1) sunk costs in plants, equipment and specialized personnel; (2) the bounded rationality of firms and imperfect information; (3) resistance to change from organizational members; (4) the presence of normative rules and standard procedures. External pressures include: (1) legal and fiscal entry and exit barriers; (2) difficulties in acquiring information about the environment; (3) a decrease of the legitimacy of organizations, due to selection forces which favour reliable and accountable organizations.

In order to grasp the complex dynamics of our present-day society the organizational ecology school tries to explain how different types of organizations survive or fail under different environmental settings.

Ecological theorists are therefore primarily concerned with vital rates: i.e. foundings and disbandings of organizations. Although ecological dynamics take place at three different levels – community, population and organization – most analyses have dealt with the population level (Carroll, 1984; Astley, 1985). Populations consist of organizations that share a specific organizational form. The populational dynamics in an ecological framework are generally based on two central concepts: competition and legitimation (Schreuder and van Witteloostuijn, 1990). Competition can be seen as the rivalry between populations for a limited amount of resources, whereas legitimacy can be described as the amount of social acceptance of a specific type of organization. The strength of competitive forces is largely determined by the so-called carrying capacity of an environment. Carrying capacity is referred to as the maximum ability of a niche[9] to support certain types of organizations, given the prevailing social, political and economic circumstances. That means that there is a restriction in the total number of organizations that can be supported by a specific resource environment (Lambkin, 1988). Based on the two central concepts of competition and legitimation, ecological theorists have built a framework for the evolution of populations over long periods of time. In order to model the effects of carrying capacity on growth rates, a logistic growth equation is used which was originally developed by population biologists (Hannan and Freeman, 1977). This so-called Verhulst-Pearl equation can be described as:

$$\frac{dN}{dt} = rN\frac{K-N}{K}$$

This equation shows that the growth rate of a population with size N is dependent on two fundamental factors. The first factor (r) represents the intrinsic growth rate, which determines the growth rate in the absence of resource constraints (Carroll, 1988). The second factor (K) represents the carrying capacity of a certain niche.[10] Because the number of organizations during the first stage of a population's development is low, resources are abundant and K (carrying capacity) is not considered to be very important. At that time the number of organizations is likely to be small: i.e. there is low density (Figure 2.1, Period 0–A).

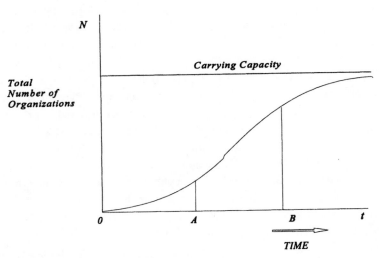

Figure 2.1 Stages of a population's growth

Over time, however, a population experiences growth and density increases. A larger number of similar types considerably improves the legitimacy of all the organizations in a specific population and therefore enhances the survival chances of similar organizations. Increased legitimacy therefore induces death rates to fall until carrying capacity is approached (Figure 2.1, period A–B). R is therefore the only meaningful factor that influences the growth rate of a population at that stage. In a later stage, when the number of organizations increases and carrying capacity is approached, the factor K is becoming increasingly important. When carrying capacity is approached, competitive forces among the organizations in a population intensify and this may well lead to a lower number of entrants and to a shake-out in the market[11] (Figure 2.1, period B–).

Organizational ecology's primary focus is on organizational diversity. Analogous to the biological question of 'Why are there so many kinds of animals?' (Hutchinson, 1959: 145) organizational ecologists have been concerned with the question of 'Why are there so many kinds of organizations?' (Hannan and Freeman, 1977: 929). Organizational ecologists have tried to answer this question by linking specific organizational types to different environmental conditions. Ecological organizational theorists have argued that some organizational forms do better under specific environmental conditions than other organizations (Hannan and Freeman, 1977, 1989;

Brittain and Freeman, 1980; Lambkin, 1988; Lambkin and Day, 1989). Hannan and Freeman (1977) distinguish among five strategy types: r-types, K-types, generalists, specialists and polymorphists. Consistent with the importance of the specific factors r and K under different stages of a population's development, ecologists have referred to organizations as r-types if they can be described as first movers. These firms are generally characterized by simple and fast-to-build organizational structures and tend to move quickly into a newly established niche. K-type organizations on the other hand are relatively slow movers which tend to rely heavily on efficient but capital-intensive and rigid organizational structures. Another closely related distinction between types of organizations is concerned with the differences between generalists and specialists (Hannan and Freeman, 1977; Tucker et al., 1990). Generalists differ from specialists in terms of the scope of the environment that is claimed by these organizations. Whereas generalists tend to occupy a large part of the environment, specialists are concerned with a more narrowly defined part of the environment. The last strategy type (polymorphists) can be seen as organizations that combine generalist and specialist strategies in order to deal with a wide range of fitness contingencies (Brittain and Freeman, 1980; Aldrich and Wiedenmayer, 1990). Polymorphists are generally characterized by a largely diversified organizational structure in combination with a holding form (Hannan and Freeman, 1989). In an attempt to generate a more detailed representation of strategy types, Brittain and Freeman (1980) combined the different strategy types into K-generalists, r-generalists, K-specialists, r-specialists and polymorphists.[12]

The division of organizations into different strategy types is not a goal in itself. It is only important if the effectiveness of these strategy types can be related to different environmental conditions. Hannan and Freeman (1977) have classified environments in terms of three features: variability, grain and uncertainty. The variability of an environment depends on the degree of change in the environment. Radically changing environments are referred to as concave, whereas incremental environments can be regarded as convex. The grain of an environment is associated with the frequency of changes. Constantly changing environments are denoted as fine-grained, whereas sporadically changing environments are referred to as coarse-grained. The third feature characterizing environments is the degree of uncertainty. Uncertainty can be seen as a derivative condition of the two other conditions (Lambkin 1988). Frequently and radically changing environments are characterized by high uncertainty, whereas sporadically and incrementally changing environments are generally characterized by a relatively low level of uncertainty.

   Table 2.1 describes the fundamental ecological propositions with respect to the fit of the organizational form under various environmental conditions (see e.g. Brittain and Freeman, 1980, Lambkin, 1988; Lambkin and Day, 1989). We refer to Section 2.4 for a more elaborated discussion of the fitness of specific organizational forms under different environmental conditions.

Table 2.1 Fitness of organizational forms under different environmental circumstances

| | | *Environment* | | |
		Fine-grained uncertain	*Fine-coarse relatively uncertain*	*Coarse-grained relatively certain*
Convex	r-generalists		K-generalists	K-generalists
Concave	r-specialists		K-generalists	K-specialists:
	polymorphists			– independent
				– captives
				– subordinates

Source: Lambkin, 1988.

2.3. AN INTEGRATED APPROACH: COMBINING EVOLUTIONARY AND ECOLOGICAL THEORIES

In the literature we find two fundamental drivers that bring about change in organizational fields: adaptation and selection. Whereas most of the organizational and strategic management literature has traditionally been dominated by the adaptation perspective, we take on a selection approach.

Although the intellectual heritage of both evolutionary and ecological organization theories is found in biology, they differ significantly in the way selection is treated. Ecologists argue that 'most of the variability in the core structure of organizations comes about through the creation of new organizations and the demise of old ones' (Hannan and Freeman, 1989: 11–12). This view is consistent with the traditional neo-classical view of Darwinian selection and is concerned with a rather deterministic relationship between firms and the environment in the sense that the 'fit' of organizations is strictly dependent on the environment. Such an approach is clearly Darwinian because organizations are stuck with their organizational characteristics and are not able to adapt to changing environmental circumstances.

Recent contributions by evolutionary economists have taken on a more Lamarckian point of view.[13] Evolutionary theories have argued that if pressures are hard enough firms can be engaged in a search process in order to increase their fit with the environment. A firm's emphasis on profit satisficing implies that firms which achieve above-average profits are not likely to be engaged in search processes, whereas firms that are deprived of satisfactory profits pursue search processes in order to increase their fit with the environment. If routines can be compared to genes in biological evolution, then the search process may well be regarded as the generator of mutations in biological evolutionary theory (Nelson and Winter, 1982). Evolutionary theorists argue that firms that are engaged in a search process do not explore all the possible directions but confine their search to the most promising ones. Nelson and Winter modelled this process using so-called Markov chains. The concept of a Markov chain is based on the assumption that 'the condition of the industry in each time period bears the seeds of its condition in the following period' (Nelson and Winter, 1982: 19). Under these conditions a probability distribution of the state at time $t+1$ can be constructed from the state of a firm's competencies and routines at time t. In general, firms are engaged in 'local search' only, which means that search is often limited to related areas. Local search and a continued reliance on their basic routines implies that firms are much better at doing more of the same than they are at adapting to change. In evolutionary economic theory the continuously changing technological environment provides a moving target. Firms with specific competencies and routines, which are appropriate in one period, are often not as successful in other periods. All the competencies and build-up of knowledge may be rendered useless in situations of change. However, as long as the combination of selection processes and competition provides a firm with signals regarding future directions of change, it might be very rewarding to pursue such a moving target (Gomulka, 1990). Recent contributions have emphasized adaptive change through learning or imitation. Dosi (1983, 1984), for example, enriched Nelson and Winter's model by introducing the Lamarckian-inspired concept of 'mutation generating mechanisms'. In Dosi's approach not only does Darwinian ex-post selection take place, but also the feedback effects on the selection of the technological paradigm are considered to be important.

We contend that describing the feedback effects of the selection environment on the behaviour of firms, i.e. taking a Lamarckian point of view, is essential for describing the strategic behaviour of organizations.[14] We think, however, that in order to describe the full dynamics of industrial systems, both Darwinian as well as Lamarckian selection should be taken into account (see also Aldrich and Auster, 1986). Inertia is an essential characteristic of organizations but by studying vital rates only we would downplay the role of changes that are due to transformation processes within organizations. Although some ecological theorists have studied the change of organizational forms over time (Aldrich, 1979; McKelvey and Aldrich, 1983; Aldrich and Auster, 1986; Baum and Singh, 1994) this change is considered to be of minor importance in ecological theories and empirical studies. It would, however, be a distortion to refer to firms as static organizations that are unable to change. The organizational ecologists' emphasis on the inertia of firms at first sight seems convincing, but lacks an explanation of the observed ability of firms to make large profits over long periods of time (even in rapidly changing environments). This makes us sceptical about the inability of firms to adapt. We contend that firms can learn from their environment and when pressures are hard enough, they try to modify their forms. Therefore, following Freeman (1991: 211) we suggest that 'at the very least any good biological model would have to be Lamarckian and not neo-Darwinian'. In general, organizations are not supposed to react very quickly to new developments. However, if organizations are confronted with persistently lower revenues they are induced to change (Singh, 1986). Therefore adaptation to the environment is considered to be an essential aspect of every dynamic theory.

Another, related point we have to make is concerned with the analysis of vital rates. In line with Winter (1990: 289) we will argue that 'it would be surprising, therefore, if a mere count of the number of firms proved to be a good indicator of the degree of pressure on the carrying capacity of the environment or other consequences of population size'. In contrast to arguments expressed by Hannan and Freeman (1977, 1989) the total size of the population seems to be a more important determinant of niche-density than the absolute number of firms.[15] An approach based on the number of firms may only be important in situations in which the growth of firms is restricted by institutional or other factors or in situations in which the population consists of small organizations (Aldrich, 1979; Bedian, 1984; Perrow, 1986; Scott, 1987). Hannan and Freeman (1977) refute this by arguing that this problem might be overcome by studying a longer time span. Over such a long time-scale even the largest companies can be dissolved. However, in our opinion some factors which are important for analysing organizational change cannot be studied over such a long time-scale. For example, the implications of a specific technological innovation cannot be effectively measured on a time-scale of, say, a hundred years. Another argument against the study of 'vital rates' *per sè* is that the selection process is often retarded by governmental influences. Social costs of liquidation of large organizations often motivate government agencies to provide firms with a substantial amount of financial aid in order to protect them from liquidation. We will argue that often exit cannot be equalled with low performance levels. Although exit is often referred to as the ultimate manifestation of organizational failure (Bedian, 1984) successful small firms can be taken over or merge with other firms. In a pure selection model these firms would be referred to as 'failures'. Therefore Winter (1990: 280) proposes to take routines as the unit of analysis: 'to distinguish survival from non-survival in a way that is not influenced by superficial institutional distinction, and to sort out the complex intermediate cases, it is necessary to identify the key routines and ask what happened to them'. It must, however, be noted that it is often very difficult to discern the key routines of an organization (Meyer, 1990). Following Hannan et al. (1990: 246) we will argue that 'The full dynamics of populations of organizations involve vital rates (of founding and mortality) as well as growth and decline of individual populations over long periods'. We propose an approach that combines rates of both founding and mortality with the growth rates of populations as well as individual organizations.[16]

Because our main concern is the evolution of high-technology industries, we should also decide upon a framework for the analysis of technological change. In organizational ecology, technological change is considered to be one of several environmental factors that affect organizations. Although technological change may spur new entries in the market, the inability to adapt to changing technologies can be a major source of organizational exit. Technological change is therefore viewed primarily as a factor which creates turmoil in the economic environment (Brittain and Freeman, 1980). Whereas ecological theorists can be denoted as technological determinists, evolutionary economic theories have stressed the interaction between forces of technological change, market structures and organizational strategies. For a detailed understanding of technological change we will therefore build on the elaborated framework developed by evolutionary economists. For the study of market structures and the importance of particular organizational types under various environmental circumstances we will take on an ecological perspective, albeit interpreted from a more Lamarckian point of view. In our approach, attention will therefore be paid both to the dynamics of populations and to the dynamics of individual organizations. From a population point of view we can study the performance of organizational forms under a diverse set of environmental circumstances, whereas the analysis of the behaviour of individual organizations generates a number of interesting propositions about firm strategies and the effects of different strategies on market structures and on technological developments. Our combined approach allows us to come up with a number of propositions about the likely success of different generic strategies over time. With these considerations in mind we put forward a number of hypotheses that can be derived from our integrated framework.

2.4. THE EVOLUTION OF INDUSTRIAL SYSTEMS: SOME HYPOTHESES

In contrast to the general conception of new life cycles born out of market needs (Sherwin and Isenson, 1967; Utterback, 1974) high-technology industries are typical examples of markets created by radical technological innovations (Mueller and Tilton, 1969; Tushman and Anderson, 1986). At the time of founding there is often substantial uncertainty about the technological feasibility of an innovation and its potential market size. Because both market and technological uncertainties are high, most commercial firms are very reluctant to support research in this stage. Moreover, social acceptance (legitimation) of potential entrants is very low, which makes it very difficult to persuade investors and financial institutions to finance these potential entrants (Bedian, 1984; Aldrich and Auster, 1986). Because markets are non-existent and technological development is to a great extent dependent on the underlying scientific knowledge base, we expect that the larger part of technological efforts is carried out by academic or other institutions under state supervision and support. These institutions are therefore expected to act as 'incubators' of radical new technological developments (Roman and Puett, 1983; Martin, 1984; Stankiewicz, 1990). Thus:

Hypothesis 1: Under conditions of high market and technological uncertainty, universities and government institutions are the first important incubators of radical new technologies.

After a short 'incubator period' the first commercial companies are likely to enter the newly born market. Because technological change is frequent and radical the market can be characterized as fine-grained and concave (Hannan and Freeman, 1977). Under these conditions the ecological model predicts that the market will be explored by small specialized fast-to-build organizations (Hannan and Freeman, 1977, 1989; Brittain and Freeman, 1980; Lambkin, 1988). The classic argument for the importance of these small firms in the introduction of new technologies was given by Arrow (1962a) who showed that a new entrant will benefit more from adopting a new innovation than will incumbent firms. For the incumbent organization a new innovation may cannibalize profits from its other products. The new entrant, however, does not experience any loss of profit as a result of the new technology or the new product. Therefore, the impetus to move into the new technology or product segment is correspondingly higher for these firms. Their flexible organizational structures and short communication lines enable these so-called r-specialist firms to respond rapidly to new opportunities in the market. At that stage of development customers focus on product performance rather than on costs (Mueller and Tilton, 1969; Parker, 1978; Dosi, 1984; Freeman, 1990). Companies can therefore expect high rewards for bringing a technologically dominant product to the market. This induces firms to follow an offensive innovation strategy in which they try to be the first on the market with new products and aim at market and technological leadership. Thus we might argue:

Hypothesis 2: A newly emerging high-technology market is first explored by r-specialist organizations pursuing an offensive innovation strategy.

In spite of the high profits and temporary monopoly gains which could be realized by offering a high performance product, the high risk involved in pursuing such a strategy brings about bankruptcy for a large number of unsuccessful firms. According to Baum and House (1990: 130–31) 'their dependence on first mover advantages makes them high-risk and, potentially, high-payoff organizations that thrive in temporarily rich and dispersed resource environments in which no firm or small group of firms dominates competition'. The combination of high risks and possible high payoffs generates a state of constant flux in which high founding rates of small firms are just enough to offset their death rates (Hannan and Freeman, 1989). The creation of new firms which try to imitate the technologies of the most successful firms is responsible for high birth rates, whereas so-called 'liabilities to newness' (Stinchcombe, 1965) are responsible for the high dissolution rates of r-specialists.

Liabilities to newness[17] refer to the observation that small new firms are characterized by higher death rates than their larger counterparts because such firms, unlike their larger competitors, are often not equipped with considerable buffers against temporary setbacks. That means that they are often not capable of dealing with temporary failures or cutbacks in sales. Moreover, social acceptance (legitimation) of the firms exploiting a new technology is often not very high in the initial stages of the life cycle (Hannan and Freeman, 1977, 1989).[18] As a result, life expectancies of these firms are generally low. Because awareness of new high-technology products is low and experience is nil, only a few consumers are willing to adopt the often high-priced products. High prices and limited usability of the new high-technology products induces most potential customers to take a 'wait and see' approach rather than buying such a radical new product directly. New-product diffusion research has shown that at this stage only about 16 per cent of the eventual adopters is likely to acquire new products (Figure 2.2). The first adopters, which make up about 2.5 per cent of eventual adopters, are (in the IT industry) often governmental institutions which buy new innovative high performance products regardless of their prices for use in military or space applications. When the technology is sufficiently developed to be introduced in the commercial marketplace another group of potential users, so-called 'early adopters', is likely to adopt the technologies or products. Early adopters fulfil the role of 'opinion leaders' and therefore have an enormous impact on the success or failure of a new product. Whereas technical and market uncertainties are very high in the initial stage of the life cycle, over time uncertainty reduces. Technological problems are often solved and institutions that are able to provide the 'best' technologies or solutions to their customers are rewarded by rapid growth. Due to the selection mechanism it gradually becomes clear which technologies will be most successful both in technological terms and in meeting customer demand. The technology, which accumulates a critical mass of consensus, may trigger off a new technological regime. Such a technological regime is often physically embodied in a product or process which stands out above others. These so-called 'basic designs' may then serve as 'technological guideposts' (Sahal, 1981) and steer the direction of future improvements in technology. The search for radical new technological changes can now be substituted by 'normal' technological progress that is represented by incremental cumulative improvements along a specific technological path or trajectory (Nelson and Winter, 1982; Dosi, 1984, 1988). We therefore hypothesize:

Hypothesis 3: The emergence of a 'basic design' leads to a substitution of radical technological development by more focused incremental cumulative improvements along a specific technological path or trajectory.

The establishment of a technological regime not only lowers technological uncertainty. Because of the adaptation of the basic design as the standard, market uncertainty is also considerably reduced. Moreover, awareness of and experience with the product increases rapidly. The overall reduction in uncertainty makes the environment less fine-grained and less concave. At this stage it is feasible for firms to enter the market on a larger scale. The prospect of a considerable market warrants large-scale advertising campaigns in order to attract the attention of potential clients. Moreover, costs decrease because of experience curve effects. Founding rates take off as a result of the growing legitimacy of organizations and the spread of know-how about the dominant product technology. The standardized direction of technological progress shifts competition away from performance and design towards price. From now on, cost factors are driving the industry. The cumulative character of technological changes rapidly expands the technological frontiers and 'research becomes increasingly specialized and sophisticated and the technology is broken down into its component parts with individual investigations focusing on improvements in small elements of the technology' (Mueller and Tilton, 1969: 576).

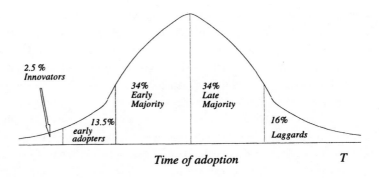

Source : Wind, 1982.

Figure 2.2 Non-cumulative pattern of adoption

The complex character of technological change at this stage clearly favours formal organizations (Dosi, 1988; Hagedoorn, 1989). Their additional advantages in terms of economies of scale and scope enable large firms to set prices below those of their smaller competitors. In such an environment, which is characterized by complex technologies and cost-based competition, large firms are clearly better off than their smaller counterparts. The emergence of a mass market and an ongoing reduction in technological uncertainty attracts a large number of so-called 'early-follower' firms into the new market. These followers are typically subsidiaries or divisions of large established firms which operate in adjacent markets. In comparison to r-specialist firms, these so-called K-generalists rely heavily on their efficient but capital-intensive and rigid organizational structures and tend to focus on a broad number of market segments. However, not all of these generalist firms enter from neighbouring markets. Some very large polymorphist firms, for which an unsuccessful entry into the new market does not threaten their survival, enter the industry at this point in time (Lambkin, 1988). These polymorphists combine their overall generalist strategy with a specialized unit approach in the new market. This enables them to deal with a wide range of fitness contingencies (Brittain and Freeman, 1980).[19] Polymorphists as well as K-generalists tend to use their efficiency advantages to leapfrog the positions of their smaller competitors (Lambkin, 1988). This leads us to the following hypothesis:

Hypothesis 4: *After the establishment of a new technological regime, K-type organizations tend to outcompete r-type organizations. This is illustrated by the start of an r to K transition in the market.*

At this stage the diffusion of technology is accelerated due to an increase in awareness and experience with the new technology. A positive evaluation of the early users may provoke another (larger) part of the potential customers to adopt the new technology or product. These adopters, who in the first instance waited for an evaluation of the early users, are referred to as the 'early majority' (Wind, 1982). They are found to account for about one-third of all eventual adopters (see Figure 2.2). The adoption of the new technology or product by such a large number of adopters can be seen as the confirmation of a successful establishment of the technological regime. Apart from awareness and experience factors, more dynamic diffusion research (e.g. Hagedoorn, 1989) has stressed the importance of cumulative improvements in the new technology. Moreover, learning effects allow prices to decline as a function of time and market growth (Dosi, 1984). The rapid increasing functionality and the improved price/performance of new technologies broadens the application fields of these technologies and gives way to a rapid increase in the number of potential users. Cost declines of 15–30 per cent per doubling of output in high-technology industries (Day, 1981) enable price decreases of the same amount. These price decreases accelerate the rate of adoption of the new product or technology. However, after a period of seemingly infinite technological progress and considerable market growth, most industries undergo a phase of more moderate technological and market development. Saturation of demand is levelling sales growth towards zero, whereas technological progress seems to approach its natural limits. At the same time, users become increasingly sophisticated and tend to demand standardization of products. The standardization of products increasingly turns products into technological commodities. Almost identical technological products are now supplied by many different competitors. As the standardization process makes it possible for users to choose between a number of competitors with virtually the same products, an increase of competition is expected. Under conditions of fierce price-based competition in which prices reflect a firm's marginal costs, an erosion of profits is likely to occur. Under these conditions firms are induced to expand their market share in order to maintain their profits. As technological change within a specific technological regime approaches its natural limits, R&D expenditure's payoff decreases rapidly. Since no satisfactory gains can be reaped by the improvement of technology, competitive strategies are to shift towards marketing, distribution and production efficiency.

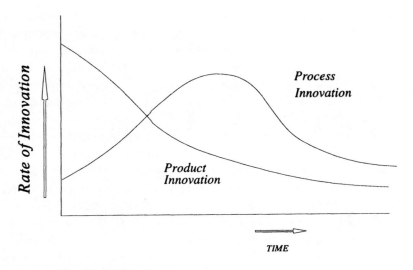

Source: Abernathy and Utterback, 1978.

Figure 2.3 Patterns of product and process innovations

A firm's competitive position in the first stage of the life cycle is largely determined by its innovative capabilities. As carrying capacity is increasingly approached and technological change becomes infrequent and incremental (convex and coarse-grained), efficiency replaces innovativeness as the strongest competitive weapon (Brittain and Freeman, 1980). Competition for scarce resources then replaces the importance of legitimation as the limiting factor on the growth rate of the population. Increasing competition in a situation in which the carrying capacity of the niche is gradually approached will lead to a state in which only the most efficient producers are able to survive (Carroll, 1984, 1985; Baum and House, 1990). Because of the price-sensitive character of competition there will be a shift of focus away from product improvements towards cost-reducing process innovations (see Figure

2.3). It is clear that in such an environment it is very difficult for small firms to compete effectively against more scale-efficient larger firms. Carroll and Hannan (1990: 109), for example, argued that 'when density is high, resources are subject to intense exploitation and few resources go unexploited. Since newly founded organizations can seldom compete head to head with established organizations the new entrants tend to be pushed to the margins of resource distribution'. By driving down costs and prices, large K-strategists are likely to outcompete the small r-strategists. This process, whereby small r-type firms are replaced by efficient large-scale firms, is often referred to in the ecological literature as the r to K transition (Brittain and Freeman, 1980).

Whereas small flexible first-mover firms were well equipped to take advantage of the high market and technological opportunities in the introductory stage of the life cycle, these same firms often fail to deal with the consolidating forces of a mature environment. The standardization of products and processes and the subsequent reduction in market and technological uncertainty induces firms to compete on a low-cost, low-margin basis. Overall, static market-entry barriers such as economies of scale and scope replace 'dynamic' entry barriers such as learning economies and preemption economies (Dosi, 1984). K-type firms which are characterized by their rigid, efficient organizational structures seem to be much better suited to compete in such an environment than r-type organizations. K-generalists with their rigid organization structures and efficient production apparatus move slowly into new niches, but once they are established they tend to out-compete r-strategists. Thus, as the carrying capacity is approached and competitive forces intensify, r-types will be replaced by K-type firms.[20] Therefore we hypothesize:

Hypothesis 5: As carrying capacity is increasingly approached and technological change becomes infrequent and incremental, efficiency replaces innovativeness as the strongest competitive weapon. This increases the rate of r to K transition in the market.

At the same time, the sophistication of users and the preoccupation of large firms with serving the overall market opens up a number of niches in which specialized, smaller firms can gain high rewards by serving the specific needs of a sophisticated customer group. This process of 'niche-elaboration' (Pianka, 1978) opens up a number of opportunities for specialist organizations. K-specialists are usually of the following types: captive producers, independent producers and subordinate producers (Brittain and Freeman, 1980). Captive producers tend to produce solely for their parent company, whereas independent specialist producers try to outcompete generalists in stable niches. Because they have little excess capacity specialists are often more efficient than their generalist competitors, at least under stable market conditions. Subordinate producers are firms that occupy a niche previously abandoned by K-generalists because the technology became outdated and the market declined. Whereas initially the market was not large enough to support multiple niches, the gradual emergence of a mass market makes a strategy of segmentation viable (Popper and Buskirk, 1992). Specialists try to bypass entry barriers and head-on competition with large K-generalists by entering market niches which are not occupied by these same firms, or which cannot be served as efficiently by generalists. Therefore we hypothesize:

Hypothesis 6: *The emergence of a mass market creates market niches, which will soon be occupied by specialist organizations.*

Eventually not only does market growth slow down but there can even be a general decline in sales. This decline can often be attributed to decreasing technological opportunities in the current paradigm (see Figure 2.4).

In this stage of development carrying capacity is reached and resources become exhausted. The lower margins that result from larger competitive pressures decrease the founding rate of new organizations and increase the dissolution rate of incumbent organizations. Therefore, the total number of organizations is likely to decrease (Figure 2.5). Whereas the first stage of the life cycle can be described as a phase where Schumpeterian enterprises play a fundamental role in the creation of new combinations, now the industry is dominated by large firms which turn innovation into routine.[21] Only the most efficient K-type producers are able to survive in such a declining market. Because of the success of the new competitive technological paradigm, the carrying capacity for the 'old' paradigm is likely to decrease (Figure 2.5). Decreasing carrying capacity implies that the environment is capable of supporting only a limited number of organizations. A further concentration of the industry seems therefore inevitable and a shake-out is likely to occur (Carroll, 1984, 1985; Pianka, 1978).

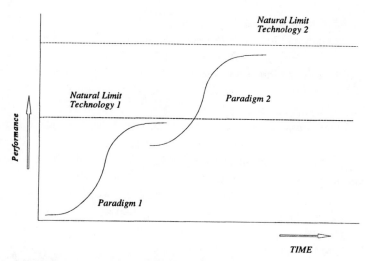

Figure 2.4 A shift of the technological paradigm

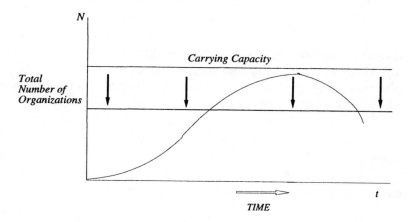

Figure 2.5 The effects of a paradigmatic shift on carrying capacity

Although technological paradigms may be very strong for a considerable period of time, it is obvious that technologies do not follow the same technological path for ever. Faced with problems of advancing current technologies, firms need to invest an increasing amount of resources in R&D to make significant technological progress. In order to speed up stagnating technological progress at this point of time, firms tend to broaden their focus in the search for alternative technologies. These search processes may eventually lead to new technological regimes or to the establishment of a new technological paradigm. Substitute technologies may offer better perspectives and may be able to trigger off new technological paths. These radical technological innovations often drastically alter the price/performance ratio of high-technology products and often act as forces of 'creative destruction' which threaten incumbent industry leaders and open up opportunities for new firms. Under these circumstances it might be sensible for any organization to shift its attention towards the new technological paradigm. However, most incumbent firms are characterized by a strong inertia which prevent them from transforming their current product and technologies. Their position as reliable and accountable organizations as well as their sunk costs in equipment and personnel prevents them from redirecting their focus to the new (more promising) paradigm. It is found that under these conditions incumbents even tend to increase investments in the old technological regime rather than switch to the new technological regime (Cooper and Schendel 1976; Foster 1986). K-strategists' elaborated and capital-intensive production structures enable them to withstand competition for a long time. The same structure, however, prevents them from moving swiftly into new resource spaces. The inability of these K-type firms to explore new markets that are opened up by the new technological paradigm initiates a K to r transition. A large number of small flexible r-type firms are able to occupy the newly emerging market, whereas a shake-out in the 'old' market raises the dissolution rate of K-types. Thus, competence-destroying innovations may lead to the demise of large established firms and to the rise of new r-type organizations. Therefore we hypothesize:

Hypothesis 7: A paradigmatic technology shift initiates a K to r transition.

K-strategists' reliance on firmly embedded routines makes the transition to a more promising technological paradigm very difficult. Firms with a relatively successful background are often even more resistant to change than other firms. This so-called 'success breeds failure syndrome' (Starbuck et al., 1978) is often observed by established industry leaders. However, the likelihood of successful switching to a new paradigm is not only a function of willingness to change but can also be seen as a factor of the competence to change. The possibility of successful switching is generally depicted as a factor of distance to the new technological paradigm (Nelson and Winter, 1982). Moreover, successful transformation is more likely if competition is weak and potential entrants are fewer (Hagedoorn, 1984; Cantwell, 1990).

Notwithstanding the difficulties that firms face to redirect themselves towards new opportunities and markets, firms eventually have to go through a period of transformation. Once a new technological paradigm takes off, it often supersedes the 'old' paradigm. Winter (1975) has argued that the only thing that is able to attract firms away from their routinized behaviour is 'trouble'. Trouble in this respect is described as performance that is below an organization's 'aspiration level' (Winter, 1975). This is in accordance with Singh's (1986) view that firms which are confronted with persistently lower revenues are induced to change. According to Winter (1971: 245) 'firms satisfice with respect to decision rules. That is if existing rules are functioning well, the firm is unlikely to change them: if not, search for better rules will be stimulated'. Under conditions of decline where sales are deteriorating, organizations will be forced to make the required step to the other paradigm. If organizations are not able to do so they will most likely cease to exist.

In the next three chapters we aim to validate the pattern of evolution of high-technology industries as described in this chapter. We will examine the full history of market and technological evolution of three major IT sectors and discuss the seven basic hypotheses at the end of each chapter.

NOTES

1. For a critical assessment of neo-classical theories we refer to e.g. Winter, 1964, 1971; Nelson and Winter, 1982; Dosi, 1984, 1988; Hagedoorn, 1989; Clark and Juma, 1991.
2. These criticisms amount to the claim that in textbook neo-classical economics the relationships are so idealized that they are unlikely to exist in reality.
3. A static equilibrium can be seen as a state of the world in which feedback mechanisms do not induce changes in a firm's behaviour.
4. This process of replication can be compared to the genetic inheritance process in biology (Winter, 1971; Nelson and Winter, 1982; Winter, 1990).
5. As Freeman (1991) has pointed out, the natural selection model should not be seen as a one-directional process, but should be seen as a process in which all three stages interact simultaneously.
6. These criticisms refer to the strong assumptions often embedded in economic models that technological change is exogenous. We must, however, not neglect the efforts of neo-classical theorists to endogenize technological change into their models.

7.	The selection environment consists of market and non-market forces which feed back the	likelihood	of	success	and profitability of certain technological innovations.
8.	Some authors have used the term dominant design to refer to the same concept (Abernathy and Utterback, 1978).
9.	The niche of a population can be defined as the 'combination of resource abundancies and constraints in which members arise and persist' (Hannan and Freeman, 1989: 50).
10.	For a more extensive review, see Hannan and Carroll (1992).
11.	The relationship between density and founding and mortality rates is elaboratedly discussed in terms of density dependence selection (Brittain and Freeman, 1988; Hannan and Freeman, 1988, 1989; Barnett and Amburgey, 1990; Hannan and Carroll, 1992).
12.	For a description of these strategy types see also Lambkin, 1988, and Lambkin and Day, 1989.
13.	Lamarck was the first biologist who described a process of adaptation in which a species survives by learning from and adapting itself to the environment.
14.	There is a strong debate in organizational ecology literature about the question of whether the incorporation of organizational change in an ecological framework is appropriate (see Perrow, 1986; Young, 1988; Singh and Lumsden, 1990; Baum and Singh, 1994).
15.	Barnett and Amburgey (1990) have tried to operationalize this perspective by measuring population mass instead of a mere count of numbers (see also Singh and Lumsden, 1990; Hannan and Carroll, 1992; Boone and van Witteloostuijn, 1995).
16.	One of the few evolutionary economic theorists who proposes a population perspective in evolutionary economic theory is Andersen (1994).
17.	Sometimes it is better to speak of liabilities to smallness because small size is often a more important determinant of failure than age (Aldrich and Auster, 1986).
18.	Empirical support for this assumption can be found in Freeman et al. (1983) and Singh et al. (1986).
19.	Polymorphists are generally characterized by a large diversification pattern in combination with a holding form (Hannan and Freeman, 1989).
20.	Some of the most successful r-strategists may succeed in transforming themselves into K-strategists.
21.	This view is consistent with Schumpeter's conception of the large firm as 'the most powerful engine of progress' (Schumpeter, 1942: 106).

3. The Computer Industry

Until the Second World War, there was no sign of what would emerge as the computer industry. The first efforts to develop a calculating device took place in the 17th century when Blaise Pascal developed a mechanical apparatus which was able to add and subtract figures. The only serious developments in the following two centuries came from the efforts of Charles Babbage. In 1822, Babbage created a device which could be seen as the precursor of today's special-purpose computer (the difference engine). Babbage's dream to create a general-purpose computer (the analytic engine) could have established a whole new technological paradigm. Unfortunately it was never completed, because of a lack of appropriate materials and construction know-how in those days. Its design, however, incorporated all the characteristics of a modern computer. Although some further experimenting with electro-mechanical calculators took place in the late 1930s, no significant contributions were made in this area.[1] The experiments in the 19th and early 20th centuries with electro-mechanical computers were interesting from a technological point of view but serious applications could not be found. As a result, a paradigm based on electro-mechanical computers did not really take off.

The groundwork for what would eventually unfold as the computer industry, was laid in 1907 with the invention of a signal amplifying device called a vacuum tube. This invention started a development which would eventually be known as 'the electronics revolution'. After a time of sitting on the fence, firms increasingly recognized the importance of these electronic components in calculating devices. However, the true foundation of the computer industry was not laid until the early 1940s, when vacuum-tube technology was sufficiently developed to play a part in electronic computers. At that time, the Second World War provided interesting prospects for the use of computers in military applications. A commercial market was, however, non-existent and most of the pioneering work in the computer area was therefore done by the major universities and their research institutes. In 1945 Eckert and Mauchly from the University of Pennsylvania introduced the first real general-purpose electronic computer. This computer, which was called the Electronic Numerical Integrator and Calculator (ENIAC), brought about a tremendous technological revolution. The ENIAC was based on a new paradigm of digital electronics, which made it possible to increase calculation performance of computers with a factor of roughly two thousand compared to its electro-mechanical predecessors (Flamm, 1988). Outside the US, developments in computer technology were primarily concentrated in those countries that were actively involved in the Second World War. During the war both German and British technicians managed to build working electronic computers for wartime applications such as coding and decoding messages. The British created the first real digital computer (the 'Colossus') which was used to decode German messages that were generated by the German code machine Enigma. After the Second World War government support decreased and the European countries gradually lost their prominent position in computer technology.

Of all the research groups that were active in the field of computer research, Eckert and Mauchly were the first to conceive a sound commercial market for their pioneering products. In 1946 they decided to leave the academic world in order to start the world's first commercial computer firm: the Eckert and Mauchly Computer Corporation. Soon a large number of small innovative firms would follow Eckert and Mauchly into the newly born industry. These first-mover (r-type) organizations made use of innovative and preemptive strategies in order to satisfy the needs of their technology-focused customers. Although their products were received enthusiastically by their clients, most of these small firms suffered from a number of liabilities to newness (Stinchcombe, 1965). They generally lacked the reputation advantages and financial resources of larger established firms. Moreover their preoccupation with high-risk, high-payoff technological products made their existence very uncertain. Because of the radical and frequently changing nature of technological developments, the environment could be referred to as concave and fine-grained. Under such environmental conditions death rates are likely to be very high. The rapid rate with which r-specialist firms could be established, however, enabled birth rates to offset the death rates of their more troubled competitors. The first large (K-generalist) firm to believe in a commercial computer market was the office equipment manufacturer Remington Rand. Remington Rand entered the computer business in 1950 by taking over the troubled Eckert-Mauchly Computer Corporation. The first computer that was introduced by Remington Rand in 1951 was Eckert and Mauchly's Universal Automatic Computer, the UNIVAC I. The UNIVAC I was built according to a concept developed by John von Neumann, who described a computer containing a central processor, memory devices, input-output devices and which made use of sequential programming (see Figure 3.1).[2]

The UNIVAC I, with its vacuum-tube technology and von Neumann architecture, would soon become a 'basic design' which set out the direction of future improvements in computer technology. The UNIVAC initiated a new technological paradigm that was based on two fundamental concepts: the von Neumann architecture and digital electronics. The direction set out by this technological paradigm led to the establishment of a technological regime which was based on vacuum-tube technology. Shortly after the introduction of the UNIVAC, Remington Rand reinforced its position in the computer industry by taking over another small innovative (r-type) firm called Engineering Research Associates (ERA). This firm, founded by former navy officers William Norris and Howard Engstrom, had strong ties with the US Navy and therefore opened up the important military market for Remington Rand.

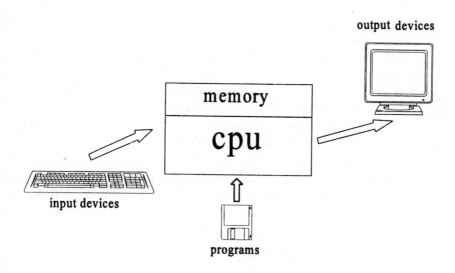

Figure 3.1 The von Neumann architecture

At that time, the computer industry was above all characterized by freely available technological knowledge and was thriving on government procurement and support. Because of the academic character of computer research, technological knowledge was exchanged at conferences and by publications in various journals. Government procurement and support made it possible for many companies to examine the feasibility and commercial prospects of computers. Moreover, the reduction in technological uncertainty that was brought about by the establishment of the new technological paradigm facilitated the entry of a number of large (K-generalist) industrial firms (including IBM) into the computer market.[3] Although direct government support declined during the 1950s, the Cold War augmented computer purchases by the United States Military. The army's preference for innovative computer products and additional government support for risky computer ventures made the computer industry a technology-driven market in which successful innovations created their own demand. As a result, many of the computer research projects focused on the innovative aspects of the computer rather than on production efficiency.

The most important reason for the growing importance of K-generalist firms in the mainframe market could be found in the product differentiation aspects associated with the reputation of the supplier (Dorfman, 1987). It is obvious that large established firms such as IBM and Remington Rand did have enormous advantages over smaller firms in that respect. Although several other large firms with enough financial resources to overcome the start-up costs in this business tried to enter the mainframe business, they usually lacked the reputation and client-base advantages of IBM and to a lesser extent Remington Rand. However, not only are reputation advantages important but also enormous investments are needed to develop and produce a complex computer system.[4] In addition an elaborate sales and maintenance network had to be set up in order to assist the client in using an unfamiliar product such as the mainframe computer. The disadvantages of small firms compared to their larger competitors led to a wave of acquisitions in the industry. At that time large numbers of small computer firms were taken over by larger firms. Notable examples in this respect are: ERA and the Eckert-Mauchly Computer Corporation, which were bought by Remington Rand; NCR, which merged with the Computer Research Corporation, and Electro-Data Corporation which was taken over by Burroughs (Brock, 1975). The acquisition of technologically advanced firms provided large firms with an important foothold in the computer industry. At that time the gradual replacement of small r-type organizations by larger K-type competitors initiated the start of an overall r to K transition of the industry.

As a typical K-type organization, IBM moved only slowly and gradually into the computer industry. After having introduced a small number of special-purpose computers in the late 1940s, IBM hesitated to enter the commercial computer market. The lack of an established commercial market for computers and the uncertainties surrounding future developments made several high-ranking IBM officials very sceptical about the computer market. However, the delivery of the UNIVAC I at the Census Bureau in 1951[5] and the growing need for computing capacity during the Korean War eventually induced IBM to move into the market for digital computers. Two years after Remington Rand's introduction of the UNIVAC I, IBM launched a large scientific computer (the 701). Despite IBM's hesitation to enter the commercial computer market, this computer turned out to be an instant success. One year after the introduction of the 701, IBM introduced a small-scale computer (the 650) which was primarily directed towards its commercial punched card machine customers. Within two years 400 IBM 650s were installed in the US. This rapid success was primarily due to IBM's large existing customer base in the punched card tabulating machine industry. With a market share of 90 per cent, and IBM's reputation and contacts, it was relatively easy for IBM to sell its customers digital computers (Brock, 1975). Only three years after its entry into the commercial computer business, IBM took over the lead in mainframe computers from its rival Remington Rand.

3.1. THE TRANSISTOR PERIOD

A major drawback of vacuum-tube-based computers was their need for continual replacement of burned-out tubes. Because unreliability was an inborn feature of vacuum tubes, and because efforts to improve the reliability and power consumption were not very successful, the technological search process was directed towards more reliable, less power-consuming devices. As a result, technological trajectories shifted towards a search for improved reliability, performance and power consumption. This shift in the direction of search would soon lead to the establishment of a new technological regime based on transistor technology. The invention of the transistor in 1947 started a profound and radical change in the computer industry. The importance of the transistor can be found in the establishment of a totally new technological regime based on semiconductor materials.[6] The (germanium) transistor, which was invented by Bardeen, Brittain and Schockly at Bell's Telephone Laboratory, was much smaller, cheaper, faster, more reliable and at the same time less power consuming than the vacuum-tube. After a period of experimenting with computers that incorporated vacuum-tube technology, the invention of the

The Dynamics of Technical Innovation

transistor in 1947, and in particular the silicon[7] transistor in 1954, radically changed the price/performance ratio of computers. The transistor, accompanied by the introduction of randomly-accessible storage media, such as ferrite core memories, made it feasible to exploit the opportunities of the computer and gave way to a considerable growth in the installed computer base (Cutaia, 1990). Large scientific mainframe computers with enormous computing capabilities could now be built at prices which could not be matched by the relatively slow and unreliable vacuum-tube computers. However, it was not until the mid-1960s (Figure 3.2), when mass-produced transistors became available, that the computer industry really took off (Harper, 1986).

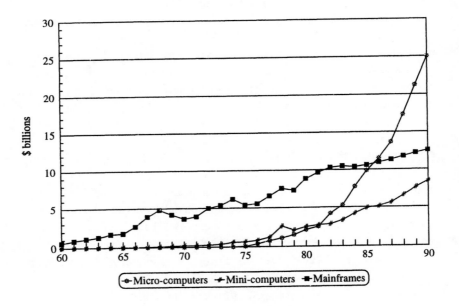

Source: CBEMA; Harrigan, 1988.

Figure 3.2 Value of shipments of major computer systems (1960-1990) (US dollars)

During the 1950s a wide variety of commercial computer products was offered by a large number of companies. Many of the commercial computers on the market were spun off from government-supported projects. Although the commercial computer market was slowly but gradually expanding, few firms invested heavily in this market. The advent of transistor technology, however, opened up opportunities for firms to compete against IBM on a technological base. The establishment of a new technological regime could render existing skills and advantages of industry leaders useless. In this light, it is not surprising that Remington Rand, facing a market share decline of 84 per cent in 4 years, was among the first commercial firms to decide upon entering the transistorized computer market (Brock, 1975). Its Solid State 80 transistorized computer which was introduced in 1958 was, however, rapidly surpassed by IBM's model 7090. The 7090 was an offspring of IBM's Stretch computer project which was undertaken in order to radically improve the performance of digital computers. Its superior features reinforced IBM's leadership in the market and established a new regime based on transistorized computers.

The importance of the commercial computer market remained modest until in the early 1960s mass-produced transistors became available. Experience curve effects and economies of scale drove down costs, and prices of transistorized components declined dramatically. Low-cost computers could now be made available for use in all kinds of business applications. Aroused by the establishment of a large commercial computer market, considerable numbers of large (K-generalist) firms entered the transistorized computer market in the early 1960s. Most of these firms came from adjacent markets such as the office equipment industry (e.g. NCR and Burroughs) or the consumer electronics industry (e.g. Philco, RCA and GE). The last important group of firms that entered the computer industry were created by technicians who worked on computers in large firms or university labs (e.g. Control Data Corporation and Digital Equipment Corporation).

Because advances that emerge from superiority and experience in the 'old' technological regime are often nullified by the establishment of a new technological regime, we would expect forces of 'creative destruction' to take place. On the basis of our integrated framework we expect an invasion of fast-to-build r-type firms which are eager to explore the opportunities in the new regime. A close examination of the computer industry, however, shows that after the establishment of the new technological regime the computer industry was still dominated by the same large firms which controlled the previous period. The eight largest computer manufacturers still occupied 98 per cent of the total market (Dorfman, 1987). IBM accounted for 74 per cent and was known as 'Snow White', whereas the others were referred to as the 'seven dwarfs'. These dwarfs included Sperry Rand, Control Data Corporation (CDC), Burroughs, Honeywell, Radio Corporation of America (RCA), National Cash Registers (NCR) and General Electric (GE). Although technological entry barriers decreased rapidly, the continued dominance of these firms clearly reflects the importance of non-technological entry barriers. Smaller companies usually did not have the resources that were needed to set up production and R&D facilities. Neither did they have the reputation and client-base advantages of their larger competitors. Clients were very reluctant to buy an unfamiliar product such as a mainframe computer from an unestablished firm, especially if this firm did not have an adequate sales and maintenance network.

In the late 1950s, IBM raised entry barriers by introducing a policy of leasing. In order to compete effectively with IBM, other firms had to set up their own leasing conditions too. Because leasing implies that it takes much longer to generate a cash flow, demand for financial resources increased enormously. Soma (1976: 26) stated that 'in the recent Industrial Reorganization Hearings, Collins testified that the first-year operation of a hypothetical firm selling its equipment would yield profits of $20 million. On the other hand, the leasing operations for the first year of that same hypothetical company would yield a net loss of $36 million'.[8] As a result, only large firms which were able to cope with major temporary losses would be able to compete effectively in this market. IBM's supremacy and the high barriers to entry during those days spurred smaller firms to find market niches in order to avoid head-on competition with IBM. One of the new entrants in the computer industry was Digital Equipment Corporation (DEC). DEC tried to bypass the entry barriers in the mainframe industry by providing low-cost small business machines. In 1960 DEC introduced the PDP-1 which became the world's first so-called mini-computer. Although he PDP-1 turned out to be a success, it was not until the advent of mass-produced integrated circuits in the mid-1960s that a considerable market for mini-computers was established.

3.2. THE INTEGRATED CIRCUITS PERIOD

The transistor-based regime was characterized by the use of discrete devices which accommodated only one device per chip. With the invention of the integrated circuit (IC) in 1959 and the discovery of the planar process,[9] a new technological regime was initiated which made possible the integration of a number of components on a single chip. Because miniaturization turned out to be a major means to achieve improved reliability and performance, miniaturization started to dominate the overall technological trajectory (see Braun and MacDonald, 1982; Steinmueller, 1987). The integrated circuit, which was originally developed at the laboratories of Texas Instruments, radically increased the diffusion of semiconductor technology in computer circuitry. As described above, the transistor was much smaller, cheaper, faster, more reliable and required less power than its predecessor. Once again these characteristics were significantly improved by the invention of the integrated circuit. The planar process facilitated large-scale, low-cost manufacturing of the integrated circuit and made it possible to integrate a substantial number of components on a single chip. The small size of these integrated circuits made it possible to incorporate them into a very broad range of products, whereas their steady declining costs made low-cost complex computer designs possible. Moreover, the gradual replacement of hardwire logic by stored program control (SPC) vastly increased the flexibility of the computer. This flexibility was further reinforced by the emergence of higher-level programming languages and the introduction of more sophisticated operating systems.

Notwithstanding substantial improvements in programmers' productivity, a major problem which confronted computer manufacturers in those days was the rapid increase in software development costs. In the mid-1960s the point was reached where software costs equalled hardware development and application costs. At that time software that was developed for one system type could not be easily transferred to another type. This considerably reduced economies of scope in software development. The potential scope and scale economies in software were, however, very high because the marginal costs of an extra copy of a software package are often negligible.[10] In its efforts to gain more from economies of scope in software development and hardware design, IBM came up with a family of computers in 1967. These so-called 360 computers featured compatible central processing units, a standard programming system and incorporated interface standards for peripherals. Although development costs of the 360 were up to five billion dollars (*Fortune*, 1966), the 360 soon became a major financial success. The ability to use the same software on all types of 360 machines provided business firms with an enormous versatility to upgrade their current 360 machines in the future. Because of its standardized components and architecture, IBM's 360 rendered economies of scope in personnel, maintenance, production, research and development and software (Dorfman, 1987). IBM's creation of a de facto standard for mainframe computers and peripherals opened up opportunities for independent peripheral manufacturers. Peripheral makers could now manufacture devices which replaced IBM's own peripherals. These peripherals were known as plug-compatible equipment (PCE) because they could be plugged into every computer of the IBM's 360 series. The newly created market for peripherals was characterized by much lower entry barriers than the mainframe computer market itself. Development costs were relatively low and IBM was not entitled to forbid their users to buy non-IBM peripherals. The combination of low development costs (due to practices of reverse engineering) and IBM's high-price strategy offered significant opportunities for plug-compatible peripheral companies to undercut IBM's prices.

Radical cost decreases which stemmed from the mass production of ICs opened up previously untapped markets. One of these markets was opened up by Digital Equipment Corporation which introduced a low-cost mini-computer, the PDP-8. For 18,000 dollars, firms which were previously unable to purchase a computer could now benefit from the advantages of electronic dataprocessing. From that time onwards, mini-computers were increasingly used in industrial applications and for communication purposes. Because initial investments and R&D costs were relatively low and head-on competition with IBM could be avoided, many firms followed DEC into the mini-computer market. The entrance of so many firms into a relatively small market, however, initiated a period of intense competition.

After a period of considerable market growth in the 1950s and early 1960s, the computer industry faced a period of more moderate technological and market growth. The further sophistication of computer users in the 1960s led to a stronger proliferation of user demand. Gradually the industry transformed from an industry that was characterized by technology-pushed technological innovation, into a demand-led industry. Over time, the integrated circuit regime had become a very strong guidepost for the further development of the computer. The combination of a large and transparent market and relatively stable technological progress made it feasible to use standardized mass-production processes. Whereas technological leadership was an important concern in the previous stages of the mainframe industry's life cycle, emphasis now shifted towards market leadership as the key to competitive success. In order to survive under such conditions, firms needed to cut costs in order to compete at lower prices. The most important cost factors of mainframe computer manufacturers were, in particular, production, marketing, development and software costs. It is clear that organizations which were able to spread these costs over a large number of products had significant advantages over other companies in such a price-sensitive market. The emphasis on large efficient organization structures and a strategy aimed at market leadership, in combination with a slowing growth rate in the computer industry, resulted in increased competition among firms. Not only did r to K transition become more important, competition between large K-type organizations also increased enormously. The assumption that continued reliance on scale economies and mass-production processes leads to a shake-out in the market was supported by the disappearance of two major mainframe manufacturers: RCA sold its computer business to Sperry Rand and General Electric sold its computer division to Honeywell. IBM's position, however, was not affected by increased competition. Its installed base and its ability to gain economies of scope from its 360 family of computers provided it with sufficient scale and scope advantages to reinforce its leadership in the market.

3.3. THE LSI AND VLSI PERIOD

Although in the previous period a large number of components could be placed on a single chip, the direction of the technological trajectory was clearly directed towards the accommodation of an even larger number of components on a chip. A breakthrough which radically increased the number of components on a chip was made by Intel in 1971. By producing a so-called microprocessor, Intel managed to build almost an entire computer on a single chip. This invention led to the advent of a new era in chip technology which would become known as the Large-Scale Integration (LSI) period. Because miniaturization was generally seen as an important characteristic of the new technological trajectory, incremental 'normal technological' progress in the semiconductor industry focused on the increase of the number of components on an integrated circuit (Table 3.1). This progress could be made because of an increase in chip size and a corresponding decrease in the size of its components. One of the first people to recognize this trajectory was Gordon Moore who observed in 1964 that the number of components within a single chip was doubling every year.[11]

Whereas previous changes of technological regimes were characterized by radical technological discontinuities which rendered existing technological competencies useless, the switch from the integrated circuit to the LSI/VLSI period was characterized by competence-enhancing technological changes. Instead of destroying the competencies of incumbent firms, the introduction of the microprocessor reinforced the position of these firms. Technological capabilities of firms in integrated circuit technology were generally seen as a prerequisite for a successful development of microprocessor-based computers. Competence-enhancing instead of competence-destroying technological discontinuities often led to a further concentration of the industry. As argued by Tushman and Anderson (1986: 37) 'competence-enhancing discontinuities consolidate leadership in a product class; the rich get richer as liabilities of newness plague new entrants'. It is clear that under these conditions it is very difficult to attack incumbent firms on a technological basis. Experience effects which arise from the cumulative production of products provide incumbent firms with clear advantages over other competitors. Given the extremely high technological and non-technological market barriers in the traditional mainframe industry, it is obvious that new firms did not manage to enter the industry at that time. Although the invention of the microprocessor could not lead to a penetration of new firms into the mainframe industry, it provided small firms with the tools to carve out new market niches which were initially disregarded by large incumbent firms.

Table 3.1 Integration of components per chip

Degree of integration	Components per chip
Small-Scale Integration (SSI)	2–50
Medium-Scale Integration (MSI)	50–5,000
Large-Scale Integration (LSI)	5,000–100,000
Very Large-Scale Integration (VLSI)	100,000–1,000,000
Ultra Large-Scale Integration (ULSI)	> 1,000,000

3.4. NEW NICHES: THE SUPER-COMPUTER AND PLUG-COMPATIBLE MAINFRAME MARKET

In the 1970s the mainframe computer market gradually developed into a highly concentrated mature market in which traditional computer manufacturers competed aggressively for market share. Because entrance into the traditional mainframe business was virtually impossible, firms tried to avoid head-on competition with IBM by entering market niches in which IBM was not (yet) active. In 1971 Control Data Corporation opened up the super-computer market by introducing a super-fast computer called the Star 100 which was aimed at the high end of the mainframe market. Although very successful from a technological perspective, commercially it was only a moderate success. The first really successful entrant in the super-computer industry was a firm called Cray Research, which was established by former CDC chief engineer Seymour Cray. By introducing a computer which was far more powerful than IBM's fastest computers, Cray created a market for totally new applications.[12] Soon, Cray Research would manage to take more than 75 per cent of the world market of super-computers (Forester, 1993).

In the 1970s we also witnessed the rise of the plug-compatible mainframe business. The idea behind the plug-compatible mainframe was to design an IBM-compatible processor unit, complement it with already available plug-compatible peripherals, and bundle it into a complete system. In 1970, Gene M. Amdahl left IBM in order to found the first plug-compatible mainframe company. In 1972 additional financial support was provided to Amdahl by the Japanese manufacturer Fujitsu. The aim was to provide high-performance mainframes for a fraction of the prices IBM charged.[13] In 1975 Amdahl delivered its first computer. The low-priced high-performance device immediately lured a large number of buyers away from IBM. Fujitsu's support for Amdahl coincided with the entrance of many Japanese firms into the international computer market. In order to avoid direct competition with IBM and to gain access to the European and US markets, Japanese companies strengthened their ties with European and US-based firms. The most common strategy in this respect was the use of Original Equipment Manufacturing (OEM)[14] agreements. Examples of OEM agreements include alliances between Siemens–Fujitsu, Bull–NEC Amdahl–NEC, Olivetti–NEC, BASF–NEC, ICL–NEC and Olivetti–Hitachi.

The invention of the microprocessor also made it feasible to introduce new types of small computers. The microprocessor equipped mini-computer makers with a powerful tool for a further decrease in the size and costs of their machines. The extremely rapidly improving price/performance (see Figure 3.3) ratio of small computers opened up a large number of previously untapped markets. Whereas in the previous period mini-computers were primarily used for manufacturing and communication purposes, the incorporation of the microprocessor made the mini-computer an attractive tool for all kinds of business applications. This led to a rapid diffusion of the mini-computer after the mid-1970s.

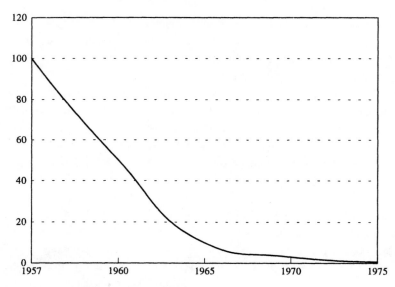

Source: Flamm, The Brookings Institute.

Figure 3.3 Price/performance improvements of computer systems.

Further development of the microprocessor in the 1970s led to even smaller computer systems, so-called micro-computers. These computers were equipped with user-friendly displays and facilitated the widespread use of computers in businesses and at home. The first commercial micro-computer was introduced in 1975 by a firm called Micro Instrumentation and Telemetry Systems (MITS). It was called the Altair micro-computer and was based on Intel's first 8-bit microprocessor. The Altair was sold as a construction kit for about $400. Its low price and innovative features made it very popular with a large number of hobbyists and technicians. Inspired by the introduction of this micro-computer, several computer clubs were initiated in the US. In one of those computer clubs, Steve Jobs and Steve Wozniak unveiled their own computer (the Apple I) which was based on parts supplied by Atari and Hewlett-Packard. Motivated by the enthusiasm of the other members of the computer club, they started production of the Apple I with a mere $1300 in cash. Although its creators at first were severely confined by a limited amount of cash, the Apple I soon became an instant success.[15] This led to a wave of new entrants into the newly created micro-computer market. Typically, IBM's reaction to the opportunities in the new market was relatively slow. Attempts are often made to overcome the disadvantages of large incumbent firms in dealing with new opportunities in the market by setting up an independent subsidiary which takes care of the new market opportunity. Free from cultural or bureaucratic forces, these ventures are able to deal effectively with new developments in the market. In the early 1980s IBM used this strategy in its efforts to bring a personal computer on to the market. IBM created an independent division which had almost complete freedom to build a personal computer. In 1981 IBM's micro-computer division came up with a technologically unsophisticated and relatively expensive computer, the IBM PC. In spite of its relatively low price/performance ratio, IBM's marketing skills and reputation enabled it once again to dominate this market. Because IBM disclosed the design features of its personal computer to encourage software development, it was relatively easy for other firms to 'clone' IBM's personal computer. By buying off-the-shelf components, hundreds of start-up firms were able to enter the 'clone' PC market with only minor investments.

However, because of the 1984–85 recession in the computer industry a shake-out was well under way. At the outset, entry barriers to the micro-computer market were almost nil. In the mid-1980s these barriers started to rise rapidly because of the growing importance of marketing and distribution networks. The crowded personal computer market unleashed a fight for shelf space at the computer stores. As a result, the micro-computer market would soon be known as the most competitive computer market of all. IBM's success in the personal computer market and its disclosure of design features induced hundreds of small firms to enter the newly created market for IBM-compatible products such as computers, programs and peripherals. Because of market-share competition and subsequent price wars a phase of consolidation and shake-out would soon characterize this part of the industry as well. In a reaction to IBM's attack on its dominant position in the micro-computer industry, Apple introduced a new computer (the Macintosh) in 1984.[16] The Macintosh featured a graphical user-friendly operating system and was much more powerful than its much more expensive predecessor, the Lisa. Due to the rapid diffusion of the micro-computer, users increasingly felt the need to connect their computers. This led to the emergence of a large number of local- and wide-area networks (LANs and WANs). LANs are types of networks that are used to share data between several types of computers within a building or a campus where information can be transmitted and received without making use of the public telecommunications system, whereas WANs are networks that connect offices in different geographical areas. The introduction of these networks made it possible to use so-called distributed processing techniques (Figure 3.4). Distributed processing can be seen as a form of parallel processing which makes use of geographically dispersed computer systems that are linked through transmission media and which make use of each other's data and processing capabilities. The need for communication between various computer systems would soon lead to a number of communication and software standards. At the same time a number of relatively cheap standardized application software packages became available. These packages reduced the need for in-house programming capabilities and made available hundreds of sophisticated software packages to the public (see also Steinmueller, 1994). Furthermore, advances in micro-electronics facilitated the replacement of magnetic core memories by much faster, high capacity integrated circuits. Because memory devices were generally seen as the 'bottleneck' of computers, the incorporation of these devices facilitated a considerable increase in the speed of computers and fostered a rapid growth of the installed base of micro-computers.

3.5. RECENT TRENDS: DECLINE OR REJUVENATION?

Ever since the development of the vacuum tube, the computer industry has been characterized by rapid technological progress and a dynamic market structure. Today, however, we are witnessing a rapid maturation of the computer industry. Signs of the maturing character of the computer industry can be found in: slower growth rates, declining profit margins, the standardization of products, an increased sophistication of users, globalization and a further consolidation of the industry. After decades of double-digit growth figures, revenue growth is currently slowing down (see Rappaport and Halevi, 1991). Saturation of demand started in the early 1980s in the mainframe industry where replacement purchases started to overtake new procurements. Today even the relatively young mini-computer market is transforming into a replacement market. The only growth potential which is left is found in the rapidly rising workstation market and to a lesser extent in the PC business. Although the rise in the total number of machines sold in the computer market is still high, this rise is mostly due to the sales of relatively low-priced PCs.Market saturation and a shift towards lower-priced computers are primarily responsible for a slowing growth rate measured in sales volume. It looks like carrying capacity is gradually being approached.

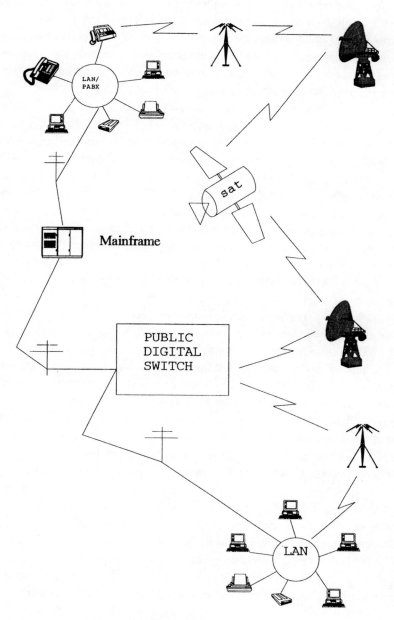

Figure 3.4 A distributed processing network

Double-digit growth rates in almost all segments in the mid-1980s have made way for single-digit and sometimes even negative growth rates in thecurrent period (Figure 3.5). Moreover, price decreases of over 20 to 25 per cent annually indicate that demand must rise by an equal amount to prevent the computer market from shrinking. A growing degree of saturation of the market, however, makes it very difficult to achieve such a growth rate.

A second indication of the maturing character of the computer industry can be found in the drive towards standardization. At present, there is a clear transition going on away from proprietary systems towards more 'open systems'. Standardization was introduced into the computer industry in the late 1960s with the introduction of IBM's 360 family of computers. Because IBM had an installed number of computers which was several times larger than that of its competitors it experienced significant cost and user lock-in[17] advantages. Since then IBM's dominant position has enabled it to impose its proprietary standard as the market standard. Because other proprietary computer makers did not have the opportunity to benefit from such a large installed base, they faced severe difficulties in contesting IBM's domination in the market. In an attempt to attack IBM's domination of the industry, several computer manufacturers joined forces in the early 1980s in order to come up with a non-proprietary industry standard. These efforts would lead to strong support for AT&T's UNIX operating system and the OSI (Open Systems Interconnection) system.[18]

The process towards standardization is further reinforced by the increasing globalization that takes place in the business community. Communication needs between different departments and divisions demand connectivity and compatibility between heterogeneous computers in different geographical areas. One of the factors which led to such a degree of globalization of the industry is found in the extremely high R&D and equipment costs that characterize the industry. Measured by R&D expenditures as a percentage of sales, the computer industry is surpassed only by the heavily government-sponsored aircraft and missiles industry (Flamm, 1988). Both equipment and R&D costs are still rising rapidly due to the growing complexity of technology and the exploitation of mass-production techniques, while at the same time, product lives are shortening due to increased competition. Hence, these costs can only be recouped by firms which are able to capture a significant share of the market. In order to achieve such a market share, firms have to expand internationally. In other words, the drive towards lower costs leads to the invasion of global markets in order to spread R&D and production costs over a larger volume of sales.[19]

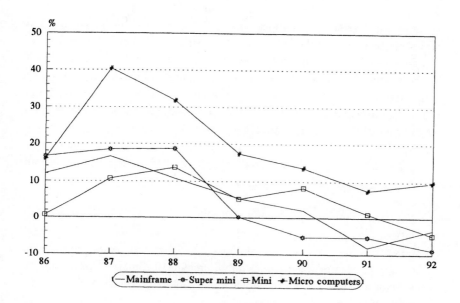

Source: Gartner Group, 1993.

Figure 3.5 Growth of revenues in annual percentages (1986–1992)

A fourth characteristic of a mature industry is the further sophistication of users. Ever since the Second World War the computer industry has been driven by technology. Technological changes which were initiated from within or from outside the industry augmented demand and opened up opportunities for new applications and for new markets. Today's computer market is, however, increasingly characterized by sophisticated users who have the ability to steer the direction of technological developments. The maturing character of the industry has important implications for the structure of competition in the computer industry. The transition towards open systems increasingly transforms computers into commodities. This transformation brings about considerable price competition in the market. Under such conditions cost structures become more important than differentiation policies. This will in particular be advantageous to large firms which are able to spread their costs over a larger number of products and which employ mass-production techniques. Whereas entry barriers are rapidly rising for broadline suppliers, the trend towards open systems also opens up a number of opportunities for smaller firms to establish themselves in niche markets. Standardization makes it possible to enter the commercial computer market without the need to sell an entire product line of computers. All kinds of small firms are able to invade the industry by selling parts, small computers, communication systems or peripherals. In such an industry large routinized firms dominate the technological and economic developments, whereas small firms survive in market niches or by providing supplementary services. Firms which are not able to gain cost leadership advantages or differentiation advantages are found to be 'stuck in the middle' (Porter, 1980, 1985) and face competition from firms that are able to gain from one of those advantages.

Continuous declining prices combined with rapid advances in speed, size and capacity in the past decades have diminished the opportunities in the current computer paradigm. Whereas technological change in the 1960s and 1970s opened up a number of opportunities for the creation of completely new markets, in the 1980s new markets have seldom been found. Ever since the construction of the UNIVAC I in 1951, computers have been built according to the rules of the von Neumann paradigm. Now, after 40 years, the limits of this paradigm seem to have been approached. This is exemplified by the fact that companies are increasingly confronted with diminishing returns from their R&D efforts. In order to achieve the same amount of technological progress an increasing amount of resources has to be invested in R&D. Slower technological growth rates are most clearly observed in the technologically most advanced and best-developed sectors of the computer industry. In the mainframe computer industry the capacity of computers in the 1980s has increased only by a mere 7 per cent, whereas in the relatively new personal computer industry capacity increased over 30 per cent annually (*Computable*, 17 August 1990). If we accept the view that the search for a new paradigm increases with the difficulties of finding satisfactory solutions in the current paradigm, we might witness a paradigmatic shift in the near future.

Signs of such rejuvenation can be found in two distinct but related areas. The origin of the first factor which might lead to a paradigmatic shift is found in the digitalization of the telecommunications network, which enables computers to communicate with each other and which provides opportunities for a whole range of new services. Digitalization of the telecommunications network implies that signals (e.g. computer data) can be transferred in digital form from one point to another through means of digital switching and digital transmission equipment. The ability to communicate with other computers will become of the utmost importance for a further acceleration of the performance of computers. A paradigmatic change away from centralized computers towards distributed computing environments in which computers share resources, data and make use of each other's processing abilities creates enormous opportunities for the computer industry. It will undoubtedly result in an increased standardization of computer and communication products and opens up opportunities for entirely new services in the digital network. With the introduction of the Integrated Service Digital Network (ISDN) an even larger number of new services will be introduced. In ISDN voice, data and graphics can be sent to other computers in digital form through new transmission media.[20] Radical improvements in technology and the use of new processing architectures will be needed in order to equip computers with the processing and storage capacities that are needed to support these kinds of applications. It was noted by Cutaia (1990: 42) that 'these forms of data require approximately 30 times the amount of information flow through the system, require 10–15 times the storage per end user, and require system processor(s) to supply approximately 64 MIPS capacity growth from 1987 to the year 2000'. The very high requirements needed to support voice/data/images applications will continually challenge the abilities of current generation computers and telecommunications equipment. In order to cope with these huge demands for computing and storage capacity, computer manufacturers are searching for new ways to improve the speed of their computers. At present, parallel computers seem to be well equipped to satisfy these needs. Hence, parallel computers might represent the second part of the new paradigm. Parallel computers can be seen as computers which incorporate a number of microprocessors, each working on parts of a problem at the same time. Most super-computer manufacturers have already successfully introduced parallel computing techniques in the past few years. A rapid acceptance of the parallel computing paradigm will, however, primarily depend on the availability of software for these computers. Because parallel computers require totally new programming techniques, past experience and lock-in advantages of current users will be rendered useless. Moreover, totally new markets will be opened up by advances in distributed computing. This may bring about forces of creative destruction which might challenge the position of current industry leaders. Undoubtedly, an effective participation in this new paradigm requires significant knowledge of communication systems, software and semiconductors.

3.6. IBM'S DOMINATION OF THE INDUSTRY

Whereas IBM continues to dominate virtually every segment of the market, its total market share is gradually declining. In the mainframe industry, the Japanese broadline suppliers (e.g. Fujitsu, Hitachi, Amdahl) have captured a significant share of the market through their efficient production and marketing of IBM-compatible systems. Their low-cost production structures, government support and the use of OEM strategies for the invasion of new markets has made these firms very successful. Whereas no Japanese firm was able to penetrate the top ten of the computer industry by the early 1980s, no less than three Japanese firms managed to enter the top five in 1992. Fujitsu ranked second, whereas NEC and Hitachi ranked third and fifth respectively (see Figure 3.6).

IBM has retained its position as the industry leader. Although the establishment of a de facto standard in the mainframe industry drastically lowered entry barriers which arose from lock-in effects, a large increase in production and R&D costs has raised financial entry barriers once again. Therefore only firms with sufficient financial resources are able to enter the industry. The enormous financial resources which are needed to overcome the huge entry barriers are exemplified by Digital Equipment's R&D spending of over $1 billion for its VAX 9000 computer system. Whereas both US and Japanese firms tend to operate on the basis of a well-developed technological base, all the major European computer makers tend to rely on foreign technological inputs (Malerba et al., 1991). Olivetti, Siemens and ICL (acquired by Fujitsu) rely on Japanese technological knowledge for their mainframe products. The French national champion Groupe Bull, relies on mainframe technology from its US subsidiary, Honeywell.

Today the mini-computer market is gradually branching out in three directions; traditional mini-computers, super-minis and workstations. Because the traditional mini-market is dominated by the industry giants IBM and DEC, small firms have started to explore new market opportunities at both the high and the low end of the mini-computer market. At the high end of the market, so-called super-mini-computers are currently challenging traditional mainframe computers. Fast growth of this segment is expected due to an increasing demand for powerful client/server applications and large graphical applications.

At the other end of the mini-computer market, specialist firms such as Sun Microsystems, Silicon Graphics and Apollo (HP) carved out new markets for so-called workstations. Workstations are increasingly used for technical applications as well as for local-area network servers. The introduction of both super-mini-computers and workstations has blurred the traditional distinction between personal computers, mini-computers and mainframes. In contrast to IBM's market share in mini-computers, its dominant position in the micro-

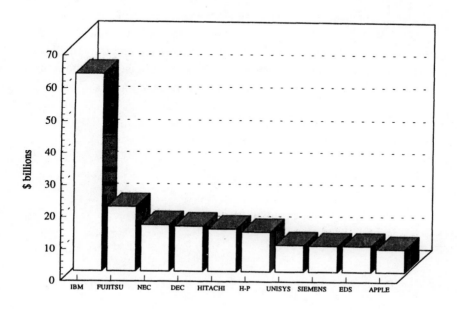

Source: Gartner Group, 1993.

Figure 3.6 Data-processing revenues of major companies (1992)

computer market is gradually decreasing (Figure 3.7). Whereas the early 1980s were characterized by a large number of proprietary PC makers, today most of these PC makers experience severe drawbacks in sales and therefore redirect their focus towards IBM compatibility. In the late 1980s technological developments in components and LCD screens made it possible to introduce portable computers. The early portable computer market was dominated by a US company called Zenith.[21] Japanese firms were particularly well placed to achieve a dominant position in the portable computer market. Their leading positions in critical areas such as LCD displays, diskdrives and memory chips, and their ability to manufacturer very small complex components made Japanese firms particularly well equipped to produce small portable computers for the newly emerging market. One of the first Japanese firms to enter the portable computer market was Toshiba. In 1990 Toshiba managed to take over the leading position in the US market from Zenith. At that time Toshiba held 21 per cent of the US laptop market followed by Zenith and Compaq each holding 10 per cent of the market. Other important competitors included Sharp and NEC, which followed closely with 9 and 8 per cent of the US market respectively (Forester, 1993). With the advent of even smaller, so-called 'notebook' computers, the laptop market experiences even more market growth and is well under way to achieve a market size comparable to the desktop micro-computer market.

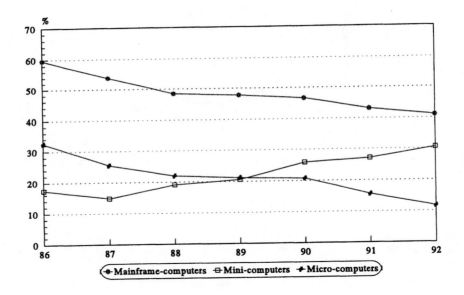

Source: Gartner Group, 1994.
Figure 3.7 IBM's market share

IBM once again failed to make use of the opportunities in the early portable computer market. In spite of its ability to gain economies of scale and scope in production, R&D and marketing, IBM turned into a bureaucratic rigid organization that was unable to meet new demands in the market. IBM seems to have retained its traditional emphasis on the relatively slow-growing mainframe and mini-computer markets. Its once dominant position in one of the most promising markets, the micro-computer market, seems to be increasingly attacked by other more flexible organizations. In another fast-growing market, the workstation market, IBM takes an intermediate position following behind specialist workstation manufacturers Silicon Graphics and Sun Microsystems. IBM's inability to participate successfully in the most dynamic (and most promising) new markets was exemplified by its major losses in 1992 and 1993. These losses have induced IBM to take on a major reorganization programme which dramatically ended IBM's commitment to lifetime employment of its employees. During 1993 more than one-fifth of its employees were laid off and more layoffs followed in 1994. IBM, however, is not alone in its inability to take advantage of newly emerging market opportunities. Whereas traditional US computer manufacturers are still a dominant force in mainframe and mini-computers, only a few of them have been able to gain a significant market share in the fastest-growing markets for workstations, portable and micro-computer markets.

3.7. DISCUSSION

In the second chapter we posed a number of hypotheses about the evolution of complex industrial systems over time. We assumed that at the time of the founding of a new industrial system both market and technological uncertainties were too high to be accepted by commercial firms. For commercial firms it will be very difficult to persuade investors and financial institutions to support their entrance into such a newly born market. Therefore, universities and government institutions are expected to play the role of incubators of the new technology (*Hypothesis 1*). In the computer industry this role was played by universities that carried out government-financed projects. The most important projects were carried out by, among others: Jay Forester of MIT, who was working on the Whirlwind I; Howard Aitken from Harvard, working on the Harvard MARK I; and J. Presper Eckert and John W. Mauchly from the University of Pennsylvania, who were building the first general-purpose electronic computer, the ENIAC. In Germany and Britain, government support was used to build computers for wartime applications. The importance of universities and government institutions at that time seems to support our first hypothesis that the role of these organizations as incubators of a new technology is very important.

After the 'incubator period' we expect that a number of flexible fast-to-build organizations (r-specialists) will enter the market (*Hypothesis 2*). This hypothesis is supported by our findings in the computer industry. During the late 1940s and early 1950s we saw the entrance of a large number of newly established organizations into the market. Most of these organizations were spin-offs from universities. The Eckert–Mauchly Computer Corporation, Engineering Research Associates (ERA), Electro-Data Corporation and the Computer Research Corporation are the most well-known exponents of these r-type organizations. Those small organizations carried out innovative government-sponsored research projects. The ease with which these organizations could be established enabled a considerable number of new organizations to enter the market at this stage. At that time competitive strategies were aimed at satisfying the needs of technology-focused customers. Military institutions, especially, showed a keen interest in the new technology. This resulted in a technology-driven industry in which some firms were able to grow rapidly and managed to reap high profits from their highly innovative products, whereas other organizations suffered from liabilities of newness and were soon dissolved.

One of the products of these r-type organizations, Eckert and Mauchly's UNIVAC I, would soon be recognized as a technological guidepost for future developments in technology. In the second chapter we assume that the establishment of a basic design leads to a substitution of radical technological development by incremental cumulative improvements along a specific technological path or trajectory (*Hypothesis 3*). In the computer industry we saw that ever since the invention of the UNIVAC I the majority of computers were built according to the rules set out by John von Neumann. The second aspect of the new technological paradigm was the use of digital components. These components are, although in a changed form, still in use today. It is remarkable to see that in such a dynamic industry as the computer industry, the two basic pillars of the technological paradigm have remained essentially unchanged for over 40 years now. This provides strong support to the hypothesis that once a technological paradigm has been established technological progress is guided by specific technological paths or trajectories.

In our fourth hypothesis we argue that the standardized direction of technological progress as set out by the new technological paradigm would open up opportunities for larger, so-called K-type organizations, which are able to benefit from the economies of scale and scope that can be gained from their elaborated and efficient organizational structures. The first K-type firm to enter the computer industry was Remington Rand. Its early success would soon lead to the entrance of a number of other K-generalist firms from adjacent markets. Our integrated framework predicts that the reduction in both market and technological uncertainty as a result of the establishment of the new technological paradigm would lead to a state in which K-generalists and polymorphists are able to outcompete r-specialists (*Hypothesis 4*). The start of the so-called r to K transition is clearly illustrated in the computer industry by a wave of acquisitions. All the major r-type organizations that we described above were taken over by large K-type competitors during the 1950s. K-type organizations are often equipped with a huge sales force and an efficient production apparatus. Moreover, their reputation and client base in adjacent markets enables them to gain rapid social acceptance (legitimation). The entrance of these K-generalist firms into the market could be seen as a confirmation of the establishment of the new industry. However, the lack of reliability and performance of the vacuum-tube components prevented the market from developing into a mass market. Inabilities to make sufficient improvements in the current technology base led a number of firms to broaden their search procedures in other directions.

The first technological regime shift in the computer industry was brought about by the invention of the transistor. We expected forces of 'creative destruction' to take place because incumbent firms could now be attacked on a technological base. Incumbent organizations are expected to have severe difficulties in redirecting their focus towards the new regime. This should give way to an invasion of fast-to-build innovative (r-type) organizations that are able to benefit from the new opportunities in the market. The computer industry, however, shows a significantly different picture. All of the major K-type firms which had dominated the previous period were able to redirect their focus to the new regime and were able to dominate the transistor period in the same way they had dominated the vacuum-tube period. The same large firms which had dominated the previous period now accounted for 98 per cent of the transistor market. Even in a so-called 'high-tech' industry, non-technological entry barriers were of more importance to the industry than technological entry barriers. Huge start-up costs, reputation and client-base advantages and IBM's leasing policy made it very difficult for new organizations to compete against the larger incumbent firms. In fact, the r to K transition which started in the vacuum-tube period accelerated in the following period.

It was not until the advent of the integrated circuit and the invention of the microprocessor that r-type organizations found opportunities to compete effectively in the computer market. Typically their importance was not found in the invasion of the mainframe computer market but in opening up new markets. Although increasing competitive pressures forced two major competitors, RCA and General Electric, to abandon the computer market, five of the seven traditional leaders retained their dominant position in the mainframe market. The mainframe market had grown into a transparent market with relatively stable technological progress. The increasing importance of static economies of scale and scope once again increased the relative importance of large established firms. This is in line with the assumption in *Hypothesis 5* that increased density raises competitive pressures and increases the r to K transition in the market. IBM proved to be a master in taking advantage of these static economies by introducing its IBM 360 series of computers. Other firms faced more problems in dealing with such a competitive environment and a first shake-out in the mainframe industry was well under way. The following period, which is referred to in the text as the LSI and VLSI period, was characterized by cumulative competence-enhancing technological progress. Because technological competence in integrated circuit technology was a prerequisite for a successful competitive position in the new period, the power of well-established incumbent firms was not challenged by new organizations. High barriers to entry in the mainframe market, IBM's power to control the market and the emphasis on price-based competition gave small new firms not a single opportunity to compete effectively in this market. As a result, the attention of new firms concentrated on promising new market niches. r-type organizations opened up the mini-computer market (DEC), the super-computer market (Amdahl) and the micro-computer market (Apple). At first, these markets were only small niches but they would soon grow into important markets themselves. In line with our expectation, as put forward in *Hypothesis 6*, specialist firms were the first to enter these specific market niches. The emergence of a mass market is generally seen as one of the preconditions that make a strategy of segmentation viable. However, in the computer industry there was another important factor that influenced the emergence of multiple market niches. The emergence of new niches was also largely due to the establishment of new technological regimes which made it possible to manufacture smaller (mini- and micro-) and faster (super-) computers.

Today's market-place is characterized by a rapid maturation of the industry. Slowing growth rates in all the industry sectors increased competition and reduced profit margins. Emphasis on standardized products induces firms to compete on price instead of performance. Because technological progress in the current paradigm seems to approach its natural limits and carrying capacity of the niche is gradually approached, firms have to broaden their search strategies in order to find new opportunities in the market. Decreasing opportunities in the existing paradigm may well lead to the replacement of the current paradigm by a paradigm based on parallel computers and distributed computing environments. Although a K to r transition has not (yet) taken place, the success of innovative r-type organizations such as Maspar, NCube, Convergent Technologies Inc., Thinking Machines Inc. and other firms[22] that ride on the success of parallel computers, and the recent losses of incumbent firms, may be an indication of the rise in r-type organizations at the expense of K-types. The research programmes of almost all of the major computer manufacturers, however, reveal that they are all involved in research on parallel computing and distributed computing architectures. Therefore it is very unlikely that they will not succeed in transforming their strategies when a paradigmatic shift takes place and a K to r transition occurs (*Hypothesis 7*).

To summarize, the integrated framework as presented in the second chapter was able to describe fairly accurately the technological and market developments in the history of the computer industry. The framework, however, seems to overstate the destructive forces of technological change and was found to underestimate the various non-technological forces that enabled firms to master changing environments. Although technological regime shifts in the computer industry were not able to initiate a gale of creative market destruction, the expected paradigmatic shift will undoubtedly challenge the flexibility and adaptiveness of incumbent organizations.

NOTES

1. The most well-known electro-mechanical computer was created by Aiken in 1944 (the Harvard Mark I).
2. This concept, known as the von Neumann design, has served as a 'technological guidepost' for the past 40 years.
3. Most of these large firms had their roots in adjacent markets such as the office equipment industry.
4. Mainframe computers were sold as complete systems. Computer manufacturers therefore had to invest in the production of CPUs, peripherals and in software development.
5. Ever since 1890, the Census Bureau was one of the major customers of IBM's punched card equipment.
6. Its relevance is underscored by the fact that semiconductor materials are still the most important material in use today.

7. The silicon transistor operated much faster and could be used under a much wider temperature range than the germanium transistor (Swann, 1986).
8. Hearings on S. 1167 Before the Subcommittee on Antitrust and Monopoly of the Senate Committee on the Judiciary, 93rd Cong., 2nd Sess. pt. 7, at 5383 (23-26 July, 1974) (The Industrial Reorganization Act The Computer Industry) (Statement by Eugene K. Collins, Director of Research, Evans and Co., NY)
9. The planar process was a revolutionary production process which could be used to produce cost-effective transistors. The planar process would soon become suited for batch processing of integrated circuits.
10. This is due to the extremely low costs of duplicating the program.
11. This observation, known as Moore's law, still holds today.
12. Cray's success was therefore in a large part due to the fact that Cray, unlike CDC, did not challenge IBM directly.
13. The first Amdahl computer had a 50 per cent better performance/price ratio than IBM's most competitive machine (Dorfman, 1987: 92).
14. Through an OEM agreement one firm supplies another firm with components or complete products, and the final product is then sold under the brand name of the acquiring company.
15. The Apple I would soon be superseded by its successor, the Apple II.
16. Ever since the introduction of the Apple I, Apple has successfully penetrated the market with the Apple II and III models.
17. User lock-in advantages arise from the considerable switching costs which are involved in switching from one make of computer to another. For a more extensive review of lock-in effects in the computer industry, see Greenstein (1991).
18. OSI provides a conceptual design which describes ways to interconnect previously incompatible computers.
19. See Chapter 8 for an elaborated discussion of the globalization process.
20. See Steinmueller and David (1994) for a more elaborated discussion on ISDN.
21. Zenith's best -selling computer (the Z–181) was, however, built by the Japanese manufacturer Sanyo (Forester, 1993).
22. After a period of fierce growth, some of these companies had to cope with some major drawbacks in terms of decreasing profits.

4. The Telecommunications Industry[1]

Although the telecommunications revolution is often referred to as a phenomenon which started after the Second World War, basic means of communication over long distances had already been in use for several thousand years. Whereas the early Indians made use of huge fires, the Romans depended on high towers for sending information to distant locations. The most well-known communication system which made use of visual telegraphy was designed by Claude Chappe during the French Revolution. Chappe constructed a system which consisted of towers containing semaphore arms to send messages. These towers covered a distance of over 3,000 miles and made available rapid communications throughout the country. Soon this system would turn out to be a key factor for the French military success in those days. Commercial applications, however, could not be found easily.

The birth of the 'modern' telecommunications industry can be traced back to the invention of the first practical telegraph in England by Cooke and Wheaterstone in 1837. Their telegraphic instrument made use of electrical signals which caused a needle to point to a specific letter (Brock, 1981). A few months later Samuel Morse patented a somewhat similar device which made use of dot-and-dash-based codes. Morse demonstrated his telegraph by transmitting messages in code from Washington to Baltimore in 1844. This event marked the start of a new technological paradigm based on the transmission of electrical signals over long distances. Morse's telegraph system would soon become a basic design which would have a major impact on future developments in telegraphy. At that time telegraphic codes were transmitted over copper wire cables. The resistance of the wires, however, made reliable long-distance telegraphy very difficult. As a result research was directed primarily towards the improvement of distance and reliability.

In contrast to regulatory policies in the rest of the world[2] the US telegraph system was operated by privately owned firms. Within 15 years after the invention of the telegraph more than 50 small (r-type) private telegraph companies were active in the United States (Belitsos and Misra, 1986). In spite of the active involvement of small firms in the industry, future demand for such an expensive service as the telegraph made larger firms very sceptical about entering the business. Early demand for telegraphic services came primarily from time-sensitive customers such as stock-market traders and newspaper agencies, and for railroad purposes. Alongside these commercial clients the government made increasing use of the telegraph for military applications. This small but well-paying group of customers provided a large incentive for further development and expansion of the systems and enabled the entrance of new organizations into the market. The newly created telegraph firms operated under a large number of different patents. In the early 1850s the Morse patent would establish itself as the most important patent. Infringement suits against competing patents resulted in the elimination of a large number of active firms (Brock, 1981). One of the largest producers and exploiters of telegraph wires and equipment (the Western Union Telegraph Company) made use of its rights on the Morse patent and its acquired system economies of scale to monopolize the market. Its exclusive railroad contracts enabled Western Union to construct by far the largest telegraph network in the entire world. In the mid-1850s extensive telegraph systems covered most of the US and Europe.[3] Although many small telegraph companies were active in the US at that time, Western Union would rapidly succeed in the establishment of an almost monopolistic position in the last half of the 19th century. However, a major challenge to its until then uncontested position was well under way in the form of a new technological innovation, namely the telephone.

4.1. THE TELEPHONE

Following the invention of the telegraph, the telecommunications industry gained further impetus through the invention of the telephone by Alexander Graham Bell in 1875. Bell filed his basic patent on the telephone only a few hours before Elisha Gray filed a similar invention. Although at first its commercial value was very low, it would eventually result in the establishment of a new technological paradigm based on analogue voice communications. This new paradigm would soon remain side by side with the telegraph paradigm for a considerable period. At the outset the telephone was regarded merely as a complementary product which could be used only in a restricted number of specific application areas. Telephone equipment was not very advanced at that time and telephone applications were severely handicapped because they could be used for short-distance services only. Whereas the telegraph was already well equipped to deal with long-distance communications, the telephone was only effective at distances of less than 20 miles.

In spite of its limited functionality and its inability to operate at longer distances, Bell's telephone soon evolved into a basic design which would serve as a technological guidepost and which would remain to a large extent unchanged for more than a century. Bell started its commercial business as a manufacturing company selling telephones to the public. At the outset private lines connected the telephones of two premises. However, soon people recognized that the value of a telephone could be enhanced tremendously by connecting existing telephone lines to each other. In order to provide switching services, so-called operating companies were franchised by Bell. In 1878 the first of these operating companies was formed in New England. During the same year telegraph giant Western Union entered the telephone industry through the formation of the American Speaking Telephone Company. In a very short period Western Union would grow into Bell's major competitor. Western Union operated on the basis of Elisha Gray's patents and took advantage of its control of a large network of telegraph lines. In spite of its relatively late start, Western Union rapidly established a prominent position in the telephone industry. This was possible because telephone and telegraph devices could be served over the same lines and because Western Union did not allow Bell's telephones to be connected to its enormous network. Moreover, its huge financial assets and reputation advantages soon enabled Western Union to outcompete Bell.

The inability to compete effectively with such a powerful corporation induced Bell to file a suit against Western Union for infringement of Bell's patents. Western Union, considering the telephone business as merely a small niche market, agreed to exit the telephone industry and gave Bell access to all its telephone patents in return for a percentage of Bell's rents and royalties. The Bell company committed itself not to enter the market for telegraphy until the expiration of its basic telephone patents in 1894. This agreement, signed in 1879, provided Bell with an almost monopolistic position in the telephone industry. The agreement is often referred to as the second of two critical mistakes in the history of Western Union. The first mistake was its refusal of Bell's offer in 1877 to buy all Bell's basic patents for $100,000. By signing the agreement with Bell in 1879, Western Union failed to recognize the opportunities of the telephone outside the limited areas in which it played a role in those days. The decision to sign the agreement was, however, not as remarkable as it seemed. At that time the telephone was barely functional and distances of 20 miles were achieved only under the best possible conditions (Wasserman, 1985). One year after signing the agreement the Bell company transformed itself into the American Bell Company. Western Union redirected its focus towards the telegraph industry and through a merger with its major competitor the American Union Telegraph company, it was able to establish a virtual monopoly in that market. In 1881 the American Bell Company strengthened its manufacturing capability by acquiring a controlling stake in Western Electric, which traditionally operated as Western Union's major supplier. One year later the American Bell Company signed an agreement with Western Electric in which Western Electric agreed to sell its products exclusively to Bell.

The first technological regime to emerge within the telephone paradigm was based on essentially the same transmission and switching technology as the telegraph. Copper wires were used to transmit analogue voice signals and switching was done manually. Because both telegraph and telephone technologies experienced the same difficulties, research on transmission equipment was also directed towards lowering the resistance of the transmission wires and improving the distance which could be achieved. At the same time efforts in switching equipment focused on the improvement of the efficiency with which signals could be routed. At first the switchboards were operated by men who were later replaced by women. This 'process innovation' proved to be very successful. According to an executive of an American telephone company in 1881, women 'are steadier, do not drink beer and are always on hand' (Rhodes, 1929: 154). However, the limits in technological opportunity of the technological regime based on manual switching would soon be reached. This is illustrated by the fact that the cost of manual switching increased enormously with each new subscriber. Every increase in the number of subscribers made it necessary to connect more circuits to one another. In many cases a call had to be routed through a number of exchanges before it was transferred. This so-called 'switchboard problem' (Mueller, 1989) was so immense that a Bell telephone manager complained that 'so far as he could see, all he had to do was get enough subscribers and the company would go broke' (Pool et al., 1977: 130). As usual in the case of diminishing returns from technological progress within a specific regime, search processes were broadened and other opportunities were explored. A solution to the pressing problems would eventually be found in a new technological regime which was based on electro-mechanical technology.

Shielded by a strong patent position and its acquired system scale economies it was not very difficult for the American Bell Company to maintain its monopolistic position in the industry. However, potential competition could be expected to enter the market after 1893 and 1894 when Bell's basic patents expired. Although entry barriers were still high because of system economies of scale, its reputation advantages and Bell's vertically integrated structure, many firms tried to enter the industry after 1894. Bell's absence in rural areas and its high tariff structure gave many independent telephone companies the chance to compete in the industry. Within 15 years after the expiry of Bell's basic patents, independent telephone companies managed to capture more than half the market for telephone subscribers (Bornholz and Evans, 1983). The newly established independent telephone companies set up local private systems and attracted customers by charging lower prices than Bell did. Bell, on the other hand, dominated long-distance services. Because Bell refused interconnection to its system, the local systems remained relatively isolated. After the expiry of its basic patents Bell tried to combat the independent telephone companies by pursuing a low-price strategy, by enhancing its service and by filing patent suits against its major competitors. However, to Bell's dismay these strategies were quite ineffective (Bornholz and Evans, 1983). After a few years Bell changed its tactics and tried to regain its grip on the telephone industry by aggressively acquiring independent telephone companies. The weak financial resources of these small (r-type) organizations made them an easy prey for Bell's aggressive acquisition strategies.

In the meantime, the American Bell Company made an attempt to escape from the strict Massachusetts laws which prevented it from achieving its expansion goals by relocating its stocks to the New York based American Telephone and Telegraph Company (AT&T) in 1899. In the following years a growing number of observers argued that AT&T abused its power and made use of aggressive acquisition strategies in order to monopolize the industry. AT&T's president, Theodore Vail, in turn argued that it was in the country's best interest to have 'One system, one policy and universal service'. Ongoing criticism about the dominant role of AT&T in the telecommunications industry, however, led to an increased call for nationalization of the telephone system. In an attempt to avoid being nationalized AT&T came to accept government regulation, which it embraced for three reasons (Brock and Evans, 1983). First, regulation was seen as a better alternative than nationalization. Second, regulatory actions could lead to a more favourable regulatory setting, and finally, regulation could lead to the elimination of competition from independent competitors. In 1913, AT&T deterred further nationalization threats by signing the Kingsbury Commitment in which AT&T agreed to stop the acquisition of telephone companies, to divest its interests in Western Union and to enable independent telephone companies to interconnect to its system. By adopting the Kingsbury Commitment, AT&T agreed to accept strict government regulation in return for a virtual monopolistic position in the US telecommunications industry.

4.2. THE ELECTRONIC VACUUM-TUBE (VALVE) PERIOD

The invention of the vacuum tube in 1907 radically changed the nature of the telecommunications industry. The vacuum tube made it possible to use thinner wires by amplifying signals through vacuum-tube repeaters. By using these repeaters the transmitting distance of wires could be more than doubled (Jewett, 1928). Moreover it gave way to so-called frequency division multiplexing, which is a technique used for transmitting several calls over a single pair of wires. The combination of vacuum-tube repeaters and frequency division multiplexing techniques paved the way for even more cost-effective long-distance telephony (Harper, 1986). Traditionally the major advantage of telegraphy over telephony was its ability to operate over much longer distances. The invention of the vacuum tube, however, started an era in which the telephone could operate over about the same distance. This enabled the telephone to replace the telegraph as the most important telecommunications device. AT&T was among the first to recognize the importance of the vacuum tube and it rapidly purchased the DeForest patents in order to preserve its prominent position in the industry. This move protected AT&T from the dangers of radical technological changes which could have led to a gale of 'creative destruction' in the industry.

AT&T would, however, soon face another threat to its monopolistic position, which came from the early development of wireless communication. Wireless communications were made possible by the further development of an invention by Guglielmo Marconi, who discovered a method of transmitting messages through the air. This so-called radio transmission was increasingly used to send telegraphic messages in the form of dot-and-dash-based codes. The success of this new transmission regime spurred inventors to examine the opportunities of wireless voice applications. Moreover, the start of the First World War provided another incentive to the use of radio communication for military applications. Military contracts to several scientists in the field of radio transmission would soon lead to the recognition of the advantages of transmitting voice over long distances through the air. Because transmission equipment was very expensive during the early days of radio operation, commercial prospects were not very promising. Radio communication was expected to be feasible only for very long-distance services. However, as soon as radio equipment became less expensive it could become a major competitor of wired telecommunications. This would pose a major threat to AT&T's monopolistic position. Because AT&T's monopoly position was in large part due to its elaborated wired network, it could render one of AT&T's major barriers to entry useless. Potential competitors would then be able to enter the market for long-distance services without the need to come up with major expenditures in wires and rights of way. The growing complexity of technological and economic forces and the regulatory problems associated with newly emerging technologies such as radio transmission, made it increasingly difficult for the US Congress to make well-balanced decisions on regulatory issues. In order to provide better regulatory actions, Congress passed a Communications Act in 1934 in which the Federal Communications Commission (FCC) was established in order to regulate interstate long-distance telecommunications and broadcasting. One of the most pressing tasks that the FCC was expected to deal with was the question of whether radio communications needed to be regulated. The newly established FCC decided to grant the common carriers exclusive access to the available frequency bands. This decision, in combination with its patents on the vacuum tube, enabled AT&T to benefit from a relatively stable monopolistic position until the 1950s. At that time AT&T firmly dominated local and long-distance telephone service as well as the telephone equipment market (Belitsos and Misra, 1986).

Notwithstanding their major impact on transmission equipment, the impact of valves on telecommunication exchanges turned out to be less successful. Experimental electronic switches that incorporated valves were too unreliable and their power consumption was too high to be effective in commercial applications. In those days continual replacement of burned-out tubes was needed and a single switching device required several thousands of energy-consuming tubes. Because fully electronic switches appeared not to be feasible at this stage, research focused on electro-mechanical switches. Between the 1920s and 1960s, these electro-mechanical switches would slowly but gradually replace the old regime based on manual switches. In the first instance electro-mechanical switches were of the Strowger and Rotary types.

Later more flexible so-called crossbar switches dominated switching technology. These smaller and faster semi-electronic exchanges featured high capacities which made it possible to remove the bottleneck in switching, which was caused by the 'switchboard problem' (Mueller, 1989). The improvements in both transmission and switching equipment made lower costs and therefore lower charges feasible, and this resulted in a significant growth in the number of installed telephones (Figure 4.1).

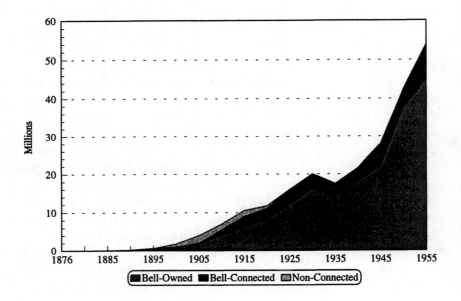

Source: Galambos, 1988.

Figure 4.1 Telephone development in the US (1876–1955)

4.3. THE TRANSISTOR PERIOD

For the telecommunications industry, the invention of the transistor in 1949 at Bell Laboratories initiated the first step into what would come to be known as the digitalization process. Whereas the vacuum tube turned out to be too unreliable for use in switching equipment, the new regime based on the transistor provided a cheaper and more reliable alternative to electro-mechanical components. It was by no means a coincidence that an important invention like the transistor took place in the laboratories of a telecommunications firm. The telecommunications industry clearly had the need for low-cost reliable components for use in their switching equipment. By incorporating transistors into their switching equipment (semi) electronic switches could be produced which featured only minor maintenance costs and which were much smaller than their electro-mechanical counterparts. In addition they provided more versatility and enabled a broad range of high-quality services (Guy, 1985). The first practical electronic exchange was installed in the US in 1960. Its use of transistors and program control made it comparable to a large computer (Harper, 1986). From that time onwards, computer and switching equipment were increasingly influenced by the same technological regime. The electronics regime that drove the electronic computer market ever since it originated in the 1940s increasingly determined the rate and direction of technological progress in the telecommunications industry. This convergence of technological regimes can be seen as the start of what would be known as the overall convergence process of information technologies.[4] The shared technological base of computers and communications implied that economies of scope could be achieved by simultaneously producing computers and communications equipment.

Although the convergence of communications and computers could have brought about important implications for AT&T's definition of its business, the 1956 Consent Decree barred AT&T from entering any business other than communications. The Consent Decree was the result of an antitrust case filed by the Justice Department in 1949 which claimed that AT&T violated the Sherman Act by monopolizing the industry for telephones and related devices. Apart from barring AT&T entrance into markets other than the regulated telephone services market, the decree also compelled AT&T to accept a policy of liberal licensing of its patents. The 1956 Consent Decree ruled that a large part of AT&T's semiconductor patents granted before 1956 had to be made available to all US firms at no charge. In addition all post-1956 patents should be made available to the same firms at a moderate fee. The decree implied a departure from one of AT&T's traditional basic means of entry deterrence but it also protected AT&T against the entrance of another industry giant, IBM, which was not allowed to enter the regulated communications industry. AT&T

had been using its prominent patent position in order to monopolize the industry ever since 1875 when Bell issued its first patent on the telephone. Although the abolition of patent protection could have evoked intense competition in the following years, federal regulatory actions had already replaced patents as the main entry barrier in the telecommunications industry. Ever since AT&T had embraced government regulation in the 1920s it had been engaged in a policy of licensing other firms at a 'reasonable cost' (OTA, 1985). By 1956, AT&T was almost completely protected from competition by federal regulation rather than by patents or other entry barriers (Brock, 1981).

Whereas digital techniques had a major impact on switching equipment, customer premises equipment and transmission equipment were not directly influenced by the digitalization process. However, the increased capacity and flexibility of switching equipment transferred the bottleneck in telecommunications from switching to transmission speed and capacity. As a result, technological trajectories were redirected in order to improve these characteristics.

4.4. DIGITALIZATION: AN ERA OF STRUCTURAL TRANSFORMATION

In the telecommunications industry, further improvements in reliability, speed, size and power consumption due to the invention of the integrated circuit paved the way for the evolution towards a fully electronic telecommunications network. Such an electronic network would be based on digital techniques and would be much faster and flexible than anything that had been invented before. The first actual introduction of digital techniques into telecommunications equipment came about through the introduction of pulse code modulation (PCM) in the 1960s. This technique, which had already been invented in the 1930s but was not economically feasible until more sophisticated solid state electronics came on to the market, could be used for the translation of analogue signals into digital form (Clark, 1991). The first electronic exchange system which made use of pulse code modulation was AT&T's Electronic Switching System no. 1 (ESS1) which was first installed in 1965. This innovative system would soon be recognized as a basic design which directed technological progress away from analogue technology towards digital techniques.[5] Another important impetus to the digitalization of the telecommunications network came from the introduction of stored program control (SPC) in electronic exchanges. Successful use of SPC in computer equipment induced telecommunication equipment manufacturers to experiment with it in their electronic exchanges. The modification of the SPC concept for use in the telecommunications industry was not very difficult because electronic exchanges at that time were already built and operated as a kind of computer. Overall the gradual replacement of hardwire logic by program-controlled digital components radically increased the speed and flexibility with which signals could be routed.[6] Meanwhile coaxial cables were gradually replacing copper wires as the major transmission medium. High-capacity coaxial cables were able to transmit large chunks of data or voice signals over a single cable. The combination of pulse code modulation, stored program control and the use of coaxial cables had an enormous impact on the speed and flexibility of the telecommunications network.

In the 1970s, the invention of the microprocessor and subsequent developments in computer and semiconductor technology once again speeded up the digitalization process in the telecommunications industry. Since then, almost every single product in the industry has been affected by digital techniques. The ongoing digitalization of telecommunications equipment made it possible to think of a network in which all signals would be transmitted, switched and received in digital form. This notion was reinforced by the emergence of satellite transmission systems and fibre-optic cables which were able to transmit pulses of light at very high speeds. Satellite systems emerged slowly in the 1960s and posed a major threat to the established position of telecommunication network operators. In contrast to wired network operators, operators of satellite systems did not have to make the enormous upfront investments which were needed to erect a global wired network. The invention of these satellite systems gave private operators the opportunity to bypass AT&T's network and to install their own private lines. Today satellite equipment is produced in three more or less separate markets: i.e. satellites, launchers and ground systems (Hills, 1986). Opportunities for telecommunication equipment manufacturers are found primarily in the ground station market. The market for satellites and launchers is closely related to defence and aerospace applications. It is therefore not surprising that aerospace agencies such as NASA, Delta and Ariane, and defence and aerospace manufacturers such as Hughes Aircraft, General Electric and Ford Aerospace, dominate the respective markets for launchers and satellites. Telecommunication manufacturers such as ITT and NEC, however, were able to grasp a considerable share of the ground station market. Today, the satellite systems market is characterized by rapidly increasing upfront costs, intensifying competition and a slowing growth rate. It is clear that under these conditions it is very difficult for new firms to enter the market successfully.

Although satellite transmission is particularly effective for very long-distance and point-to-multipoint transmission it faces competition from another relatively new transmission medium, namely optical fibres. Although the possibilities of fibre-optic technology had already been demonstrated by Kao and Hockham in 1966, commercial application started only in the late 1970s (Harper, 1986). Radical price decreases and the emergence of single-mode optical fibres in the 1980s have made fibre-optic cables the single most important new transmission regime. Fibre-optic cables are characterized by a large bandwidth coupled with reliable data transmission at very high transmission speeds. During the 1980s, optical fibres developed into cost-effective high-capacity transmission media that slowly but gradually penetrated specific application areas in which satellite transmission tended to dominate. Today, optical fibres are much cheaper, have a higher capacity and speed and are very reliable for both long- and short-distance transmission. As a result fibre optics are used extensively in local- and wide-area networks (LANs and WANs) that require high-capacity lines. Moreover, optical fibres are likely to play a very important role as the basic transmission element in the emerging Integrated Services Digital Networks (ISDN).[7] Competition between optical fibres and satellites is most likely to take place in long-distance communications, with on the one hand traditional telecommunications carriers such as AT&T and ITT which are rapidly integrating optical fibres into their long-distance lines, and on the other hand the major satellite system operators such as SBS and Intelsat.

It is obvious that, to make developments in transmission speed and costs fully effective, they have to be accompanied by similar developments in the field of switching equipment. In the 1970s the first completely digital time-division switches were introduced. These digital switches could be seen as special-purpose computers that were able to handle the high data transmission speeds which were made possible by developments in transmission equipment (Morgan and Sayer, 1988). Their enormous capacity enabled them to switch sound, data and images. The combination of high-speed broadband transmission, very fast digital switches and the invention of mini- and micro-computers in the computer industry made it economically feasible to link computers in distant locations. The ability to share computing and data resources is evolving into a whole infrastructure of LANs and WANs which are connected to the public network. The software used by these 'hybrid networks' also enables the supply of various 'new interactive services' or value-added services such as electronic mail, electronic banking and data storage, retrieval and processing. Such 'intelligent network' allows users to share processing capacity and information sources in distant locations and opens up a whole set of new application areas in computers and telecommunications.

4.5. DEREGULATION AND LIBERALIZATION

The increasing use of digital components in telecommunications products and the establishment of large digital networks gave way to shifting boundaries between the computer and telecommunications market. The blurring boundaries between the regulated communications and the unregulated computer market caused confusion about the parts of the market that were regulated and those that were competitive. In an attempt to deal with these problems, the FCC started its 'Inquiry into regulatory and policy problems presented by the interdependence of computer and communication services and facilities', the so-called Computer I inquiry. In 1971 the FCC ruled that regulation applied to pure communications and hybrid services with a dominating communications component, whereas pure dataprocessing and hybrid services in which the dataprocessing component dominated would remain unregulated.

However, as both voice and data communications were increasingly transmitted in digital form, the distinction between voice and data communications became artificial (see Hills, 1986). It became increasingly difficult to discriminate between services that were dataprocessing related and those that were primarily directed towards communications. In order to clarify matters, the FCC initiated a second inquiry, Computer II, in 1976. In the results, which were issued in 1980 the FCC discriminated between two types of services, 'basic and enhanced'. Basic voice services would remain regulated whereas those services that added value to the basic service (enhanced services) would be deregulated. In addition the Computer II decision ruled that the market for terminal equipment would be deregulated. These deregulatory actions paved the way for a large number of firms to enter the terminal equipment market. AT&T itself was now allowed to offer both voice and data terminal equipment and to offer enhanced services through a subsidiary which would be created under the name AT&T Information Services (ATTIS).

The decision to open up the market for terminal equipment ended a long and heavy dispute between AT&T on the one hand and its large users and potential competitors on the other. The first confrontation in the market for terminal equipment and attachment products occurred in 1948 shortly after the Second World War when a company called the Hush-A-Phone Company requested the FCC to allow it to sell a telephone attachment that diminished noise interference. AT&T had never allowed attachment products to be connected to its telephone network because it argued that they could cause damage to the system. After a seven-year legal battle the FCC decided that the product did not harm the system and Hush-A-Phone was granted the right to sell its product in the market. Another competition-evoking action which was undertaken in order to crack AT&T's monopoly in the customer premises equipment (CPE) market came about in 1966 when the Carter Electronics Corporation filed an antitrust suit against AT&T. Carter Electronics demanded the right to market its Carterfone.[8] In 1968, the FCC ruled that AT&T was not allowed to prevent competing firms from selling their attachment products to the public. The attachment product should, however, be connected to the network through an interface device which protected the network from damage. The FCC decision instantly created a new competitive market for CPE. Within a few months after the Carterfone decision hundreds of small, often newly established, firms entered the market. The absence of strict regulatory and financial entry barriers would soon make it a very competitive market in which firms competed by selling a broad range of innovative new products. In 1978 the FCC finally removed the last regulatory barrier by allowing direct attachment of CPE to the network.

Today the CPE market is characterized by intense competition. Low-priced products are offered in particular by Japanese, Korean and Taiwanese firms, whereas large US and European telecommunications manufacturers dominate the higher end of the market. Their dominant position, however, is increasingly attacked by the aggressive expansion strategies of large diversified (K-generalist) Japanese manufacturers. At present the CPE market is entered primarily from two related markets: the office equipment and the consumer-electronics market. According to Charles et al. (1989) there are two reasons for office equipment suppliers to enter the CPE market. The first reason is that both CPE and office equipment products are based on the same underlying technology base, which might render economies of scope in R&D and manufacturing. The second reason is that CPE products are increasingly integrated into the products of these manufacturers. In spite of the possible economies of scope and other advantages that these producers might have, the CPE market is still dominated by the major telecommunication giants such as AT&T in the US, Alcatel, Siemens and Ericsson in Europe and NEC in Japan (Charles et al., 1989).

The CPE market was, however, not the only market of AT&T that was under attack. In the transmission market, the invention of microwave systems made it feasible for organizations to bypass AT&T's network and to erect private systems (Hills, 1986). In response to many requests from both large users and equipment manufacturers, the FCC started an investigation in 1956 whether or not to grant private companies the right to establish their own microwave systems. After three years, the FCC ruled that private microwave lines above 890 Herz could be exploited by organizations other than the common carriers. AT&T argued that this decision would lead to 'cream skimming' on the market and argued that the concept of 'universal service' was at stake (Temin, 1987). Ever since the 1934 Communications Act, AT&T has been required to provide high-quality telephone services to all the residents of the United States at a reasonable price (Simon, 1985). AT&T would be disadvantaged by the 'above 890' decision because competing companies would now be allowed to erect private lines only in the most profitable areas. The FCC, however, did not revise its decision and the only thing AT&T could do was to drastically decrease its tariffs in order to deter potential competitors.

Although the 'above 890' decision did not lead to an immediate weakening of AT&T's dominant position in the industry, it opened up opportunities for potential competitors to fight AT&T's regulatory monopoly position. One of the first firms that grabbed the opportunity to attack AT&T's position after the 'above 890' decision was a firm called Microwave Communications Inc. (MCI). In 1965 MCI requested the FCC to build a private microwave system between St Louis and Chicago. In 1969, the FCC finally granted MCI the right to establish its microwave system. Aroused by MCI's success, numerous firms requested the FCC to establish similar services. The enormous number of applications induced the FCC in 1971 to take the Specialized Common Carrier Decision which allowed non-common carriers to operate private line services. In 1974, AT&T was forced to allow specialized carriers like MCI interconnection to its local exchanges (Breyer, 1982). Soon MCI would be joined by Southern Pacific, Western Union, ITT and Satellite Business Systems (Simon, 1985). These so-called other common carriers (OCCs) gradually captured a considerable share of the, by now, highly competitive market.

4.5.1. The Divestiture of AT&T

The ongoing pressures on AT&T's monopoly position accumulated in 1974 in an antitrust suit filed by the US department of Justice. In this suit, AT&T was accused of using its vertically integrated structure to raise barriers to entry and of cross-subsidizing its unregulated activities by the profits from its regulated activities (Crandall, 1989). After a legal battle of more than seven years the suit was settled by a Consent Decree on 8 January 1982. The original suit was aimed at the divestiture of AT&T from its manufacturing arm (Western Electric), its long-distance service (AT&T Long Lines) and its research facilities (Bell Labs). The final settlement, however, called for the divestiture of AT&T from its 22 local Bell Operating Companies (BOCs). These 22 organizations would be grouped into seven independent Regional Bell Operating Companies (RBOCs) which were coordinated by a Central Services Organization (CSO). By separating AT&T from its operating companies, the Justice Department managed to eliminate the opportunities for AT&T to cross-subsidize its competitive services from its monopolistic position in the local exchange market (Bruce et al., 1986). The RBOCs would offer local telephone services, whereas AT&T would provide interstate and long-distance services. AT&T was also granted the right to enter overseas markets[9] and was allowed to enter other (non-regulated) markets. Finally AT&T was freed from the restrictions of the 1956 Consent Decree. The operating companies on the other hand were limited to the supply of local services. The settlement came into effect on 1 January 1984 and led to the breakup of the largest corporation in the world (Figure 4.2).

In 1980, AT&T had $150 billion in assets and more than one million employees. It was 'as large as the next three largest corporations combined. Nineteen of its operating companies and Western Electric were large enough, individually to make the Fortune 500, and four of its operating companies, as well as Western Electric, were large enough, individually to make the Fortune 100. Its yearly sales were larger than the gross national products of Finland, Greece, Norway and Columbia' (Evans and Grossman, 1983: 96). On 1 January 1984 the settlement reduced the size of AT&T to only one-quarter of its original size. Soon after the settlement, AT&T directed its focus towards international markets, meanwhile trying to maintain its dominant position in the US market by selectively reducing prices and by offering new services (Davies, 1991). Competition was, however, well under way by firms that were eager to enter the lucrative US market. One of the first entrants into the US market was

ITT, which bought AT&T's international interest in 1920 and now tried to re-enter the US market. ITT would soon be joined by a number of Japanese, European and Canadian organizations. Because of the regulated character of the international communications market AT&T's only chance to enter foreign markets was by aligning itself with domestic firms. AT&T started its international operations by a joint venture with Philips in the Netherlands. Soon other alliances with, for example, Olivetti in Italy and CGE in France, would follow. The divestiture of AT&T in the US not only altered the American marketplace but it also led to deregulatory actions in the rest of the world.

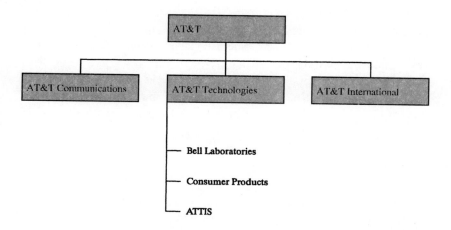

Figure 4.2 AT&T's organization structure after divestiture

4.5.2. Japan

In Japan telecommunications services were traditionally provided by the Japanese Ministry of Communications. In 1952 a public organization (NTT) was created, which took over the provision of domestic telecommunications services in Japan. The international telecommunications services were granted to another organization, Denshin Denwa Company Ltd (KDD). KDD operated on a commercial basis whereas NTT was a public corporation. Further deregulatory actions came about in 1985 when two laws came into effect that aimed at a further deregulation of the Japanese telecommunications system. The first law, the 'Telecommunications Business Law', discriminated between two types of carriers: Type I and Type II. Organizations which owned their own telecommunications facilities were referred to as Type I carriers, whereas organizations which provided services but did not own their own facilities were referred to as Type II carriers. A restricted number of regulatory rules applied to Type I carriers whereas Type II carriers were almost completely free from regulatory restrictions. The second law that came into effect in 1985 was called the Nippon Telegraph and Telephone Corporation Law. This law called for the privatization of NTT. Today NTT faces competition in all of its core markets.

After 1985, a number of newly established Type I carriers entered the market. The high capital investments involved in order to install telecommunications facilities implied that only very large businesses could enter from related fields (K-generalist). In 1989 two major new competitors entered the market for long-distance telecommunications: International Telecom Japan Inc. and International Digital Communications (*Telecommunications*, September 1990: 29–38). Type II carriers, on the other hand, did not have to cope with large start-up costs because they did not own transmission facilities. The lower regulatory and financial entry barriers for these firms gave way to the entrance of hundreds of small (r-type) organizations in the value-added services market.[10]

4.5.3. Europe

European PTTs have enjoyed a steady monopolistic position ever since telephone services were integrated into the state-owned Postal Telegraph and Telephone administrations (PTTs). In the structure of the European telecommunications industry there was no room for private companies to challenge the position of the PTTs or that of their preferred suppliers. After the divestiture of AT&T, however, some European countries started slowly but gradually to remove the barriers to free competition. Some years before the divestiture of AT&T, Britain had already taken the first steps towards liberalization of the telecommunications market. Liberalization in Britain started in 1981 when the British Telecommunications Act came into effect. The Act established British Telecom (BT) as a public corporation and called for the liberalization of the telephone equipment market (e.g. phones, modems, answering machines). In 1984, BT was privatized and the Office of Telecommunication (Oftel) was established in order to watch over BT and to advise the government on the future development of the telecommunications marketplace. In the same year a licence was granted to a corporation called

Mercury to provide telephone services in competition with BT. Another year later Mercury was granted the right to fully interconnect with BT's network. Further liberalization of the UK market came about through the 1991 'White Paper' issued by the UK government. In this paper almost complete liberalization of the networks and services market is foreseen in the near future (OECD, 1992a). In spite of these turbulent developments in Britain, the PTTs on the continent of Europe were able to deter most of the threats to their dominant position. In every country on mainland Europe, telecommunications transmission and voice telephony remained regulated. On 30 June 1987 the European Commission documented its vision on the future of the European telecommunications industry in what would be called the 'Green Paper'. In this paper it was argued that the technological convergence of information technologies made available a large number of new services. In order to take advantage of these new services it was necessary to make changes in the regulatory framework in order to improve the efficiency of the European industry. Implementation of the Green Paper proposals led to a liberalization of the markets for CPE and value-added services in most European countries. There is, however, little evidence that the role that is played by the PTTs in the future telecommunications networks is decreasing (Mansell, 1993).

4.6. REGULATION, DEREGULATION AND AFTER

Ever since its initiation, the telecommunications industry has been described as a typical example of a natural monopoly (see e.g. Baumol et al., 1982). A natural monopoly is referred to as an industry which is characterized by economies of scale and scope of such importance that one firm is able to serve the market more efficiently than several firms:[11] i.e. an industry which is characterized by a cost function which is subadditive (Baumol et al., 1982). In terms of 'normal' economies of scale, however, the early telecommunications industry did not qualify as a natural monopoly. Although some economies of scale could be gained by stringing multiple wires on a single pole (Brock, 1981), switching equipment was clearly characterized by diseconomies of scale. By and large, technical economies of scale in transmission could not compensate for the loss of scale economies in switching equipment. Thus, in terms of technical economies of scale one could hardly speak of a natural monopoly. The importance of scale economies in the telecommunications industry was, however, found in so-called system economies of scale. The value of a telephone or telegraph network was increased dramatically by an increase in the number of users.[12] Apart from these system economies of scale, economies of scope can also be of particular importance. Economies of scope can be realized whenever it is less costly to produce two or more products simultaneously than to produce them separately (Goldhar and Jelinek, 1983). Economies of scope can be seen as one of the most important rationales behind the integration of Postal, Telegraph and Telephone services in the European countries (Davies, 1991). In these integrated PTTs, duplication of facilities could be reduced by the joint provision of telegraph and telephone services over the same lines. The success of the independent telephone companies soon after the expiry of AT&T's basic patents and more recently after the divestiture of AT&T, however, suggests that the traditional monopoly position of AT&T has never been 'natural' but was due either to regulatory practices or to patent protection. In fact, the expiry of Bell's basic patents in 1894 gave way to the entrance of thousands of independent telephone companies and led to an explosive growth in the number of installed telephones.[13] Advocates of free competition have pointed out that a monopoly may lead to higher prices and retards technological progress. Figure 4.3 shows that the rental costs of a private leased line are much lower in liberalized countries such as the US and Britain than in other, more regulated, countries.

In line with Schumpeter (1934) a number of authors have argued that a monopoly position generates funds for innovative activity. However, most authors agree that although there has to be some sort of incentive in terms of a temporary monopoly position from innovation, the absence of competition often retards technological progress. If, for example, we compare the regulated telecommunications industry with the competitive computer industry, we find that there are large differences in the speed of technological progress. Flamm (1989), for example, has shown that there are significant time-lags between the incorporation of electronic components in computers and communications. In many respects the communications industry seems to lag behind the computer industry more than a decade (see Appendix I). Whereas computer products are characterized by life cycles of about six years, telecommunications switching equipment traditionally had life cycles of 20 to 40 years and transmission equipment was only replaced every 10 to 20 years. There are basically two explanations why regulated industries are characterized by slower technological innovation than their unregulated counterparts (Flamm, 1989). The first explanation can be found in the so-called 'Arrow-effect'. Kenneth Arrow (1962a) was one of the first to recognize that monopolistic firms such as

AT&T have less incentive to undertake innovative activities than firms that compete in a competitive environment. The second explanation is found in the use of rate-of-return regulation by the US government. Rate-of-return regulation refers to the system in which a regulated firm is not allowed to make profits that exceed a certain fair rate of return. Such a regulatory system encourages so-called 'gold plating' of plants and equipment. In a seminal paper on the effects of regulation on firm behaviour, Averch and Johnson (1962) showed that rate-of-return regulation induced firms to behave inefficiently (see also Train, 1991). Under conditions of rate-of-return regulation carriers are induced to invest in more expensive equipment, which depreciates much more slowly, than they would otherwise do. This led to a system which featured high tariffs, long-lived plants and low emphasis on services (Martin, 1977).

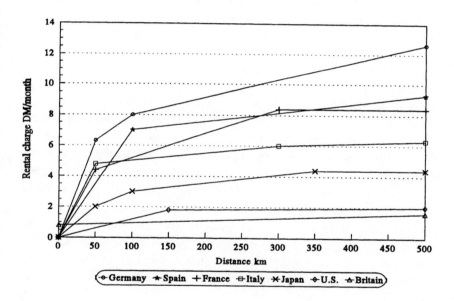

Source: Volkswagen (*Economist*, 5 October 1991).

Figure 4.3 Rental cost of a private leased 64 kilobit/second line (January 1991)

Although a monopoly may seem uneconomic in terms of public interests, there are a number of non-economic reasons which played an important role in the arguments in favour of regulation. In particular, the goal of 'universal service at an average price' seems to be very important in this respect. The term universal service is used to describe the goal that all people should be able to make use of telecommunications services at a reasonable price. A monopolistic market structure was thought to be the best framework in which to offer such services. Therefore, the general opinion was that regulatory actions were needed in order to secure universal service. In the telecommunications industry we found two different regulatory approaches (see Ergas, 1988). In the US, the regulatory approach was characterized by a structure in which private companies competed in the marketplace, although they were subject to regulatory agencies. In Europe and Japan, on the other hand, telecommunications services were provided in a more or less autonomous way by a public enterprise.

In the late 1970s and early 1980s, the digitalization process made it increasingly difficult to maintain the traditional divide between regulated voice and unregulated data transmission. At the same time pressures from large users and potential competitors increased to open up the market for telecommunications services and equipment. Today deregulation and liberalization are high on the agenda in most countries. Deregulation and liberalization are seen as a means to speed up the process of technological innovation, to boost new services, to increase competition and to establish a global digital broadband telecommunications network.

Whereas technological changes and deregulatory actions continue to alter the telecommunications marketplace, there is a growing debate among theorists and practitioners about the shape of tomorrow's market. As put forward by Mansell (1993), there are two distinct views on the future relationship between technological innovation and the institutional environment. The first perspective, which was labelled the 'idealistic model', envisages an increase in competition and a decreasing need for regulatory actions. The second view, which is represented by the 'strategic model', foresees the establishment of an oligopolistic market that is dominated by a few very large global operating firms, who possess the power to influence the structure of the future public network. The latter model would call for further regulatory actions in order to protect public interests. Deregulation in the US, subsequent movements in Japan and Great Britain and slow but gradual deregulatory actions on mainland Europe have led to further globalization of the market and initiated increased competition in the international telecommunications marketplace. Today the competitive process in the CPE and services market can be seen to approach the rules of perfect competition and therefore closely resemble the expectations of the idealistic model. Empirical evidence from the switching and transmission markets, however, shows that these markets are increasingly dominated by a small number of large globally operating companies. The structure of these markets is determined by enormous upfront costs which are needed to develop a new generation of switching equipment, satellite systems or optical fibres. The growing importance of economies of scale in combination with shrinking product life cycles brings about particular advantages for those firms that succeed in capturing a larger share of these markets.[14] These conditions might lead to a setting which is characterized by oligopolistic rivalry among a few large firms and therefore closely resembles the view put forward by the 'strategic model'.

Radical technological discontinuities did not affect the dominant position of the leading telecommunications firms. Their technological competencies and integrated structures enabled them to retain their lead in the world market. In the US the major telecommunications services supplier AT&T still dominates all of its core markets[15] and is still vertically integrated with its main supplier, Western Electric. Although in Europe the relationships between PTTs and their preferred suppliers are becoming less tied, the need for backward compatibility between old and new equipment has forced network suppliers to retain most of their quasi-vertical relationships with their traditional suppliers (Mansell, 1993). It must, however, be stressed that these so-called 'national champions' are currently slowly losing their relatively protected market to larger foreign competitors. The relatively fragmented market and the dependence on their home country makes it very difficult for the relatively small national firms to deal with the ever increasing R&D outlays needed to develop new generations of equipment. It therefore seems that the 'strategic model' describes the core of the telecommunications industry more accurately.

4.7. DISCUSSION

In the second chapter we put forward an integrated framework for the analysis of complex industrial systems over time. It might be very interesting to evaluate whether such an integrated framework, which is primarily based on the assumption of competition, can be applied to an industry which has above all been characterized by its regulated character. In our framework we assume that in the first stage of an industry's evolution both market and technological uncertainty are very high and that (because of these uncertainties) only a very limited number of firms are willing to support research at that stage. It was thought to be very difficult for firms to persuade potential investors and financial institutions to provide the required financial resources. Therefore we assume that most of the research in this stage will be undertaken by universities and government institutions (*Hypothesis 1*). The role that is played by these institutions in the telecommunications industry, however, has been very modest. Both the telegraph and telephone market were opened up by independent inventors who could be regarded as 'entrepreneurs' in the Schumpeterian sense. In the telegraph market this role was played by Cooke and Wheaterstone and Samuel Morse. In the telephone market Graham Bell and Elisha Gray played a similar role. The fact that these small entrepreneurs were able to come up with such important inventions was probably due to the fact that their devices were relatively simple and easy to build. Neither expensive sophisticated equipment and materials nor thorough scientific knowledge was needed in order to build these devices.

The entrepreneurs who were responsible for the invention of the first telecommunications devices would soon establish their own private companies in order to bring their inventions to the market. In their efforts to market their products they would soon be joined by a large number of newly established small organizations. Early demand came from time-sensitive customers such as stock-brokers, newspaper agencies, railroad owners and from the government. This well-paying group was more interested in the quality of the service and the distance that could be achieved than in the costs of the services. Therefore competition in this period focused on the technological capabilities of the equipment rather than on costs. This is in line with our assumption (*Hypothesis 2*) that a newly emerging market is likely to be explored by small r-type organizations which pursue offensive innovation strategies in order to gain technological and market leadership. Their flexible and fast-to-build organizational structures and short communication lines enable these firms to respond rapidly to new opportunities in the market. In the telecommunications industry the attempts to gain market leadership by bringing a technologically dominant product to the market led to a state of technological flux where each company marketed its own design. We assumed, however, that after some time the establishment of a basic design would lead to a period of more stable technological progress along a specific path or trajectory (*Hypothesis 3*). In the telegraph industry Morse's device would soon become one such 'basic design' on which future developments were based. Bell's telephone played a similar role in the telephone market.[16] The importance of these basic designs is demonstrated by the fact that both devices were able to rule their respective markets for more than a century. This observation clearly confirms *Hypothesis 3*. The establishment of these basic designs and the emergence of a technological regime based on copper wires and manual switching led to a considerable reduction in the uncertainty about the future direction of technological developments. Technological developments now followed the paths which were set out by these basic designs.

In Chapter 2 we argued that the standardized direction of technological progress shifts competition away from performance and design towards price. A relatively stable technological environment is assumed to favour large efficient (K-type) organizations over their smaller less efficient r-type competitors (*Hypothesis 4*). In the telegraph industry the market would soon be dominated by the Western Union Telegraph Company. In the telephone industry Bell would eventually establish itself as the dominant organization. Although both organizations started out as small r-type organizations they were able to grow into well-established large (K-type) organizations. Both Western Union and Bell managed to grow into K-type organizations by taking advantage of their patents and rights of way.[17] Bell's strategy was particularly aggressive. By acquiring most of its small r-type competitors, Bell was able to establish a virtual monopoly in its market. Western Union did not use aggressive acquisition strategies but achieved a similar position by outcompeting its competitors. In line with *Hypothesis 4* we saw that the dissolution of r-type organizations in favour of Bell and Western Union started an r to K transition in the market. Bell, however, was only able to make the transition from an r-type organization into a K-type because its major K-type competitor (Western Union) failed to recognize the opportunities in the newly emerging paradigm. Western Union did not realize that the largest threat to its dominant position did not come from its direct competitors but from a new technological innovation, namely the telephone. Western Union even refused Bell's offer to buy its basic patents for $100,000. Although Western Union entered the market for telephone services and equipment it withdrew a few years later by settling a patent infringement suit with Bell, which allowed Bell to survive from the pressures of competition. Its inability to compete with a giant like Western Union had already weakened Bell's financial position. Bell, at that time a relatively small r-type organization, was simply not able to compete against an already well-established (K-type) organization. Western Union had all the tools that were needed to outcompete its smaller competitor, Bell. It could have benefited from its technical and system economies of scale, its large and well-established maintenance and service network, its affluent financial resources and rights of way. It failed, however, to recognize the opportunities of the telephone market. Its success in the telegraph industry made Western Union 'blind' towards the emerging opportunities in the telephone market. This so-called 'success breeds failure syndrome' (Starbuck et al., 1978) made it possible for Bell to thrive in the newly established market, whereas the telegraph market would gradually decline in favour of the telephone market. This is in accordance with *Hypothesis 7*, which argues that a K to r transition takes place after a paradigmatic technology shift. The decision of Western Union to leave the telephone market and Bell's commitment not to enter the market for telegraphy created a spheres-of-influence position in which Western Union dominated the telegraph industry and Bell ruled the telephone market.

The emergence of a mass market in the early 20th century at first did not lead to the expected entrance of new organizations into market niches. This is due primarily to the regulatory framework in the US which prevented organizations from entering the regulated telecommunications market. Until the 1950s, AT&T enjoyed a relatively stable monopolistic position in virtually all its markets. Since then, AT&T increasingly has faced potential competitors which tried to invade its regulated markets. Although AT&T was able to deter most of these threats it gradually lost some of its market share to other organizations. Threats to AT&T's dominant position came in particular from new entrants into the customer premises equipment and into the microwave services markets. In 1984 AT&T's divestiture opened up most of the other previously regulated markets. AT&T's divestiture led to a wave of deregulatory and liberalization actions in other countries in the world. Remarkably these actions did not lead to the expected de-concentration of the telecommunications market. Although swarms of new firms entered into niche markets, such as the customer premises equipment and value-added services, new firms were not able to challenge the dominant positions of the traditional telecommunications companies in their core markets (transmission and switching). This confirms *Hypothesis 6*, which argues that mass markets open up opportunities for specialized organizations to enter niche markets. The integrated structure and technological competencies of the incumbents enabled them to retain their dominant position in the market. Today these core markets are characterized by enormous minimum R&D thresholds and an emphasis on static economies of scale. Oligopolistic rivalry between a small number of very large organizations has intensified price-based competition and makes it very difficult for other organizations to enter these markets. In fact the performance of an organization is to a large degree related to its share of the market. It is obvious that in such a market there is no room for r-type organizations any more (see *Hypothesis 5*).

Although a new paradigm based on digital electronics is increasingly altering the marketplace there are no real indicators that the incumbent telecommunication companies are losing their dominant positions to new small organizations. Newly built r-type organizations took advantage of the opportunities which arose in the market for value-added services and customer premises equipment. The growth of these markets is likely to increase much more rapidly than the markets for transmission and switching equipment. We might, therefore, witness a power shift away from the traditional suppliers towards new services and CPE suppliers.

To summarize, it seems very difficult to apply our integrated framework to an industry which has been ruled by patent laws and regulatory actions. In the competitive stages of the market, the framework is, however, well equipped to predict the evolution of the market. The role of universities and government institutions is found to be much lower in the telecommunications industry than expected. Because the industry is currently transforming technologically from analogue to digital systems and market structural changes are brought about by deregulatory actions and liberalization of the markets, it is very difficult to assess whether the paradigmatic shift which is currently taking place leads to a 'creative destruction' in the industry.[18] Until today, the incumbent telecommunications manufacturers managed to deter most of the threats to their dominant position in their core markets.

NOTES

1. Because of the heterogeneous character of the telecommunications industry and the absence of international competition before the 1980s, this chapter will be concerned primarily with the evolution of the largest of all domestic telecommunications markets: the US telecommunications industry.
2. In most European countries the telegraph system was rapidly placed under the same regulatory regime as the postal systems. This inaugurated an era dominated by huge national institutions which, after the introduction of the telephone, would be called Post, Telegraph and Telecommunications administrations (PTTs).
3. Among the countries with the most sophisticated systems in Europe were Great Britain, France and Germany.
4. Chapter 6 is concerned with a more elaborated analysis of the convergence process.

5. Even today pulse code modulation is still in use in the latest telecommunications equipment.
6. Another important feature of SPC-controlled digital switches was that they enabled a large number of 'intelligent services' to the public.
7. ISDN can be seen as an agreed development path towards a future digital broadband telecommunications network. An ISDN will feature broadband transmission of voice, data and images at high standardized transmission speeds and will provide the basic infrastructure for a broad range of 'intelligent services'.
8. The Carterfone was an attachment product that enabled the interconnection of mobile radio systems to the public network.
9. Ever since AT&T had sold its overseas operations to ITT in 1920 it had not been present abroad.
10. The number of new carriers actually increased from 85 in 1985 to 968 in 1990 (OECD, 1992a).
11. One of the foremost economists who put forward this argument for telecommunications regulation was Alfred Chandler (1977). Alfred Chandler's opinion was used in court by AT&T in the late 1970s when AT&T's monopolistic position was under attack.
12. System economies of scale became particularly important when the so-called 'switchboard problem' was solved by the invention of larger capacity electro-mechanical switches.
13. The growth rate of installed telephones increased from an average of 9 per cent a year in the period between 1881 and 1895 to an average of more than 27 per cent a year by the turn of the century (Wasserman, 1985).
14. Whereas the costs to develop a new generation of exchanges have grown above $1 billion increasing competition reduced the life cycles of digital exchanges from 20 to 40 years to less than ten years. With R&D costs in excess of $1 billion for the current generation of digital exchanges and a world market of only $14 billion in 1986, a supplier needs at least 10 per cent of that market to generate adequate returns over the life of the product (*Economist*, 1987).
15. AT&T's domination in its core markets is, however, not all-encompassing. AT&T's position in, for example, switching equipment is constantly challenged by Northern Telecom and a number of non-North American firms.
16. The establishment of these devices as 'basic designs' was not due to their technological superiority or market success but primarily to their strong patenting position.
17. System economies of scale in the telephone market became important only after 1915, when local networks were technically integrated into a national system (Galambos, 1988).
18. We should, therefore, also take into consideration that apart from technological change, changes in the policy environment can also induce transitions in the market structure.

5. The Semiconductor Industry

The micro-electronics industry was born out of the invention of the triode vacuum tube by Lee DeForest in 1906.[1] The triode vacuum tube was a device composed of three electrodes, which was able to amplify electrical signals. At first, the characteristics of the vacuum tube were poorly understood and its commercial value was rather low. Only after considerable improvements at AT&T,[2] the troublesome tube was transformed into a somewhat more reliable component (Morris, 1990). In the 1930s the vacuum tube was sufficiently developed to be used in all kinds of electronic equipment, such as radar, tv and radio equipment. Although significantly improved, the vacuum tube still suffered from a number of serious drawbacks. Its high power consumption, large size, heat dispersion and inherent unreliability made the vacuum tube an extremely troublesome device. Because efforts to improve the basic characteristics of the vacuum tube were not very successful, a number of vacuum-tube producers started to search for more reliable, smaller components. Large-scale research programmes were directed towards new materials on which future components could be based.

Soon attention would be drawn towards the specific properties of semiconductor materials. Semiconductors were found to be neither good insulators nor good conductors. Their conductivity depended on factors such as temperature, impurity and optical excitation (Malerba, 1985). Because of their ability to act as either conductors or insulators they could be used as 'active components' which were able to modulate, rectify or amplify electrical currents (Dosi, 1984). Although in the 1930s and early 1940s several attempts had been made to incorporate semiconductor materials into electronic components,[3] semiconductor devices were still not sufficiently developed to be regarded as viable alternatives to the vacuum tube. Widespread interest in semiconductor technologies was, however, regained on 23 December 1947 by the invention of the point-contact germanium transistor at Bell Laboratories in Murray Hill. The point-contact transistor was a rather simple semiconductor device that was capable of switching or amplifying electrical currents.

93

Commercial production of the germanium transistor started in 1951 at AT&T's manufacturing arm, Western Electric. Within a few years, AT&T was joined by a large number of other companies who managed to bring their own germanium transistors to the market. Most of these companies operated under licence of AT&T, who had actively encouraged the licensing of its transistor technology to other firms. In the spring of 1952, AT&T held a symposium on transistor technology which was attended by 35 firms from all over the world. Those attending paid an entrance fee of $25,000, which could be deducted from a possible licence fee. The symposium turned out to be an enormous success and speeded up the diffusion of transistor technology tremendously. At first, transistors were not very successful in driving the much cheaper vacuum-tube components out of the market. The only commercial customers who valued size and power consumption more than price were hearing-aid manufacturers.[4] Somotome, one of the leading hearing-aid manufacturers, brought the first transistorized hearing aid on to the market in 1953. Somotome's device incorporated five germanium transistors and was known for its small size and low power consumption. The use of germanium transistors for other commercial products, however, was not a great success. Germanium transistors were superior to the vacuum tube in terms of speed, size and power consumption, but were still troublesome in terms of life expectancy, applicability, reliability and manufacturing yields (Braun and MacDonald, 1982). Although its successor, the junction transistor, was superior to the point-contact transistor in many respects,[5] it was not until the invention of the silicon transistor that most of the problems were solved.

The invention of the silicon transistor by Texas Instruments in 1954 gave way to more reliable and faster components that could be used over a much wider temperature range (Swann, 1986). The need for devices that were able to operate over a broad range of temperatures was especially great in military and space applications. In the years after the invention of the silicon transistor, demand from NASA and the US military grew exponentially. The emergence of a large and highly profitable military market for silicon transistors vastly improved the viability and profitability of these devices. The success of silicon transistors in the military market established the first technological regime in a paradigm based on semiconductor materials. The regime was based on small, fast and reliable silicon devices. Silicon replaced germanium as the most important semiconductor material and the technological trajectory was directed towards further improvements in speed, size, reliability and manufacturing costs. The obvious advantages of transistors over their vacuum-tube predecessors (see Table 5.1) gave way to a rapid substitution of vacuum tubes by solid state devices.

Table 5.1 Characteristics of transistors and vacuum tubes

	Weight G	Size cm	Power Dissipation W
Standard Tube	120	200	3
Miniature Tube	55	60	2.5
Subminiature Tube	35	40	2
Transistor	15	10	0.2

Sources: Steutzer, 1952; Morris, 1990.

The replacement started in military and space equipment but as soon as prices started to decline, transistors were increasingly incorporated into a wide variety of commercial products. In 1959, for the first time in the history of the semiconductor industry, shipments of semiconductor devices were higher than those of vacuum tubes (see Figure 5.1).

5.1. THE BIRTH OF A NEW INDUSTRY

Although at the outset manufacturing costs of transistors were much higher than those of vacuum tubes, the particular advantages of the transistor posed a serious threat to the dominant position of the incumbent vacuum-tube manufacturers. A very high elasticity of substitution between the transistor and its predecessor forced vacuum-tube producers to watch the developments in transistor technology very closely (Dosi, 1980). In the early 1950s, eight major vacuum-tube manufacturers were active in the United States: CBS, General Electric, Philco, Raytheon, RCA, Sylvania, Tung-Sol and Westinghouse.

Because the transistor made vacuum-tube technology obsolete, incumbent firms were forced to enter the transistor market in order to maintain their

The Dynamics of Technical Innovation

existing market shares. General Electric, Raytheon and RCA started production of transistors in 1951. Soon they were followed by the other five major vacuum-tube manufacturers. Within three years all eight companies had managed to enter the new market (Tilton, 1971). Their vast technological, production and marketing resources enabled them to gain market leadership in the new market. Not only did these firms manage to dominate the transistor market in terms of market share, they would also account for the majority of the new technological developments at that time. Together with Bell Laboratories they accounted for approximately 57 per cent of total R&D expenditures and were granted 66 per cent of total patents over the period 1952–61 (Tilton, 1971).

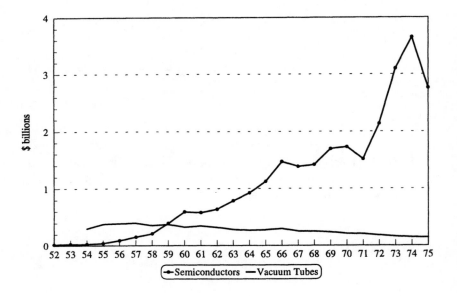

Source: Webbink , 1977.

Figure 5.1 Value of industry shipments of vacuum tubes and transistors (1952–1975)

In Europe and Japan, large-scale production of transistors started under licence of Western Electric in the early 1950s. A dominant role in both markets was played by large vertically integrated vacuum-tube-producing companies. In the

1950s the number of transistorized components in consumer products was rapidly rising. Because merchant producers were non-existent at that time, consumer electronic manufacturers were forced to enter the transistor market in order to satisfy their own in-house needs. At that time the technological capabilities of European firms were much higher than those of their Japanese counterparts. Ever since the invention of the vacuum tube, European firms had been working on the leading edge of technology. Because of their technological sophistication, European firms were able to enter the market for transistors very rapidly. The Dutch multinational Philips, German Siemens, and the British firms GEC and Thomson-Houston were already producing transistors in the late 1940s (OECD, 1968, cited in Malerba, 1985). Philips even reported the production of a transistor a few weeks after Bell's announcement of the invention of its germanium transistor (Dosi, 1981; Malerba, 1985). In spite of their relatively weak technological capabilities all of Japan's major vacuum-tube producers managed to enter the transistor market before 1957. A dominant role in the Japanese market was played by, among others, Hitachi, Kobe Kogyo, Matsushita, Nippon Electric, Mitsubishi and Toshiba. Their dominant position, however, was soon attacked by new entrants such as Sanyo, a former washing-machine producer, Fujitsu, a well-known manufacturer of communication equipment and Sony, who managed to become the first producer of transistors in Japan (Tilton, 1971). In spite of overseas developments, US producers were able to retain their dominant position in the semiconductor world market. In comparison to Europe and Japan, the US had a larger market, a more sophisticated scientific and engineering base and financing capital was more readily available. In addition, the position of US producers was boosted by a very strong military market and considerable government support. In Europe, the role that was played by the military was negligible and in the case of Japan even completely absent.[6] The absence of a military market for their products clearly disadvantaged Japanese firms in terms of innovativeness.

The importance of transistors grew rapidly in the mid-1950s when the silicon transistor was brought on to the market. Its introduction was accompanied by two major process innovations: the oxide-masking and the diffusion process. These process innovations radically increased the quality and yield rate of transistors. Before that time, manufacturing of transistors had been very troublesome. Large-scale production of transistors was not possible and yield rates were particularly low. Braun and MacDonald (1982: 54) referred to the production process as a 'manufacturer's nightmare'. It was not until the invention of the oxide-masking and diffusion process that batch processing of transistors became possible. At that time there was a strong link between scientific and commercial activities. Technology was above all embodied in people and was almost freely available from Bell Laboratories[7] and a variety of well-known university institutes. Relatively low barriers to entry and the prospects of highly profitable government contracts led to the entrance of a large number of new firms into the transistor market. Many of these start-up companies were created by scientists or engineers who left incumbent organizations in order to establish their own firms. These so-called 'spin-off' companies were often backed by venture capitalists and thrived on the knowledge of former employees of large incumbent transistor manufacturers. Because technological knowledge was primarily people-embodied it was relatively easy to transfer this knowledge from the incumbent to the new company. One of the first new entrants which was able to grasp a considerable share of the transistor market was the inventor of the silicon transistor, Texas Instruments (TI). Its invention gave TI a vast lead over its competitors. High prices and considerable learning curve advantages enabled TI, a previously small geophysical company, to grow into one of the largest competitors in the transistor market. In 1957, TI became the world's largest semiconductor manufacturer.[8] Another new entrant, Transistron, would manage to grow into the second-largest producer of transistors.[9]

By the end of the 1950s, new companies had conquered almost all of the leading positions that were previously held by large vacuum-tube-producing companies. Although most of the major technological innovations were still introduced by large established companies, smaller firms were often more successful in the commercialization of these innovations. A relatively low appropriability of technological innovations enabled new firms to benefit from innovations that were introduced by their much larger and more research-intensive competitors. Because new firms had no commitments to a specific technology, they were often able to move into new technological fields much faster than their incumbent competitors. In 1957 at least 50 companies were able to enter the semiconductor market (Morris, 1990). The overall market structure, however, remained rather concentrated. In 1958, the twenty largest companies accounted for 97 per cent of the total US market (Braun and MacDonald, 1982). The high degree of concentration in the market clearly reflects the importance of dynamic economies of scale, such as learning-curve advantages, during this period (Dosi, 1981).

Most of the semiconductor-producing companies made use of highly offensive innovative strategies. Their innovative products fulfilled the need of the US military for faster and more reliable components and created temporary monopoly positions for the most successful innovators. At that time, government-financed research programmes and military procurement provided the main source of income for most of the active transistor manufacturers. Military agencies were well prepared to pay a premium price for highly sophisticated devices. Demand and R&D subsidies of military organizations allowed firms to explore new technological opportunities and establish a large sophisticated market. The military's emphasis on technological performance instead of price gave way to a rapid expansion of the technological frontier and drove the technological trajectory towards a reduction in size, weight and increased reliability (Braun and McDonald, 1982).

A considerable overlap between the military and the civilian trajectory enabled US manufacturers to reinforce their leading position in the commercial world market (Dosi, 1984). Innovative components developed under military contracts enabled companies to establish temporary monopoly positions in the commercial market. Those temporary monopoly positions were particularly important because the production of semiconductor devices was characterized by steep learning curves. Firms with larger production runs were able to learn fast through experience and were rewarded by much higher yield rates than other organizations. Those firms that were able to go down the learning curve fast enough faced lower costs and correspondingly larger market shares. In order to 'buy' market shares a number of companies made use of a strategy known as 'forward pricing'. In this strategy the company sets a price lower than average costs in order to recover its marginal costs. By setting its prices below those of its competitors the innovator is able to seize a large part of the market and may succeed in deterring or postponing the entry of other companies. A strategy of forward pricing is, however, only viable if the marginal costs of the innovator decrease faster than those of its competitors due to its greater cumulative volume[10] (Jelinek and Schoonhoven, 1990).

5.2. THE INTEGRATED CIRCUIT

Although transistors replaced vacuum tubes in most devices, they were increasingly challenged by new devices that were known as integrated circuits (ICs). The first germanium integrated circuit was invented by Jack Kilby at the laboratories of Texas Instruments in 1959. Compared with discrete devices, which consisted of only one device per chip, integrated circuits joined at least two components on a single chip. The first integrated circuits contained only two interconnected transistors, but since then the number of transistors per chip has doubled every single year.[11] This rapid increase in chip density was made possible by a significant reduction in the size of the components and an increase in overall chip size (Swann, 1990; van Zand, 1990). Shorter paths between the various parts had a positive effect on the reliability, speed and power consumption of these electronic components (Swann, 1986). In spite of the improved functionality of these devices, the production of integrated circuits turned out to be very troublesome.

In 1959, Fairchild Camera and Instrument introduced a process innovation which radically improved the batch processing of transistors. This so-called 'planar process'[12] not only improved the existing production techniques of transistorized devices, but also facilitated large-scale production of silicon integrated circuits. Shortly after the invention of the planar process the first silicon integrated circuits were brought on to the market by Fairchild and Texas Instruments. Their small size and low weight made these ICs extremely well-suited to be used in small electronic devices. It was, therefore, not surprising that the first commercial ICs, like their predecessors, were increasingly incorporated into hearing-aid equipment. However, as soon as prices started to decline, ICs were incorporated into a broad range of other commercial products. During the 1960s mass-produced ICs started to replace transistors in commercial as well as in military applications. The successful introduction of silicon ICs speeded up the replacement of germanium by silicon as the most important semiconductor material in use. This substitution process was accompanied by changes in the basic manufacturing technologies. At first IC manufacturers made use of bipolar technologies such as transistor transistor logic (TTL). In the late 1960s developments branched out in two directions; faster bipolar technologies (ECL) and parallel developments in lower-power-consuming technologies (p-channel MOS).[13]

Promising developments in integrated circuits, and faster bipolar and MOS-technologies led to the entrance of a large number of companies which were eager to explore the opportunities in the new technologies. In the early 1960s barriers to entry for new firms were relatively low. Knowledge was spread freely by universities and AT&T, and the mobility of engineers and scientists was extremely high. Small new firms were often much more able to explore the new technological opportunities than their larger well-established competitors.

Vested interests in transistors inhibited incumbent organizations from responding quickly to new developments in IC technology. New firms, on the other hand, were much more flexible and particularly eager to explore new technological directions. As a result, small firms were often much faster on to the market with their integrated circuits than were their larger competitors.

Initially the IC market was stimulated by large-scale NASA and Air Force programmes which aimed to promote the development of ICs.[14] The stimulating role of the US government gradually decreased during the late 1960s (Figure 5.2). At that time, the computer industry took over the role of the US military as the most important customer of integrated circuits (Malerba, 1985). The shift from a military to a commercially oriented market radically increased the importance of price as a competitive factor. Although innovativeness remained very important, large-scale efficient production became an important success factor in the IC market. During the 1960s, static barriers started to rise rapidly. Some of the new entrants managed to survive by selling innovative devices to computer manufacturers. The growing importance of price as a competitive factor, however, drove many of the new organizations out of the market. Company turnover became particularly high during the late 1960s when competitive forces intensified and the market became increasingly concentrated. In the late 1960s the market was dominated by only five major companies: Fairchild, Motorola, Signetics, Texas Instruments and Westinghouse. Together these five firms accounted for more than 80 per cent of the total integrated circuit market (Tilton, 1971).

Because a sophisticated computer industry was absent in most of Europe and Japan, semiconductor companies from those regions did not feel the need to be engaged in innovative digital ICs. European and Japanese manufacturers retained their interest in transistors and were relatively late to enter the IC market. Japanese companies, however, succeeded in catching up with their European competitors in terms of technological sophistication. In 1965, eight major Japanese producers were able to manufacture ICs: Fujitsu, Hitachi, Matsushita, Mitsubishi, NEC, Oki, Sony and Toshiba (Morris, 1990). At that time European semiconductor firms were already far removed from the technological frontier that was set by US companies. European electronics firms had been interested primarily in the use of relatively unsophisticated bipolar integrated circuits for use in their consumer electronic and heavy electrical devices, whereas US companies focused on digital ICs for use in advanced computer systems.

Dosi (1984) argued that there were three factors which were primarily responsible for Europe's lag *vis-à-vis* its US competitors in semiconductor technology. First, the number and size of companies in Europe which undertook research efforts in semiconductors was much lower than in the US. Second, minimum R&D thresholds could be met by only a very limited number of European firms (Philips and Siemens). The third factor is associated with the availability of so-called bridging institutions in the US which closed the gap between scientific research and the commercialization of inventions. In addition, Dosi (1984: 50) stressed 'the mobility of scientists and engineers, the availability of venture capital, and the size and sophistication of the American market'. The cumulative nature of technological developments in the 1960s was responsible for the stability in the time lag between US firms and their European competitors. Because venture capital was very scarce and the mobility of engineers was very low, new firms did not play an important role in the European semiconductor industry. Therefore, a process of 'creative destruction' as found in the US market did not take place. The very same firms that dominated the vacuum-tube industry in the 1940s and 1950s were still the dominant players in the integrated circuit market of the 1960s. Because the market for innovative IC technologies was growing much faster than the market for the unsophisticated transistor devices, European firms did not only lose their prominent technological position but also lost a considerable part of their world-wide market share. The price war of 1970–71 drove all but five European companies out of the mass semiconductor markets (Dosi, 1980). At that time a number of European companies started to move into more specialized markets. In the US, large vertically integrated vacuum-tube producers, like their European counterparts, remained focused on the production of relatively old-fashioned components such as transistors and linear integrated circuits. After the recession of 1970–71 none of the leading companies in the mid-fifties had been able to retain its dominant position. The top five positions were now taken by IBM, TI, Motorola, Western Electric and Fairchild (Braun and MacDonald, 1982).

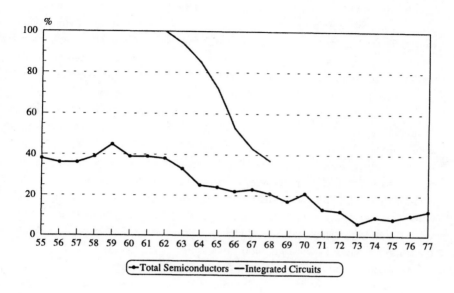

Sources: Semiconductor procurement from Wilson et al., 1980: 146, noted in Okimoto et. al. 1984: 84; IC procurement from Dosi, 1984: 44.

Figure 5.2 Military procurement of semiconductors and ICs

5.3. THE LSI/VLSI PERIOD

The integrated circuit regime was marked by a strong trajectory that aimed to increase the number of components on a chip. Although initially this trajectory proved to be very successful, it ran into a growing number of difficulties. The ongoing increase in the number of components per chip gave way to increasingly specialized devices. Because semiconductor devices lost their general-purpose character it became increasingly difficult to reap economies of scale in the manufacturing process. The rapidly growing design and production costs of the highly complex devices were now increasingly difficult to recoup by the relatively small production runs that were characteristic for such complex devices. The difficulties associated with the existing technological regime gave way to a search for more attractive alternatives. Again the search was led by small new organizations. One of those firms (Intel) managed to bring a radically new product on to the market. Intel's new device, which was first described as a 'computer on a chip' but would soon be known as a 'microprocessor' came on to the market in 1971.[15] The device was essentially a central processing unit on a chip.[16] In the microprocessor, software replaced the hardwire logic which was characteristic of earlier components. The use of software gave the microprocessor an unsurpassed flexibility. The same mass-produced microprocessor could now be used for completely different applications simply by making changes in the software. Intel's 4-bit microprocessor established a new technological regime and offered new organizations the chance to attack the dominant positions of incumbent organizations. Of the established IC producers, only Motorola managed to enter the early microprocessor market successfully. Other established firms were not able to bring viable products to the market until 1975 when TI and Fairchild introduced their own microprocessors.

Although static barriers to entry rose rapidly during the 1960s, they remained relatively modest until the mid-1970s. Riding on the waves of new technologies, a large number of new companies entered the market with only a modest amount of capital. National Semiconductor entered the market in 1967 with a mere $1 million in cash, whereas Intel[17] managed to invade the market two years later with only $3 million (UNIDO, 1981; Ernst, 1983). During the second half of the 1970s, technology became increasingly embodied in equipment instead of in people. Scientific advances which had played a critical role during the early years of the semiconductor industry became less important. The ever-increasing densities of semiconductor devices required highly sophisticated equipment rather than scientific advances (Morris, 1990). Extremely high R&D and manufacturing outlays were needed to design and manufacture the highly complex devices. Because of the rising capital requirements, R&D and production thresholds were raised and barriers to entry became more important. These conditions clearly favoured large firms which were able to amortize costs over a larger number of products. As a result the number of newly created spin-off companies decreased rapidly during the 1970s (Dosi, 1980).[18] The lack of sufficient resources in combination with an inefficient production scale made it increasingly difficult for small specialized companies to survive under the, at that time, highly competitive conditions.

Braun and MacDonald (1982) have shown that from 35 semiconductor companies which started production of semiconductor components in the period 1966–75, only seven companies were still independent in 1980. Only those companies that were able to combine innovativeness with excellence in manufacturing managed to survive. A typical example of such a company was Intel. Only one year after the introduction of its 4-bit microprocessor, Intel managed to produce a much more powerful 8-bit equivalent. Intel, as well as other organizations, followed a strong trajectory which focused on an increase in processing capacity, a larger bit-size, increased functionality and further reductions in costs (Swann, 1990). In 1973, even before most firms had been able to enter the 4-bit microprocessor market, Intel introduced an improved version of its 8-bit microprocessor, the 8080 (Wilson et al., 1980). Its technological superiority gave Intel a leading edge against potential competitors. Within three years of the introduction of its first microprocessor, Intel had been able to achieve an almost monopolistic position in the rapidly growing microprocessor market.

Because at that time software packages started to replace custom-programmed applications, the availability of software packages became an increasingly important success factor in the microprocessor market. Intel's domination of the market encouraged a large number of companies to write software for Intel's microprocessors. Very soon a large number of software packages became available for Intel's microprocessors. Because Intel did not want to jeopardize such a large stock of software, compatibility among the various generations of microprocessors became Intel's most important strategy. IBM's choice to incorporate Intel's microprocessor in its PC line once again boosted Intel's sales and established the MS DOS/Intel/IBM standard in the PC market (Blair, 1991).[19] The availability of a large stock of software, combined with the innovative capabilities of Intel's microprocessors and the support of IBM, left little room for other organizations in the market. In the 1980s, Intel came up with a number of backward compatible microprocessors. Intel's presence in the 16-bit market started with the 80286 microprocessor. In 1986 this microprocessor would be replaced by the 32-bit 80386, followed in 1989 by the much more powerful 80486. Recently, Intel introduced an even more powerful device, the so-called 'Pentium' microprocessor. Intel, the by now undisputed leader, used to be a well-known practitioner of the 'cream-skimming' strategy. It sold its innovative products at a premium price and decided to leave the sector as soon as competition became fierce and prices went down. Intel then moved on to other (more profitable) markets. Today

Intel chooses to stay in its 'old' markets and harvests profits which it invests in more promising new markets.

Until recently most of the technological developments in the microprocessor market have been competence-enhancing, thereby increasing the domination of the existing market leaders. Today's microprocessor market is characterized by a virtual duopoly of Motorola and Intel.[20] Their microprocessor architectures are, however, under increasing pressure. In the late 1980s and early 1990s a growing number of radically new designs have been brought onto the market. Whereas traditional complex instruction set computer (CISC) microprocessor producers tried to increase the number of components and instructions on a single microprocessor, a number of non-leading competitors and new entrants started to focus on a completely different trajectory. Instead of increasing the number of instructions embedded in a microprocessor, they radically reduced the instruction set of their microprocessors. These so-called reduced instruction set computers (RISC) incorporate only the most important instructions. The relatively simple structure of these devices gave way to much faster and more reliable components as compared to the traditional CISC-based microprocessors.

The opportunity to attack Intel's dominant position in the microprocessor market has attracted a large number of new and established companies into the emerging RISC market. The RISC market was opened up in the late 1980s by two producers of workstation computers: MIPS Computer Systems[21] and its arch rival, Sun Microsystems. As soon as their microprocessors proved viable, they were followed by a number of larger computer companies. Hewlett Packard formed the Precision RISC Organization (PRO) to promote its PA-RISC architecture, and more recently industry giants IBM and Apple joined forces with Motorola to develop the so-called PowerPC microprocessor. In 1993 they were followed by DEC who brought its Alpha RISC processor to the market. The apparent advantages of RISC technologies over the traditional CISC microprocessor forced Intel to come up with its own RISC processors. Until now no single RISC architecture has been able to establish itself as the industry standard. Competition between the various competitive designs is, however, extremely fierce.[22]

5.3.1. Semiconductor Memories

The growing importance of the computer industry not only affected the microprocessor market but was also illustrated by the initiating role it played in the development of memory chips. Until the 1970s, magnetic core memories were the most important random access memory devices in use. Magnetic core memories were relatively slow and were able to store only limited amounts of information. The advent of highly sophisticated von Neumann computer designs in the 1960s rapidly increased the need for more advanced memory chips. Because semiconductor materials were already in use in most micro-electronic devices, research was directed towards memories based on semiconductor materials. The first semiconductor memory chips were brought on to the market in the mid-1960s. Their impact, however, was limited until 1970, when Intel brought the 1K DRAM on to the market (Gill, 1990). Intel's device was based on sophisticated MOS technology and managed to drive the traditional magnetic core memories out of the market. Their smaller size and much higher speed made semiconductor memories particularly suited to be incorporated into sophisticated computer systems. In the early days of the DRAM market the leading positions were occupied by small innovative US companies such as Intel and Mostek. Established firms, with the exception of Texas Instruments, failed to recognize the opportunities in the semiconductor memory market (Wilson et al., 1980). In 1975 the first Japanese competitor (NEC) entered the DRAM market. NEC would soon be followed by a number of other Japanese firms. Their entrance into the memory market was primarily provoked by the effects of the 1974–75 recession. After a boom in the early 1970s the US semiconductor market was struck by a major recession in 1974–75. US firms were forced to halt investments in R&D and new manufacturing plants and laid off thousands of people during the recession. Because of the cutbacks in plant and labour most US firms were unable to meet demand when the recession came to an end. Japanese companies, on the other hand, were particularly eager to fill this gap by bringing large quantities of low-priced mass-produced memory chips to the US market.

The Japanese involvement in the US semiconductor market started in 1959, when for the first time in the history of the semiconductor industry Japanese companies shipped large amounts of (germanium) transistors to the US (Braun and MacDonald, 1982). Ever since the 1960s, Japanese companies have made vigorous attempts to increase their technological capabilities by practices of reverse engineering. The Japanese government allowed them to build up production in a protected home market and once they established a firm position on the Japanese market they started to attack foreign markets by pursuing a low-price strategy in order to buy market share. Price competition would turn out to be a particularly viable strategy in the DRAM market because memory devices were all near-perfect substitutes. The diversified nature of Japanese firms enabled them to cross-subsidize their component divisions in order to sustain investment in plant and R&D during periods of temporary cutbacks in sales. Moreover, their high levels of vertical and horizontal integration ensured a large captive market. After several years of catching up with the US, Japanese companies succeeded in cracking the dominant position of US firms in the early 1980s. Japanese firms had lagged behind in the introduction of 1-, 4- and 16K DRAMs but succeeded in bringing the first 64K DRAM to the market. While US firms were struggling to develop a new very complex 64K RAM chip, Fujitsu managed to come up with a larger version of its 16K RAM device.[23] Fujitsu was soon followed by a number of other Japanese firms that used a similar strategy. The Japanese design was not only faster to the market, but would also prove to be much more reliable than its more complex US counterpart (Weinstein et al., 1984). Learning-curve advantages stemming from the rapid introduction of the 64K RAM enabled Japanese companies to seize a considerable market share. US firms, on the other hand, entered the market relatively late and were facing rapidly decreasing returns. These decreasing returns made it very difficult for a large part of those companies to invest in a new generation of DRAMs. In 1982, Japanese companies managed to capture 70 per cent of the 64K RAM market (Weinstein et al., 1984). At that time, all of the leading positions that were previously held by small pioneering firms were now taken over by much more efficient, large, vertically integrated competitors (see Table 5.2). Because technological change became increasingly cumulative and moved along strongly focused trajectories, it became increasingly difficult to catch up with the leaders. Dosi (1981) has argued that in such a strong and cumulative regime the position that is currently occupied determines the ability to keep up with the movements of the technological frontier. As a result, the market gradually changed from a dynamic marketplace which was dominated by innovative small start-up companies into a highly concentrated market structure in which only the most efficient producers managed to survive.

The Japanese domination of the DRAM market was not only important in terms of profits, but was also of strategic importance to the Japanese IT industry. DRAMs were generally considered to be one of the most important technology drivers. Production and technological experience in DRAM technology was considered to be a prerequisite to the entrance of higher-end markets. The strategic importance of DRAMs was well understood by the Japanese Ministry of International Trade and Industry (MITI). Ever since the

1960s, MITI had been trying to improve the competitive position of Japan. MITI protected the Japanese market from foreign imports and actively encouraged the diffusion of technological knowledge among the various Japanese companies. In 1975, MITI and the telecommunication giant NTT initiated a large-scale collaborative research programme which was aimed at the investigation of VLSI technology. Active members of this programme included all the major electronic companies such as Fujitsu, Hitachi, Mitsubishi, NEC and Toshiba. In the following years six major research labs would be established in Japan. The VLSI programme, which ended in 1979, radically improved the technological capabilities of Japanese firms. The project resulted in no less than 100 patents and about 460 technical papers (Uenohara et al., 1984).

5.3.2. Semiconductor Cycles

In order to secure themselves from a shortage of vital components, firms often tend to order components in excess of their short-term needs (Blair, 1991). Component manufacturers respond to these needs by increasing their capacities during periods of high demand, but once the new plants start operating they often face overcapacity. This leads to the typical semiconductor cycles. According to Gordon Moore 'The balance of supply and demand in this industry lasts for about 35 minutes' (Forester, 1993: 62). Since 1977, the semiconductor market has been hit by a recession about every four years.[24] It is therefore not surprising that a major boom in 1984 was followed by the worst recession of all times. US semiconductor companies lost approximately $500 million in the 1985–86 recession. This recession, which was largely due to a recession in the computer industry, led to the exit of all US companies except Texas Instruments from the DRAM market. In spite of the overcapacity which characterized the industry during the recession years, Japanese companies managed once again to maintain their investments in plants, R&D and equipment. The ability of Japanese companies to outperform US firms during and shortly after recessions is widely discussed in the literature (see e.g. Okimoto et al., 1984; Hobday, 1989; Gill, 1990; Jelinek and Schoonhoven, 1990; Forester, 1993). Most authors have argued that Japanese companies are particularly successful because of their specific industry structure in which Japanese companies are linked to large conglomerates of other companies and financial institutions.

The Dynamics of Technical Innovation

Table 5.2 Vertical integration in the semiconductor industry

	1970	1976	1982
Vertically Integrated Manufacturers	ITT Motorola Raytheon RCA Texas Instruments	AEG- Telefunken Ferranti General Instruments Harris Hughes ITT Motorola NEC Plessey Philips/Signetics Raytheon RCA Rockwell Sesosem Siemens Texas Instruments	AEG-Telefunken Bourns Exxon/Zilog Ferranti Fujitsu GE/Intersil General Instrument Gould/Ami Harris Hitachi Honeyw./Synertek Hughes ITT Matsushita Mitsubishi Motorola NEC Oki Philips/Signetics Plessey Raytheon RCA Schlum./Fairchild Sharp Siemens Sprague Thomson-CSF Texas Instruments Toshiba TRW Unit Tech./Mostek
Independent IC Manufact.	AMD AMI AMS Electronic Arrays Fairchild Intel Intersil MMI Mostek National Semi. PMI SGS-Altes Siliconix	AMD AMI Electronic Arrays Fairchild Intel Intersil MMI Mostek National Semi. SGS-Altes Siliconix Synertek Zilog	AMD Inmos Intel Nat.Semiconductor SGS-Altes

Source: Mackintosh, cited in Gerybadze, 1984.

These conglomerates, which are often referred to as 'Keiretsus' can be described as systems in which organizations have a large number of horizontal and vertical links to other organizations in the system and to specific banks. Firms in the Keiretsu favour each other by preferential contracting and sub-contracting, whereas the banks in the Keiretsu generously provide capital on a long-term, low interest basis (Hobday, 1989, 1990; Todd, 1990; Forester, 1993). The Keiretsu structure allows for long-term strategies as opposed to the US situation where firms feel constant pressure from their stock-holders to produce short-term results. The large size, long-term low interest loans and deep pockets of Japanese firms enables them to deal effectively with temporary cutbacks in demand. These advantages, combined with their excellence in manufacturing and quality control, account for the success of Japanese firms in virtually all commodity IC markets.

US firms were clearly not able to compete effectively against their Japanese competitors in high-volume commodity IC markets in which success is to a large degree dependent on market share (production volume). In a market where capital and R&D investments have increased dramatically with every new generation of DRAMs, only very large efficient organizations are able to survive. Because new generations of DRAMs are introduced every three or four years, a very high market share is needed in order to recoup the rising capital and R&D costs. During the 1985–86 recession, all of the major Japanese firms maintained their investments in plants and equipment and some of them even managed to expand their production capacity. Japanese companies were particularly successful in the memory market because software capabilities, services and close links with the computer industry were not very important. In this market it was manufacturing capability that counted most. In 1986, at the end of the recession, Japanese companies managed to overtake US companies in terms of world-market share in the semiconductor industry and established an almost monopolistic position in the memory market. A large number of American firms, including the former industry leaders Intel and Mostek, left the high-volume commodity DRAM market and directed their attention towards (semi-) custom ICs and microprocessors. At that time only Texas Instruments and the small producer Micron Technology remained active in the DRAM market.

In spite of their inability to compete effectively in the DRAM industry, US firms were well known to be ahead of Japanese companies in terms of design and software skills. Because of their close contacts with world-wide leading US computer firms, they were also superior to their Japanese competitors in terms of user-producer interactions. The exit from high-volume commodity markets drove US firms into new markets where efficient production was subordinate to design and software skills. One of the markets which was invaded by a large number of US semiconductor manufacturers was the emerging market for semi-custom ICs. Semi-custom chips were designed as a reaction to the inefficient production runs of custom chips, and are based on the same basic chips. These basic chips are modified at a later stage in order to tailor the chip for use with a specific application. The use of the same basic chips enables companies to reap economies of scope in the manufacturing process. Semi-custom chips are not only much cheaper to produce but also pay off in terms of design lead times and costs (Ernst, 1983).

The relatively new and rapidly growing market for application specific ICs (ASICs) gave small US start-up firms the opportunity to bypass the major barriers to entry into commodity markets. Success in the ASIC market is not dependent on large-scale production efficiency but on design skills and customer relationships. Although manufacturing costs remained very high during the 1980s, design costs have decreased enormously because of the availability of relatively low-cost CAD equipment and software. A large number of new entrepreneurial firms which employed highly skilled designers started so-called 'fab-less' firms which concentrated on design and contracted out their manufacturing. In the US, firms such as Chips and Technologies, Weitec and Maxim have successfully pursued this strategy. Other new entrants abandoned the design part and specialized in the manufacturing of ASICs. A large number of these so-called 'silicon foundries', however, suffered from a chronic lack of funds. Fixed costs in terms of plants and equipment have increased tremendously with every new generation of semiconductors. Jelinek and Schoonhoven (1990: 35) have argued that 'production technology for semiconductor products is easily the most complex process ever adapted to mass production'. Today a new generation chip line would cost about 1 billion US dollars. A very large market share seems necessary to recoup these extremely high capital outlays.[25]

Apart from economies of scale in the production of electronic components, economies of scope (Goldhar and Jelinek, 1983) are gaining increasing importance. As demonstrated above, high costs of R&D and production equipment call for very large production runs in order to amortize these costs. The rapid rate of succession between various generations of products, however, makes it increasingly difficult to achieve a sufficient scale of production for one product. An efficient number of products can often only be achieved by using the same equipment to produce various different products. Jelinek and Schoonhoven (1990: 37) have argued that the growing share of ASICs in total production has considerably increased the need for such economies of scope. They argued that because of the semi-custom character of ASICs 'no single user will order enough of any product to cover the heavy investment in production equipment'. Therefore equipment must be able to produce a broad scala of designs. During the 1980s, US firms have invested heavily in state-of-the-art FMS equipment which allowed them to move swiftly between the production of different ASIC designs. Even in Europe, where traditional vacuum-tube producers have always dominated the marketplace, small firms started to enter the ASIC market. Hobday (1989) reports start-ups in countries like Belgium (Mietec), Holland (Advanced Silicon Corporation) and Switzerland (Lassaray), as well as pan-European initiatives (European Silicon Structures). In spite of the noted disadvantages of Japanese companies in high-end applications such as ASICs, Japanese firms started to enter the ASIC market in the mid-1980s. Within a few years, they even managed to become the world leaders in the low-end ASIC market (Morgan and Sayer, 1988). A recent article on Japanese start-ups (*Solid State Technology*, September 1990: 45–6) showed that nine out of eleven newly established semiconductor companies aimed to enter the market for ASICs.

5.4. RECENT INTERNATIONAL DEVELOPMENTS

The relatively modest position of European firms in the international semiconductor industry is indicated by their world market share (Figure 5.3). European firms have lagged behind in advanced MOS and microprocessor technology (Hazewindus, 1982). They specialized in relatively old-fashioned discrete components. In-house needs were generally valued more than merchant production. In order to catch up with the US and Japan, the EC initiated European-wide collaborative pre-competitive R&D projects in the mid-1980s. Although these R&D projects were successful in technological terms, they did not lead to an improved position of European companies on the world market (Hobday, 1990). The predicted rapid growth of the European semiconductor market, however, may be an important stimulus to the European manufacturers to improve their competitive position.

In 1991, Japanese firms captured 46 per cent of the semiconductor market whereas the share of US firms decreased to 39 per cent. Today six out of the top ten semiconductor manufacturers are Japanese firms. In the DRAM market, Japanese companies face serious competition only from competitors from the so-called newly industrialized countries (NICs).[26] Companies from those countries have specialized in low-cost production of commodity chips. US firms, on the other hand, are particularly successful in high-end components and in application- and system-specific ICs. Increasingly worried about the deteriorating competitive position of US firms, the Semiconductor Industry Association (SIA) initiated a government industry R&D consortium called Semiconductor Manufacturing Technology Project (Sematech). Sematech was established in 1987 by 14 leading semiconductor companies and was funded by those companies and a subsidy of $100 million from the US government. Its aim was to regain world-wide semiconductor manufacturing leadership. Members of Sematech include AMD, AT&T, DEC, Harris Corporation, HP, Intel, IBM, LSI Logic, Micron Technology Inc., Motorola, National Semiconductor Corporation, NCR, Rockwell International and Texas Instruments. At that time Japanese companies had captured between 80 and 90 per cent of the world DRAM market (Hobday, 1989) and were a dominant force in equipment manufacturing. In 1989, a second consortium was established in order to facilitate the re-entrance of US firms into memory chips. The participation of US firms in the memory market was of strategic importance because profound knowledge in DRAM technology was seen as a prerequisite for the successful participation in other sectors of the semiconductor market. However, the consortium, which was known as 'US memories', never really took off, and collapsed in January 1990. At that time a number of US firms had already been able to re-enter the DRAM market. In line with the US consortia, Japanese firms established their own collaborative research project (TRON) which aimed to attack the US lead in microprocessors. This strategy was in line with previous attempts to attack high-end markets from an established base in low-end markets. In spite of persistent Japanese efforts to crack the hegemony of US microprocessor manufacturers, US domination of the market is still all-encompassing.

In 1991, the two largest US competitors, Intel and Motorola, accounted for more than 90 per cent of the market for advanced microprocessors (Molina, 1992). The existing market structure, however, might be severely destroyed by the advent of new powerful RISC-based microprocessors. Although RISC microprocessors pose a serious threat to the dominant position of both Motorola and Intel, this does not seem to jeopardize the position of US firms in the microprocessor market. Both Japan and Europe have only a minor presence in the emerging RISC market (Molina, 1991). Most of the threat comes from other major US companies, such as Sun Microsystems, DEC, Hewlett Packard and the alliance of IBM, Motorola and Apple. Therefore we believe that in spite of the ongoing 'creative destruction' in the market-place (see Table 5.3), the existing duopoly of the US (microprocessors) and Japan (commodity markets) will remain basically unchanged in the near future.

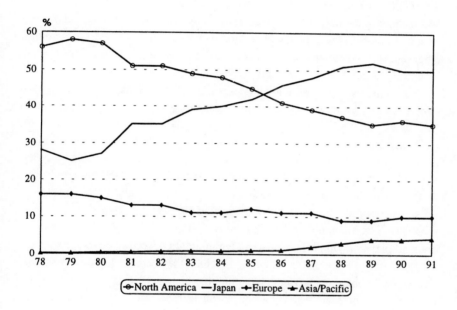

Source: Dataquest, December 1991.

Figure 5.3 World-wide semiconductor market share (1978–1991)

5.5. DISCUSSION

The semiconductor industry can be seen as the driving force of technological change for virtually all sectors of the information technology industry. The semiconductor industry is of strategic importance, not only in terms of market size, but also because its outputs are vital components in a wide range of other products. In *Hypothesis 1* we stressed the role of universities and government institutions as the most important incubators of new technologies. The role of these institutions would be particularly important because emerging markets were often characterized by a great deal of uncertainty about the technological feasibility of innovations and their potential market size. In contrast, the first semiconductor device was a relatively simple device that could be used as a replacement of an existing device (the vacuum tube). Therefore, both market and technological uncertainties were rather low. The extremely high elasticity of substitution between the transistor and its vacuum-tube predecessor and the emergence of a large and profitable military market raised the interest of large incumbent vacuum-tube producers.

Not only in terms of market size, but also in terms of technological sophistication, large well-established firms were a dominant force during the first decade of the newly born semiconductor industry. One organization in particular, Bell Laboratories, played a vital role in the creation and diffusion of new semiconductor technologies. Its liberal licensing policies enabled a large number of companies to explore the opportunities in the early semiconductor market. Although our first hypothesis cannot be confirmed by our analysis, government procurement and support played an extremely important role at a time when commercial demand was almost non-existent. In particular, military demand played a vital role in shaping the direction of technological progress.

Relatively low barriers to entry and the prospects of highly profitable government contracts induced a large number of small specialist companies to enter the newly established market. Because the largest customer, the US military, clearly favoured innovativeness over price, efficient production was less important than the ability to improve the existing technological characteristics. Because small new organizations had no commitments to existing technologies, they were able to respond rapidly to the new opportunities in the market. This is in line with *Hypothesis 2*, which states that a new market is likely to be explored by small specialist organizations that pursue an offensive innovation strategy. It must be stressed, however, that in the US small companies were relatively late to enter the semiconductor market. As described above, the early market was dominated by large, well-established firms. In 1960, however, nearly all the major vacuum-tube producers were driven out of the market by smaller new specialist competitors. In Europe and Japan, a very low mobility of engineers and the lack of venture capital inhibited the emergence of small start-up companies. Therefore *Hypothesis 2* cannot be confirmed for these regions.

Texas Instruments' invention of the silicon transistor established a technological regime that was based on small, fast and reliable semiconductor components. From that time onwards silicon became the most important material in use. The importance of radical product innovations decreased after the invention of the silicon transistor. Process innovations, on the other hand, became more important after the establishment of the transistor regime. Two major process innovations were particularly important during this period: i.e. the diffusion and the oxide-masking process. The decreasing importance of radical product innovations supports *Hypothesis 3*, which argues that the emergence of a 'basic design' leads to a substitution of radical technological developments by incremental cumulative improvements along a specific technological path or trajectory. In general, a more standardized direction of technological progress shifts competition away from performance and design towards price. In the semiconductor industry this process was speeded up by the replacement of the US military by the computer industry as the most important source of demand. The emergence of a commercial market increased price-based competition. In the semiconductor industry costs per unit were not only dependent on static economies of scale in the production of these devices, but also on more dynamic scale economies such as learning economies. It was therefore particularly important for firms to stay close to the technological frontier. Those firms that were able to combine static economies of scale and learning economies were most successful in the semiconductor industry.

This is in concordance with *Hypothesis 4*, which asserted that after the establishment of a new technological regime, large K-generalists start to outperform smaller r-specialists. In line with *Hypothesis 5*, which proposed an r to K transition during times of fierce competition, we found that large firms with a high-tech orientation were best equipped to thrive under such environmental conditions. Although newly established firms entered the market on a very large scale after the invention of the integrated circuit, the IC market would soon be dominated by only five major firms that accounted for more than 80 per cent of the total IC market (Tilton, 1971).

Table 5.3 League table of micro-electronics manufacturers (1945–1990)

	1945	1955	1960	1965	1975	1980	1984	1990
RCA	1	7	5	6	8			
Sylvania	2	4	10					
General Elect.	3	6	4	5				
Raytheon	4			10				
Westinghouse	5		8					
Ameperex	6							
National Video	7							
Ranland	8							
Eimac	9							
Landsdale Tube	10							
Hughes		1	9					
Transistron		2	2	8				
Philco		3	3	8				
Texas Instruments		5	1	1	1	1	1	7
Fairchild		8		2	2	6		
Motorola		9	6	3	5	2	3	4
Clevite		10	7					
General Instruments				4	7	10		
Sprague				7				
National Semiconductor					3	3	5	5
Intel					4	4	6	
Rockwell					6			
Signetics/Philips					9	8	8	10
American Microsystems					10			
AMD						9	10	
NEC						5	2	1
Hitachi						7	4	3
Toshiba						10	9	2
Fujitsu							7	6
Mitsubishi								8
Matsushita								9

Sources: 1990: Dataquest; all other years: Craig, 1986.

In the early 1970s a paradigmatic shift took place in the semiconductor industry. Microprocessors started to replace integrated circuits in a large number of applications. As we have argued in *Hypothesis 7*, a paradigmatic shift often undermines the position of large well-established companies in favour of small newly established companies. From the established IC-producing companies only Motorola managed to enter the early microprocessor market successfully. At about the same time, semiconductors started to replace magnetic core memories as the basic memory units in computers. Again new firms rapidly invaded the new market, whereas the incumbent organizations retained their focus on the 'old' technologies. This confirms our earlier expectation which was put forward in *Hypothesis 7*. Once the basic technologies were well understood and the market turned into a well-established mass market, production efficiency became more important. Technological progress turned out to become increasingly incremental and radical changes were very rare.

Once a mass market is established, windows of opportunity are likely to occur and firms tend to invade multiple market niches *(Hypothesis 6)*. During the second half of the 1980s, application-specific memory devices, custom chips and RISC microprocessors created opportunities for firms to bypass the enormous barriers to entry in production and research. This confirms the proposition that was put forward in *Hypothesis 6*. Specialization not only took place within market niches but also within the value chain. Some organizations specialized in the production of semiconductors whereas other organizations restricted their attention to the design part. Such a pattern of vertical specialization was particularly found in the (semi-)custom IC market.

To summarize, the integrated framework as presented in the second chapter was able to predict fairly accurately the technological and market developments in the history of the semiconductor industry. Two hypotheses, however, could not be validated: *Hypothesis 1* and *Hypothesis 2*. *Hypothesis 1*, which stresses the role of universities and government institutions as incubators of new technologies, could not be validated by the existing evidence because, in contrast to what was expected in Chapter 2, technological and market uncertainty was not very high during this period. Low market and technological uncertainties and a very high elasticity of substitution between the transistor and the vacuum tube would soon arouse the interest of large incumbent vacuum-tube-producing companies. The role of small companies in the early semiconductor industry was therefore much lower than was expected in *Hypothesis 2*. The importance of small companies, however, rose rapidly during the 1950s in the US. Virtually, every change in technological regime in the semiconductor industry was accompanied by forces of 'creative destruction' and the emergence of new companies in the market-place.

NOTES

1. On 25 October 1906, Lee DeForest applied for a patent on its famous three-element vacuum tube.
2. AT&T had bought the radio receiver rights for the triode vacuum tube.
3. The first point-contact diode, which allowed electrical signals to flow in only one direction, had already been invented in 1938 at General Electric.
4. Until the late 1950s, hearing-aid manufacturers would remain the most important commercial customers of transistors.
5. In comparison to the point-contact diode, the junction transistor was capable of dealing with much higher currents, did not generate much noise, and was much easier to manufacture (Morris, 1990).
6. Government support in Japan took off in 1972 and was substantial until 1980 (Uenohara et al., 1984).
7. The Consent Decree of 1956 forced Bell Laboratories to pursue a policy of liberal licensing.
8. It was able to retain this dominant position until 1985.
9. Transistron had successfully improved and marketed the gold bounded diode, which was invented at Bell Laboratories.
10. In general production yields are a function of cumulative production experience. Over time costs per unit decrease rapidly due to learning effects (Abernathy and Wayne, 1964).
11. This pattern was first recognized by Gordon Moore at Fairchild Semiconductor, and is therefore referred to as Moore's law.
12. The planar process builds upon the oxide-masking and diffusion processes and, although in modified form, is still in use today.
13. In spite of its low speed, pMOS was much easier to manufacture, was denser and had a much lower power consumption than bipolar technologies. It was not until the 1980s that low-power-consuming MOS technologies matched bipolar technologies in terms of speed (Swann, 1986).
14. In 1962 the US government procured the entire US production of ICs.
15. Although Texas Instruments invented the first microprocessor, Intel managed to bring the first commercial microprocessor to the market.
16. By adding memory and input-output devices, one could build a complete computer out of this single chip (Dorfman, 1987).
17. Intel was one of the so-called 'Fairchildren', which were spin-off companies from the large US manufacturer Fairchild. In the 1960s, Fairchild spun off a large number of new companies, such as AMD, Amdahl, Apple, DEC, Intel, Mostek and Zilog.
18. Another factor for the decreasing number of spin-off companies in the 1970s is that less venture capital became available due to high capital-gains taxes in the US (Hazewindus, 1982) and because investors became more cautious after some serious industry crises in the 1960s.

19. For a long time, the only serious competition in the PC market came from the Apple Motorola alliance.
20. Together, Intel and Motorola are reported to account for more than 90 per cent of total advanced microprocessor sales (Molina, 1992).
21. MIPS Computer Systems is now part of Silicon Graphics Corporation.
22. For a more detailed description of the RISC market see Duysters and Vanhaverbeke (1996).
23. The only US exception was Motorola, which pursued a somewhat similar strategy to its Japanese competitors.
24. Since 1977, the industry has been hit by four major recessions, in 1977, 1981, 1985 and 1990–91 (Okimoto et al., 1984).
25. The importance of market share is indicated by Forester (1993) who has shown that every doubling of production volume decreases manufacturing costs by 30 per cent.
26. Especially from Korean firms such as Samsung, Hyundai and Goldstar.

6. Technological Convergence: An Empirical Analysis

In the previous chapters we have argued that technological convergence is gradually removing the sectoral boundaries between the various IT industry segments.[1] Such a process of convergence can be ascribed to a growing similarity among the technological foundations of the different IT segments. For a very long time technological developments in telecommunications and computers have followed very distinct trajectories. Today, the basic design parameters which form the core of technological regimes (Georghiou et al. 1986) have become increasingly similar, not only in terms of the material properties but also with respect to the manufacturing process involved. Although the convergence process started in the late 1950s it was not until the early 1970s that it really took off. At that time large numbers of powerful digital components were brought on to the market at relatively low costs. In the following years subsequent improvements accelerated the rate of adoption of these components in all kinds of electronic equipment.

Today almost every single electronic device is based on the same digital technology. Digitalization of telecommunications and computer equipment has broadened the existing technology base and facilitated the emergence of large-scale communication networks that carried voice, data and images. As computers were increasingly accommodated within those telecommunications networks, previous existing technological and market boundaries became vague. The blurring boundaries between the computer and telecommunications markets soon challenged the core competencies of the traditional suppliers and induced 'lateral entry': i.e. entrance of firms from adjacent markets. In the telecommunications industry the first signs of convergence appeared through the introduction of stored program control (SPC) in the field of digital switching.[2] The second wave of convergence took place during the mid-1980s when analogue telephone systems were gradually transformed into fully digital networks (Davies, 1991). The rise in distributed computing and the digitalization of the telecommunications network induced a number of telecommunication firms to accumulate skills in software and micro-electronics and raised the interests of computer manufacturers in telecommunication technology. At that time a number of authors and industry practitioners argued that the IT industry would eventually offer a continuum of products, which could not be referred to as either telecommunication or computer products. They envisioned that all the different IT markets would melt into one giant 'information and entertainment industry' and that firms would react to the new opportunities by lateral entry into each other's markets (de Jonquieres, 1989; *Business Week*, 25 May 1992: 69–71).

After decades of stable development, the existing institutional and technological structure of the telecommunications industry was suddenly challenged by a wave of new technologies. The digitalization of telecommunications networks made it impossible to think of computers and telecommunications as separate technologies. The convergence process created a huge potential for new products and services and turned out to be a large impetus to deregulatory forces in the industry. All over the world technological convergence induced governments to re-examine the existing regulatory frameworks and to implement deregulatory and liberalizing actions. Although computer and telecommunications equipment are now based on the same enabling technologies they have traditionally been produced by different companies. A relatively stable environment which characterized the computer industry and more in particular, the telecommunications industry, induced firms to develop a stable set of routines to deal with their environment.

Today such routinized behaviour does not seem sufficient to deal with the technological convergence process in information technologies. The required technological competencies in adjacent technologies are often not present within the existing technology base. For those companies several options are open to acquire the essential technological knowledge. Technology can be developed in-house or it can be acquired on the market by arms'-length transactions (e.g. using R&D contracts) or through the acquisition of technological sophisticated companies. Between these two extremes, acquisition or internal development, several options are open to a company. Companies may perform R&D together with a partner, license-in technology or use other forms of cooperation. Internal development is costly but often necessary to achieve the required technological base. Cooperative strategies, on the other hand, involve less capital and are particularly suited to monitor new technological developments. In the past decade the number of cooperative agreements by firms has rocketed (see Chapter 7). The use of cooperative agreements, however, is often only effective in combination with internal development. Haklisch (1989) has argued convincingly that interdependence is often used as a viable strategy to strengthen independence.

In the early 1980s, many industry observers expected that the convergence process would provoke a battle between the industry giants IBM and AT&T (Tunstall, 1986). After its divesture in 1984, AT&T was allowed to enter other (unregulated) markets and bought MOS Technology and more recently NCR. IBM on the other hand grasped the opportunity to strengthen its presence in the telecommunications market and bought telecom equipment makers Rolm Corporation and SBS Satellite. AT&T turned its focus on the computer industry by acquiring a stake in Olivetti. Although acquisition of knowledgeable companies seems to be an attractive option for companies that have to deal with convergent technologies, acquisition strategies are hampered by at least three main problems (Aldrich and Auster, 1986). The first problem is associated with information distortion and opportunism, which may mislead the acquiring company. A second problem is that creative and innovative companies which are incorporated in a large and bureaucratic structure often lose their flexibility and therefore lose much of their original creativity and innovativeness. The third problem is related to the externalities which are connected to the acquisition of a company. It is often difficult to divest those assets which are not sought for in the first place. An additional problem that is associated with acquisitions occurs if a company does not have an already sufficiently developed level of technological knowledge in a specific field. Then it turns out to be extremely difficult to absorb the acquired knowledge into its own technological core. It is often noted that a firm's absorptive capability is to a large degree dependent on the degree of knowledge in a specific field (Dodgson, 1989; Cohen and Levinthal, 1990; Levinthal, 1994). Therefore we might argue that if the core of a company's technology base is not sufficiently adapted to the new technology, then the absorption of acquired technological knowledge within the technological core of a company is very difficult.

The combination of those factors may explain why most of the acquisitions were (until today) not very successful. In the late 1980s IBM moved out of telecommunications by selling its share in Rolm, whereas a large number of telecommunications companies sold their interests in computer equipment (Malerba et al., 1991). In the early 1990s, it gradually became clear that the expected 'lateral entry' between the telecommunications and computer markets had not taken place (Mansell, 1993). Two factors seemed to be responsible for the low degree of lateral entry that was found in the telecommunications and computer markets, i.e. economies of scope that turned out to be lower than expected and the continuing importance of scale economies (Malerba et al., 1991). Economies of scope which were gained by the joint production of telecommunication and computer equipment were simply not able to offset the loss of economies of scale. In this chapter we will argue that there is a third, maybe even more important, factor that influenced the low degree of convergence within firms, namely inertia. Following evolutionary and ecological theory we will argue that both external and internal inertial forces significantly reduce the ability of firms to deal with changes in their technological cores. Firms are often simply not able to adapt swiftly to their changing technological environments.

6.1. RESEARCH QUESTIONS

Although most of the attention has been dedicated to the technological convergence between telecommunications and computers, such processes are not restricted to those two markets. The pervasive effect of micro-electronics and software can be found to drive convergence between virtually all the major IT markets – consumer electronics, broadcasting, instrumentation, military electronics, software, computing and telecommunications. Until the late 1970s the boundaries between those markets were clearly defined, but since then the convergence process has blurred the once existing boundaries. Patterns of convergence are found to occur at a number of different levels: the product-market level, the technology level and the firm level (von Tunzelmann, 1988). At the product-market level we find well-known examples, such as 'multi-media' products, which bring together software, computers and consumer electronics and a whole range of new products, referred to as 'telematics' products, which embody the convergence between computer and telecommunications technology. At the technology level we find a change away from analogue devices towards completely digital devices. Today virtually all segments of the IT market have been affected by the pervasive effect of micro-electronics and software.

Although in this book (so far) a great deal of attention has been paid to the product and the technology level, considerably less has been directed towards the third level of convergence, that within firms. In order to account for the full implications of the convergence process, however, it also seems relevant to pay somewhat more attention to this level of convergence. What we wish to examine, therefore, is whether and to what degree firms from different markets are affected by the technological convergence process. The major aim of this chapter is to examine whether the so-called convergence of information and communication technologies has led to a growing similarity of firms which are active in different IT markets. Although telecommunications and computer equipment are based on the same enabling technologies, it can be argued that the convergence process has taken place much more slowly than was expected in the early 1980s (Malerba et al., 1991; von Tunzelmann and Soete, 1987; von Tunzelmann, 1988). The few empirical studies on the convergence process within firms (von Tunzelmann and Soete, 1987; von Tunzelmann, 1988) showed that patterns of convergence had not significantly affected the core competencies of the major IT firms.[3] Their analyses were based on US patent data which covered the periods 1969–84 and 1969–86. Most industry observers and practitioners agree, however, that the convergence process accelerated in the late 1980s and early 1990s.[4] Therefore an analysis that is based on data until 1986 is likely to underestimate the current magnitude and importance of the convergence process. Extending the time-frame might therefore be an important step forwards in understanding the broader implications of these patterns of convergence in IT markets.

In terms of the methodological aspects, the aim of the chapter is to provide an analysis of patterns of convergence in the IT industry which combines quantitative and semi-quantitative methodologies. In this chapter we will apply a combination of descriptive and analytical approaches to study trends in the by now familiar industries: computers, telecommunications and semiconductors.

6.2. HYPOTHESES

In this book we abandon the common shared (strategic management) view of organizations as rapid, flexible adapters and stress the importance of inertial forces that prevent organizations from transforming their strategies and structures according to new demands of the environment. Following evolutionary theorists, we argue that apart from a stochastic element in the choice of decisions and their outcomes, most of the behaviour of firms is relatively predictable and repetitive. Such standard patterns of behaviour are often labelled 'routines' (Nelson and Winter, 1982) or 'comps' (McKelvey, 1982). Routines can be compared to biological genes because they govern a firm's behaviour and are heritable in the sense that future behaviour is largely based on today's characteristics (Nelson and Winter, 1982). A firm's reliance on basic routines severely reduces its speed of adaptation. It would be a caricature, however, to characterize firms as static organizations that are unable to change. Firms can be engaged in a 'search' process in an attempt to increase their 'fit' with the environment. Change mechanisms, however, are only triggered if the performance of an organization is well below its aspiration level (Cyert and March, 1963; Lant and Mezias, 1992). Firms with a relatively successful past are therefore often even more resistant to change than other firms. This so-called 'success breeds failure syndrome' (Starbuck et al., 1978) is often observed with established industry leaders. Evolutionary theorists argue that firms which are engaged in a search process do not explore all possible directions but confine their search to the most promising directions. Firms are often engaged in 'local search' only, which means that search is often limited to related areas. Local search and a continued reliance on their basic routines implies that firms are much better in doing more of the same than they are in adapting to change. We therefore expect that companies stick to their core businesses and therefore patterns of convergence are not likely to be found. The first and probably most important hypothesis is thus:

Hypothesis 8: Ongoing patterns of technological and product-market convergence have not significantly affected the technological cores of the participating companies.

The second issue we will deal with in this chapter is concerned with the question of whether convergence is taking place more persistently in firms that are active in some particular market segments than in others, and will also be concerned with an analysis of patterns of strategic technology alliances over time. Although the existing empirical studies on the convergence process did not study strategic alliance data, von Tunzelmann (1988: 3) suggested that 'various "stopgap" arrangements like strategic alliances were being sought to grapple with circumstances where this was proving a major competitive liability'. Because of increasing capital and surging R&D costs in combination with shrinking life cycles in all IT segments, firms are no longer able to monitor all the technological developments in the IT industry. Therefore, access to knowledge from other players in adjacent markets is becoming increasingly important (Economic Commission for Europe, 1987; Korzeniowski, 1988). The convergence process causes the blurring of traditional technological and sectoral boundaries and therefore increases the need for companies to keep up with many different technologies (van Tulder and Junne, 1988). Broadening the existing technology base by internal development would call for a considerable increase of the already heavy R&D cost burden. The combination of rising R&D costs and shorter life cycles induces firms to search for alternatives to internal development. Cooperation is often considered as a viable means to monitor several technological developments at relatively low costs. Given the problems with acquisitions as noted above, it therefore seems interesting to consider whether strategic technology alliances are increasingly used to deal with patterns of technological convergence (see van Tulder and Junne, 1988; Leban et al., 1989; Raphael, 1989; Charles et al., 1989). In other words we try to find out whether firms prefer to use strategic alliances as a basic means of dealing with the process of technological convergence. Therefore we argue:

Hypothesis 9: Firms tend to converge through means of strategic technology alliances, in the sense that the number of strategic technology alliances in neighbouring sectors have increased significantly over time as compared to the alliances in 'core' sectors.

6.3. DATA

For our analysis we make use of two types of data: patent data and data on strategic technology alliances. The patent data is based on a database that is compiled by the European Patent Office (EPO), which was established in 1978 on behalf of 13 European countries. Inventors who desire the protection of their invention can apply to the EPO for a patent in one or more of the 13 associated countries. The use of patent statistics has been criticized on many different grounds (Cohen and Levin, 1989; Griliches, 1990; Archibugi, 1992). The first and probably most important criticism is related to the use of patents as a measure of innovative output. It is argued that firms differ considerably in their propensity to patent. Some firms consider patenting as a viable means of protecting their innovations whereas others make use of other methods to safeguard their technological improvements. There are also wide country-specific differences in the approach towards patenting. Japanese firms, for example, tend to patent every claim, whereas US companies are more likely to bundle several claims into one patent (see Cohen and Levin, 1989). The propensity to patent not only differs across firms but also across industry sectors. Patent protection, for example, seems to be fairly effective in the semiconductor industry but to a lesser extent for computers (Nelson, 1987).

Another problem of patent statistics is related to the large differences that exist in the economic and technological importance of individual patents. Although some patents can be associated with major technological breakthroughs, a far larger number of patents are of considerably less importance and many patents are not even commercially exploited[5] (Dorfman, 1987; Graoutzi et al., 1988; Cohen and Levin, 1989). A related problem is that the majority of patents applied for are for product improvements. Although process innovations are usually not less significant in both economic and technological terms they are often not patented. In the case of process innovations, secrecy often turns out to be a viable alternative to patenting. For process innovations lead time and learning curve advantages also seem to be sufficient to protect the innovation (Nelson, 1987; Dosi, 1988).

However, there are also a number of advantages of using patent statistics. One important advantage of patent data over innovation input data is that patents are assigned to different technology classes which in turn can be (partly) translated into different economic sectors (Pavitt, 1988; Acs and Audretsch, 1989). Another important factor is that the chances of a patent being granted are closely related to the technological sophistication of a product and its innovative features. We might therefore argue that patents are a relatively good indicator of the level of technological sophistication of a company (Nystrom and Edvardsson, 1980). We must, however, keep in mind that patent statistics can not be used to measure the complete set of technological variables. Patent statistics can not be used to measure issues such as tacit elements of technology, they can measure only the codifiable part of technology. A more serious problem for the analysis of the IT sector is that for a long time software was not patentable and even today, software is being patented on a very limited scale only.

In this chapter patent statistics will be used to measure changes in the technological cores of major IT companies. In order to guarantee the 'global' character of our sample we incorporated all the leading companies in each sector: i.e. computers, telecommunications and semiconductors. We deliberately did not assign companies to a certain sectoral category on the basis of their profile but on the basis of their sales level in a specific sector. That means that we did not a priori label companies as being either computer firms, telecommunications firms or semiconductor firms according to their past or present profile. If we had only included firms that fit a certain profile we would not have accounted for the convergence that existed at the beginning of the time period. Company-level aggregation of subsidiaries was performed for every year of the analysis.[6] Information on company subsidiaries was taken from annual reports and from multiple volumes of *Who Owns Whom* (Dun and Bradstreet, 1970–1994). Company structures therefore differ with respect to the year in which they are analysed. Such an approach enables us to include also that part of the convergence which can be attributed to take-overs in adjacent markets. Changes in the technological cores of major IT-producing companies were measured by analysing the distribution of patents among three major IT sectors: computers, telecommunications and semiconductors. We assume that shifts in the core (technological) competencies of firms are reflected in changes in the relative number of patents that are applied for in a specific sector.

The data on strategic technology alliances was taken from MERIT's CATI database (see Appendix II). The CATI database contains information on over 10,000 agreements (of which some 5,000 agreements are related to the information technology sector). All the alliances in the database are either related to technology transfer or to some sort of joint innovative effort. In the present chapter we will use the term alliance to refer to those cooperative agreements that are not connected through majority ownership. An alliance can normally be seen as an agreement which is positioned between two extremes: arm's-length transactions on the market on the one hand and the complete merger of the two firms on the other. Our present study focuses on those alliances that were established in the period 1980–93. As in the case of patents, we have to use the strategic alliances with care. The CATI database is somewhat biased in terms of: 1) a skewness in the distribution of modes of organizations towards those that are more often reported in the literature; 2) a possible over-representation of large firms; 3) the underestimation of certain technology fields which do not belong to the core technologies; and 4) a possible bias towards Anglo-Saxon organizations. Our preoccupation with rather large companies and IT markets, however, implies that our analysis is unlikely to be seriously biased by these drawbacks.

Data on strategic technology alliances was used to measure the degree to which alliances are used to cope with the convergence process. As in the case of patents, we measured for each company the distribution of alliances among three major IT sectors: computers, telecommunications and semiconductors. In order to safeguard the strategic element in our sample we will study only those alliances which are undertaken for strategic reasons. Following Hagedoorn (1992: 164) we will refer to alliances as being strategic if they 'can reasonably be assumed to affect the long-term product market positioning of at least one partner'. Because alliances between government or academic institutions and private companies are frequently undertaken for different economic reasons than the alliances between two or more private companies[7] (see e.g. Haklisch, 1986), we will restrict our attention to those alliances which are established between private companies. For the same reason we do not pay attention to government-initiated or EC-wide R&D cost-sharing programmes such as ESPRIT, EUREKA or JESSI.

6.4. ANALYSIS

A first indicator of the degree of convergence within leading information technology companies is the presence of companies in more than one table of leading companies (see Appendix III). In our sample of leading IT manufacturers eight companies are among the leading producers of all three types of equipment: i.e. computers, telecommunications and semiconductors. With the exception of AT&T (and IBM if one includes captive production) all those players have a European (Philips, Siemens) or Japanese background (Fujitsu, Hitachi, Matsushita, NEC, Toshiba). This is not remarkable because it is well known that Japanese and European multinationals have a more diversified character than their US counterparts.[8] For each of the sectors we describe the overall distribution of patents and strategic technology alliances in semi-quantitative and quantitative terms respectively. All the data in the graphs are shown as three-year moving averages, in order to correct for yearly fluctuations that might attract too much attention away from the overall trends. Figure 6.1 shows the distribution of patents of leading computer companies as a percentage of their combined number of patents in all three sectors. Convergence seems to be an essential feature of these firms ever since the early 1980s. Involvement in telecommunications has always been very high and this high level of telecommunications patents turns out to be relatively stable over time. The data, however, indicate a decreasing trend of semiconductor patents in favour of computer patents.

Figure 6.2 displays a more diffuse pattern. It shows the distribution of strategic technology alliances of leading computer companies. In general the percentages of alliances in the different sectors seem to be somewhat inversely related to the percentages of patents. Computers seem to take an intermediate position, whereas semiconductor alliances account for a relatively large share of all alliances. Telecommunication alliances, on the other hand, seem to play a relatively modest role. The data does not indicate any significant trends except for a rise in semiconductor alliances during the period 1988–90 and a corresponding decrease of computer and telecommunication alliances during the same period. In order to test our main hypotheses we will now turn to a more quantitative approach. The first step in our analysis is to test *Hypothesis 8* which assumes that ongoing patterns of technological and product-market convergence have not significantly affected the technological cores of the participating companies. We therefore assume that there is no positive relationship between time and relative sectoral patenting.

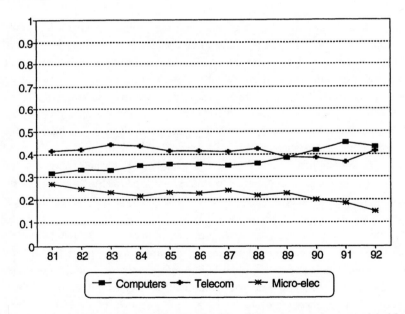

Figure 6.1 The distribution of patents of leading computer companies (three year moving averages,1980–1993)

A simple linear regression was used to measure the correlation between time (coded as 1–14) and the relative importance of patents and alliances in a particular sector. We made use of linear regression technique because we expected a linear relationship between patenting behaviour and time and also because the graphs that were presented above did not indicate a non-linear pattern. Because we assumed that the number of patents or alliances in one period could be related to the number of patents in the immediate preceding periods we tested the results for autocorrelation. In only one case (telecommunication patents for semiconductor firms) was autocorrelation found to exist (Durbin Watson: 0.93880). We therefore decided to use an autoregression analysis for that particular case in order to correct the results for autocorrelation.

We will now test *Hypothesis 8* which assumes that there is no linear relationship between time and relative sectoral patenting for major computer companies. Table 6.1 shows the results of a study on the trends in relative patenting and alliancing behaviour over time.

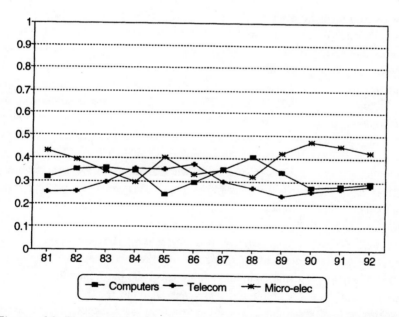

Figure 6.2 The distribution of strategic technology alliances of leading computer companies (three-year moving averages, 1980–1993)

Table 6.1 Results of the regression analysis on alliances and patents of major computer companies

	B	SE B	T	sig T	R^2	SE	F	Const
Computers								
Patents	1.036	0.244	4.243	0.011	0.599	3.686	17.99*	29.040
Alliances	-0.171	0.698	-0.245	0.811	0.005	10.538	0.060	33.729
Telecom								
Patents	-0.191	0.288	-0.664	0.519	0.035	4.346	0.441	42.750
Alliances	-0.171	0.699	-0.245	0.811	0.005	10.536	0.060	33.729
Micro-elec.								
Patents	-0.845	0.193	-4.380	0.001	0.615	2.911	19.18*	28.206
Alliances	0.330	0.790	0.417	0.684	0.014	11.919	0.174	36.380

* $p < 0.01$.

The overall measure of goodness of fit for the linear model is represented by the coefficient of determination (R^2). High R squares are found for computer patents and semiconductor patents. R squares for all the other variables are very low. In the case of computer patents almost 60 per cent of the variance is accounted for by the regression, whereas in the case of semiconductor patents this figure is about 62 per cent. The F values that are used to test the significance of the R^2s and for the significance of the dependent variable in the equation show that both computer patents and semiconductor patents are significantly dependent on the independent variable (time). The Beta for computer patents shows a positive sign whereas the Beta for semiconductor patents is represented by a negative sign. This implies that computer companies have significantly decreased their relative interest in semiconductors in favour of a growing number of patents in their 'core business'. These results indicate that *Hypothesis 8*, which asserted that patterns of technological and product-market convergence have not significantly affected the technological cores of the participating companies, can be confirmed for computer companies. For the relative distribution of strategic technology alliances we did not find any significant trends except for the constant in the equation which is significant for all cases. This indicates a strong stability in the relative distribution of alliances over time. It is therefore very unlikely that firms converge through means of strategic alliances as put forward by *Hypothesis 9*, at least in the analysis of leading computer companies. This means that *Hypothesis 9* cannot be confirmed on the basis of our analysis.

For leading telecommunication equipment companies we found quite a different pattern (see Figure 6.3). Convergence processes seem to have had only a modest impact on these companies. By far the largest number of technological activity measured by patents takes place in the telecommunications field. Overall there seems to be only a slight interest in computer technology and a decline in the number of semiconductor patents.

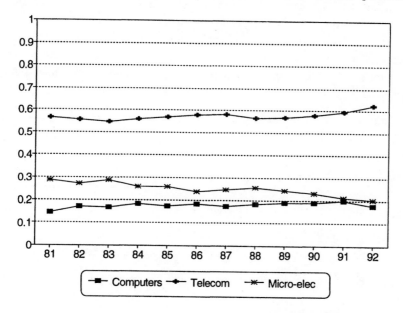

Figure 6.3 The distribution of patents of leading telecommunications equipment companies (three-year moving averages, 1980–1993)

The distribution of strategic alliances as shown in Figure 6.4 shows a similar low degree of involvement in computer technology. Alliances in the field of semiconductors now account for a significantly larger share. The share of semiconductor alliances as a percentage of the total number of alliances, however, does not seem to be rising over time. Since the mid-1980s telecommunication alliances account for most of the IT alliances of telecommunications companies.

The results of the linear regression (Table 6.2) show relatively high R^2s for patents in telecommunications and semiconductors. Corresponding significance levels of 0.05 in the case of telecommunications patents and 0.01 in the case of semiconductor patents indicate major shifts in the distribution of patents among different technological sectors. The results of the analysis for computers, however, do not indicate a significant trend in the relative importance of computer patents for telecommunication equipment producing companies. Again we find a growth in the relative importance of 'core' telecommunications patents ($p<0.05$) and a significant decrease in the relative importance of semiconductor patents ($p<0.001$). This, once again, confirms *Hypothesis 8* that convergence has not been able to change the relative importance of the core technological competencies.

The results for strategic alliances resemble the previous findings for alliances in the sense that they do not indicate a growing degree of convergence through means of strategic technology alliances. That means that once again *Hypothesis 9* cannot be confirmed by our analysis.

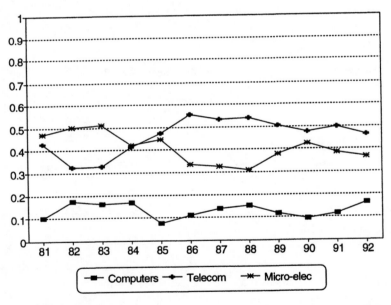

Figure 6.4 The distribution of strategic technology alliances of leading telecommunications equipment companies (three-year moving averages, 1980–1993)

The third analysis is concerned with the patents and strategic technology alliances of major semiconductor companies. The results of this analysis cannot be used to confirm or reject our basic hypothesis because technological convergence affects semiconductor companies in a different way. In this case the relationship with the other sectors is vertical instead of being horizontal. Leading semiconductor companies are affected by the convergence process basically by a change in the degree of diffusion of their components in the end products of the computer and telecommunications industry. Because micro-electronic components have become the single most important parts of both telecommunications as well as computer equipment and because micro-electronics components are increasingly customized to the end-products, we expect that semiconductor firms are urged to acquire technological knowledge in both fields. We therefore expect to find an increasing involvement of semiconductor firms in telecommunications and computer equipment.

Table 6.2 Results of the regression analysis on alliances and patents of major telecommunications equipment companies

	B	*SE B*	*T*	*sig T*	R^2	*SE*	*F*	*Const*
Computers								
Patents	0.291	0.180	1.618	0.132	0.179	2.717	2.617	15.015
Alliances	0.266	0.534	0.498	0.628	0.020	8.048	0.248	11.616
Telecom								
Patents	0.431	0.198	2.171	0.050	0.282	2.992	4.712*	54.765
Alliances	0.752	0.724	1.039	0.319	0.083	10.918	1.080	40.633
Micro-elec.								
Patents	-0.722	0.154	-4.681	0.001	0.646	2.326	21.91**	30.220
Alliances	-0.901	0.701	-1.286	0.223	0.121	10.570	1.654	46.457

* $p < 0.05$.
** $p < 0.01$.

For the leading semiconductor firms, telecommunication patents seem to be of particular importance (see Figure 6.5). More than half of their patents are applied for in the telecommunications field. There is, however, only a modest, but steadily growing interest in computer patents from major semiconductor companies. The relative amount of semiconductors seems to be relatively stable over time.

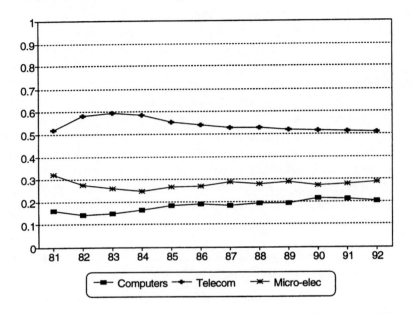

Figure 6.5 The distribution of patents of leading semiconductor companies (three-year moving averages, 1980–1993)

For strategic technology alliances Figure 6.6 shows quite a different picture. Alliances in the core-field semiconductors account for the majority of all alliances. Alliances in the telecom field are, in contrast to telecommunications patents, quite insignificant. During the mid-1980s we find a brief upheaval in the number of telecommunications alliances. This upheaval is, however, reversed in the following years. The relative importance of computer alliances is modest and seems to be rising marginally during the period 1985 to 1988. The results of the regression analysis as shown in Table 6.3 indicate that there is only one significant trend. The relative importance of patents in the field of computers seems to be rising over time. Although not significant, the results of the patent analysis indicate also a higher degree of vertical quasi-integration in the case of telecommunications patents. The results of the analysis on technological alliances indicate a relatively stable pattern over time. Again, no significant trends are found for the strategic technology alliances of major semiconductor companies over time.

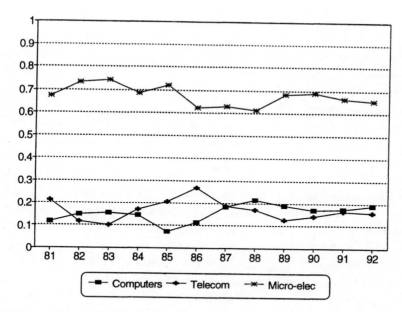

Figure 6.6 The distribution of strategic technology alliances of leading semiconductor companies (three-year moving averages, 1980–1993)

Table 6.3 Results of the regression analysis on alliances and patents of major semiconductor companies

	B	SE B	T	sig T	R^2	SE	F	Const
Computers								
Patents	0.398	0.146	2.714	0.019	0.380	2.210	7.364*	15.217
Alliances	0.556	0.471	1.181	0.261	0.104	7.108	1.394	11.642
Telecom								
Patents	0.108	0.498	0.217	0.204	0.501	4.062	4.350	51.516
Alliances	−0.423	0.579	−0.730	0.479	0.042	8.736	0.532	20.818
Micro-elec.								
Patents	−0.156	0.247	−0.631	0.540	0.032	3.724	0.398	29.568
Alliances	−0.134	0.664	−0.201	0.844	0.003	10.020	0.041	67.540

* $p < 0.05$.

6.5. DISCUSSION

In this chapter we analysed how major computer and telecommunications equipment companies have been affected by the technological convergence process. The results of the regression analyses have shown that firms are basically unaffected by technological convergence during the period 1980–93. The results indicate a confirmation of *Hypothesis 8* which argued that firms are still doing more of the same instead of being involved in a process of redefining their 'core' business. *Hypothesis 9*, which argued that firms tend to converge through means of strategic technology alliances, could not be confirmed on the basis of our analysis. In spite of a significant growth in the absolute number of alliances in all sectors, cooperative agreements do not seem to be used extensively for dealing with technological convergence. We may therefore conclude that technological convergence, although apparent on the technological and product/market level, does not seem to have affected the 'core' competencies of major IT companies. Firms seemed to have maintained their original technological form. According to Stinchcombe (1965), there are three reasons which can be responsible for the persistence of traditional forms. The first reason is that the original form is still the most efficient form. The second reason is that the original form may be retained by institutional forces, vested interests or a strong ideological position. The third reason is based on the existence of a natural monopoly or an assured funding base. We believe that in today's deregulated and liberalized market structures, institutional forces are not strong enough to induce firms to take on a particular form. For manufacturing companies, the argument of a natural monopoly or assured funding base does not seem to be relevant any more. That means that it is very likely that for many organizations the original form is still the most efficient form. Despite the observed technological convergence we are therefore still able to discern different forms of organization instead of one converged form.

Aldrich (1979) has argued that different organizational forms can coexist only if they are dependent on different environmental resources. That means that although they are influenced by the same technological regime, computers and telecommunications constitute a different niche. It is remarkable to see that despite the noted convergence at the start of the period, both computer and telecommunications firms have retained most of their interest in their 'old' technological regime and have basically neglected the important developments in the new regime. Given the cumulative nature of technological development, this implies that firms which do not invest in a specific technological field soon enough have the chance to become 'locked-out' of a specific technological path (Cohen and Levinthal, 1990). This means that for companies which are active in one particular sector it becomes increasingly difficult to acquire the required knowledge in another field. The likelihood of successful switching to a new regime is therefore not only a function of willingness to change but can also be seen as a factor of the competence to change. The possibility of successful switching is generally referred to as a factor of distance to the new technological regime (Nelson and Winter, 1982; Cantwell, 1990). The inability to benefit from new opportunities might, however, also have to do with so-called 'liabilities of age and size' (Aldrich and Auster, 1986), which assert that organizations become increasingly inert as their age or size increases. The relatively old and large organizations which constitute our population, tend to develop a relatively stable and bureaucratic structure that does not leave room for flexible adaptive behaviour to new opportunities. Instead of changing, these firms increasingly rely on the retention and replication of existing routines. Once a set of routines has become embedded within a firm, those firms tend to change only gradually. Existing routines often determine the direction of possible future paths. It is, however, not very likely that new small organizations are able to attack the leading positions of the industry leaders. New organizations often suffer from liabilities to newness as well as from liabilities of smallness. In the IT industry they face huge barriers to entry which are due to increased R&D and production cost. In addition, the cumulativeness of the technological regimes significantly reduces the changes of success for new organizations. It is often very difficult for new organizations to acquire skills in production and R&D which have been mastered over decades by their larger competitors.

Overall our findings do not indicate a pattern of increased technological convergence within firms. The ongoing process of technological convergence at the product-market and the technology level has not been accompanied by a significant rise in the relative number of patents or alliances in adjacent technologies. From an evolutionary perspective such patterns of resistance to change are not unexpected. We believe, however, that in the near future companies will have severe difficulties in achieving their aspiration levels of performance. Therefore we think that at that time companies will be forced to redefine their 'core' business and adapt their existing technology base according to the demands of the new technological regime. Strategic technology alliances in combination with internal development can be an important means to achieve that goal. Although strategic technology alliances do not seem to be used extensively to deal with the convergence process we believe that given the rapid increase in the number of newly established strategic technology alliances these alliances can still play a very important role in high-technology sectors. In the next chapter, therefore, we aim to find out what the specific contribution of strategic technology alliances is for companies that are active in the information technology industry.

NOTES

1. For a multi-market competition perspective on technological convergence see van Wegberg (1994).
2. The introduction of stored program control (SPC) in electronic switches made it possible to replace mechanical control systems by much more flexible software-based control programs.
3. In this chapter the term 'core competencies' is used to describe the traditional focus of the companies in our analysis.
4. Harper (1986) observed that in the early 1980s only a very limited number of products embodied both communications and computing functions.
5. Differences in the importance of patents can be assessed by using data on patent renewals or by means of a patent citation analysis (Cohen and Levin, 1989). Another alternative is to assign a value to individual innovations (Dorfman, 1987). This is, however, an extremely time-consuming undertaking.
6. The full list of companies which are analysed in this chapter can be found in Appendix III.
7. We assume that alliances between government or academic institutions and private companies are often less profit seeking and are to a lesser extent used for product development.
8. For a further analysis of structural and strategic differences among companies from various home countries, see Chapter 8.

7. Inter-Firm Relationships in Major IT Networks

In traditional business literature, organizations were typically described as independent self-contained units (Contractor and Lorange, 1988). Only recently have organizational theorists devoted more attention to the connections among organizations. The concept of interorganizational relationships has been introduced in organizational literature in the late 1960s by, among others, Evan (1966) and Warren (1967). These authors put forward a view in which organizations were described in terms of their relationships with other organizations (e.g. key suppliers, buyers or competitors). In the following years, only a few articles on this subject were published in the leading journals. The attention that was aroused by these publications, however, remained rather modest. Although relationships between companies have been ignored in business literature for a long time, a rapid increase in the number of alliances in the 1980s (Harrigan, 1985b; Haklisch, 1986, 1989; Contractor and Lorange, 1988; Mowery, 1988; Hagedoorn, 1990) gave way to a growing body of literature on both the use and structure of such agreements. Today cooperative agreements have become an important and recurrent issue in strategic management, international business and industrial economics as well as in organization studies. With a few notable exceptions (see e.g. Hagedoorn and Schakenraad, 1990, 1991, 1993; Nohria and Garcia-Pont, 1991; Nohria and Eccles, 1992) agreements have been studied from a dyadic or firm-level perspective. In this chapter we will argue, however, that the strategic value of strategic alliances can be assessed only by paying attention to the overall structure of the network in which a firm is embedded. From a network perspective the number of links of a particular company is only one of several basic variables. Knoke and Kuklinski (1982: 13), for example, noted that 'the structure of relations among actors and the location of individual actors in the network have important behavioral, perceptual, and attitudinal consequences both for the individual units and for the system as a whole'. Therefore the evaluation of the power of organizations in a network requires an extensive analysis of an organization's position in the network and its connection to other players, as well as its ability to control flows of information.

7.1. RESEARCH QUESTIONS

Before the 1980s, cooperative agreements (usually joint ventures) were typically undertaken between somewhat smaller companies. During the 1980s large multinational enterprises (MNEs) also came to play a role in the establishment of strategic alliances (Hladik, 1985). Traditionally most of these alliances were undertaken in order to gain access to foreign markets or to bypass government regulations (Contractor and Lorange, 1988; Hamel et al., 1986; Haklisch, 1989; Porter and Fuller, 1986). Today we observe an increasing number of multinational corporations, more or less comparable in size, which link up with each other. The scope of these alliances is usually global and the modes of cooperation can take numerous forms: e.g. consortia, cross-licensing agreements, joint ventures, research partnerships, franchising and so on. Whereas cooperative agreements used to be undertaken on the basis of short-term objectives, today firms are increasingly recognizing the strategic importance of these agreements (Harrigan, 1985b; Porter and Fuller, 1986; Contractor and Lorange, 1988).

In today's global markets in which technological progress is extremely rapid, boundary-spanning strategic technology alliances have become an important factor for the overall competitive position of a company. Firms are now often engaged in multiple strategic alliances with different partners at the same time. Therefore it seems necessary not only to focus on the alliances of one specific organization, but also to consider all ties between the players in a specific sector. A one-firm or dyadic level of analysis seems simply inadequate to study industry sectors where virtually all companies are linked to each other. This chapter is therefore concerned with an empirical analysis of the evolution of cooperative networks. More in particular we aim to enhance our basic understanding of cooperative behaviour in three major high-technology sectors: i.e. computers, telecommunications and semiconductors. Before the mid-1970s there appeared to be an inverse relationship between R&D intensity and cooperative alliances (Stopford and Wells, 1972; Friedman et al., 1979; Haklisch, 1989). Today, high-technology sectors account for the majority of all newly established alliances (Fusfeld and Haklisch, 1985; Osborn and Baughn, 1990; Mytelka, 1991; Hagedoorn 1993). Changes in the relative importance of strategic technology alliances for high-technology sectors are above all due to fundamental shifts in the structure of the global environment and in the process of technological change (Haklisch, 1989). Fierce competition, the homogenization of markets and ongoing globalization tendencies account for most of the structural changes, whereas rapid growing capital and R&D costs, the ever-increasing complexity of products and a significant increase in the speed of technological developments are important drivers from a technological point of view (Haklisch, 1989). The rapidly changing technological and competitive settings induced firms to search for new ways to increase their flexibility. In the late 1970s and early 1980s, a number of companies started to trade their traditional practices like mergers and foreign direct investment for new forms of cooperation such as joint ventures, joint development agreements and various types of technology-sharing agreements. These new forms of agreements gave firms a previously unknown degree of flexibility in terms of the acquisition of technology and for market-entry purposes (Vonortas, 1989). Given the increased need for flexibility and the rapidly changing structural and technological conditions in high-technology markets, we assume:

Hypothesis 10: *High-technology industries are characterized by a large increase in the number of strategic technology alliances during the 1980s and early 1990s.*

A second related hypothesis is concerned with the above-mentioned drive towards flexibility which occurred during the 1980s (see e.g. Harrigan, 1985a; Schreuder and van Cayseele, 1988; Vonortas, 1989). If firms are indeed trying to increase their overall flexibility this might be reflected in a trend towards more flexible forms of cooperative organization. We would then expect a reduction in the relative importance of equity agreements in favour of more flexible non-equity agreements during the 1980s and early 1990s.

Hypothesis 11: *The equity/non-equity ratio of strategic technology alliances has decreased considerably over time.*

Ever since the 1980s, all of the major IT sectors have been subject to major structural and technological turbulence. IT sectors have increasingly been characterized by rapidly rising costs of equipment and R&D, accompanied by steep learning curves and ever-shortening product life cycles. These developments urge firms to cooperate in order to share development costs and to reduce lead times for innovative products. A reduction in lead times allows firms to preempt the market and enables them to move faster down the learning curve. Another very important development came through the emergence of new technological regimes and the ongoing complexity of technology, which raised the need for flexibility in order to respond quickly to changing market needs and to new technological opportunities. Because of the rising costs of R&D in all sectors of the IT industry, no single organization seems able to monitor such a broad range of technologies by itself. Given these specific characteristics of the present-day information technology industry we assume that traditional motives for the establishment of strategic technology alliances have made way for rationales that are related to a reduction in lead times, technological complementarity, or the reduction of the costs of R&D. *Hypothesis 12* is therefore formulated as:

Hypothesis 12: Although the traditional rationale for the establishment of strategic alliances (market access) is still evident, its importance has decreased during the 1980s in favour of other rationales such as a reduction in lead times, technological complementarity and a reduction of the costs of research and development.

After we have established some basic understanding of historical trends of strategic partnering over time we will pay attention to the overall network structure of the different IT sectors. Our basic assumption is that networks of strategic partnering reflect a sector's underlying competitive structure. Therefore we try to find out whether differences among technological and competitive drivers in each of the sectors has led to differences in network structures and in differences among the network positions of major players. We will deal with this issue by focusing on two levels of analysis. The first is concerned with the overall network characteristics, whereas the second focuses on the differences among focal companies in terms of their network centrality. At the overall network level we will try to elaborate on *Hypothesis 10*, which assumed that high-technology industries are characterized by an increasing number of alliances during the 1980s and early 1990s. We argue that the increase in the number of alliances is not only due to an increase in the number of firms that undertake alliances, but to a greater extent is also due to an increase in the relative number of alliances by the focal players. Therefore we hypothesize:

Hypothesis 13: *The networks of strategic technology alliances in all major IT sectors under study have evolved from sparse networks during the early 1970s into very dense networks in the following periods.*

Another question that will be addressed in the network analyses is concerned with the relationship between patterns of strategic technology alliances and market structural aspects of the major IT sectors.[1] In the literature, strategic partnering has often been described in terms of oligopolistic rivalry among large multinational companies (Casson, 1987; Chesnais, 1988; Mytelka, 1991). In contrast to Porter's (1990) assumption that strategic partnering is used primarily by 'second-tier competitors' to catch up with the leading companies, most of the literature has argued that networks of strategic partnering are dominated by the leading companies in the market. In this chapter we will try to assess whether market structural changes are reflected in changes in network positions of the companies involved. One of the most important trends in terms of the market structural positions of the major companies is found in the increasing involvement and domination of Japanese competitors in all IT segments. This trend is shown in the large-scale entrance of Japanese companies in the international IT industry during the mid-1970s and their dominant position in the industry in the most recent period. Japanese firms were not very active in the international IT industry until the mid 1970s. We therefore would expect Japanese firms to be absent in the first period (1970–77) but that they would show up in the second period (1978–85). In the last period (1986–93) we would expect Japanese firms to have moved out of their peripheral positions in the second period to more central positions. This leads to the following hypothesis:

Hypothesis 14: *Japanese firms have become apparent in cooperative networks during the period 1978–85 and have moved into central positions during the late 1980s and early 1990s.*

Apart from these 'generic' features of the networks we will pose a number of hypotheses about the evolution of networks in the specific industry sectors. In the computer industry we expect to find a network structure that closely resembles its oligopolistic market structure. This network is expected to be built around a small number of focal players. In this 'oligopolistic' network, IBM is likely to stand out as the single most dominant player. Thus:

Hypothesis 15: The cooperative network in the computer industry is dominated by IBM and a small number of large well-established companies. Differences in network centrality of those companies compared to other companies in the network are very high.

In the semiconductor market we would expect to find quite a different network structure. Extremely high expenditures on production and R&D (even compared to the computer industry) have induced virtually all firms in this market to establish strategic alliances. Joint development of products has become a necessity to survive under the extremely high competitive pressures that are characteristic for this sector. We therefore would expect to find a very dense network which is characterized by a much more equally spread distribution of centrality values:

Hypothesis 16: The cooperative network of the semiconductor sector is characterized by a large number of more or less equally distributed links among virtually all active companies.

For the telecommunications industry we would expect to find very sparse networks in the 1970s and early 1980s at a time when competition was relatively low and technological progress was not very fast. During these periods the number of cross-border alliances is limited due to the inward direction of the (national) companies. In the third period deregulatory and liberalizing actions have led to increased international competition, rapid technological progress and the need to access other markets. Therefore we would expect to find an increase in the number and international orientation of strategic technology alliances during this period.

Hypothesis 17: Cooperative networks in the telecommunications sector are very sparse during the first and second periods and international links are almost completely absent. In the most recent period we find a large increase in both the number of alliances as well as in terms of their international orientation.

7.2. RESEARCH METHODOLOGY AND DATA

In order to test the hypotheses that are put forward in the previous section we will have to examine both the evolution of the overall number of IT alliances and the evolution of these alliances within each specific IT sector. The next section is therefore concerned with an empirical analysis of historical patterns of strategic technology alliances over time. On the basis of time-series data on the growth of newly established alliances we will be able to validate or reject *Hypothesis 10. Hypothesis 11* will be dealt with in Section 3, which analyses the relative changes in the equity versus non-equity ratio of cooperative agreements ever since 1980. After we have assessed the major trends in the number and forms of alliances we will turn to the underlying rationales for strategic partnering. We will focus more in particular on those rationales that are important for companies participating in high-technology industries. From an empirical perspective we will try to validate *Hypothesis 12* by looking at the relative importance of the different rationales during the 1980s. After we have established some basic understanding of historical trends in strategic technology alliances we will try to identify the basic networks of strategic alliances and their development over time. The structure of the networks in each IT sector and the positions of the major actors in these networks are analysed by means of a statistical technique that is known as network analysis. Network analysis tries to capture the social structure of a network by focusing on the role and structure of the relationships among the various actors. Network analysis treats relationships between organizations not as isolated links but as part of a larger social structure. In this chapter we will consider networks of alliances from two distinct levels of analysis. We will start with a description of the basic characteristics of the overall network and will then proceed with an examination of the role and importance of the individual players in the network. This enables us to reject or validate our 'generic' as well as our more sector-specific hypotheses (*Hypotheses 14–17*).

The data presented in this chapter are based on the MERIT—CATI database (see also Appendix II). In this chapter we study over 2,200 strategic technology alliances that are related to either computers, telecommunications, semiconductors or software.[2] Alliances in the field of software account for 32 per cent of total IT alliances. Semiconductors account for 26 per cent, whereas cooperation in telecommunications and semiconductors account for 25 per cent and 17 per cent respectively (see Figure 7.1).

As in the previous chapter, the expression inter-firm cooperation is used

The Dynamics of Technical Innovation

to refer to those cooperative agreements between partners who are not connected through (majority) ownership. Although cooperative agreements can take numerous forms, such as marketing, production and research agreements, we will limit our analysis to technology-inclined agreements. Before 1975 this type of agreement was virtually unknown (Hladik, 1985). In the 1980s, however, several authors started to report a strong and steady increase in the number of strategic technology alliances (Hagedoorn and Schakenraad, 1990; Hergert and Morris, 1988). In order to safeguard the strategic element in our sample we will study only those alliances that are undertaken for strategic reasons. As in Chapter 6, we will refer to alliances as being strategic if they 'can reasonably be assumed to affect the long-term product market positioning of at least one partner'. Because alliances between government or academic institutions and private companies are often undertaken for different reasons from the alliances between two or more private companies (see e.g. Haklisch, 1986), we will restrict our attention to those alliances that are established between private companies. For the same reason we do not pay attention to government-initiated or EC-wide R&D cost-sharing programmes such as ESPRIT, EUREKA or JESSI.

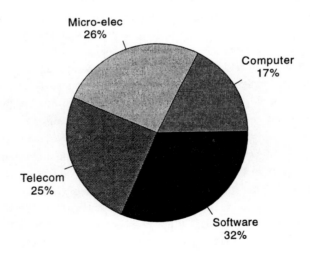

Figure 7.1 Number of cooperative technology agreements (as a percentage of total IT agreements)

7.3. HISTORICAL PATTERNS OF COOPERATIVE AGREEMENTS IN MAJOR IT SECTORS

In order to assess the importance and magnitude of strategic alliance activity we calculated the number of newly established strategic technology alliances as they appear in our CATI-database. Figure 7.2 shows the total number of newly established strategic technology alliances in four major IT sectors: i.e. computers, semiconductors, telecommunications and software. All numbers are calculated as three-year moving averages in order to smooth yearly fluctuations that might attract too much attention away from the overall trend.

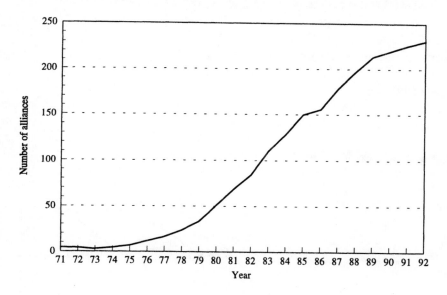

Figure 7.2 Number of newly established strategic technology alliances in IT sectors (three-year moving averages, 1971–1992)

During the first half of the 1970s cooperative activity remained at a rather modest level in the information technology industry. During the second half of the 1970s, as companies were slowly becoming more aware of the advantages associated with the use of strategic alliances, the number of newly established alliances started to increase gradually.[3] It was, however, not until the late 1970s that the rise in the number of alliances really took off. Apart from a short period of stabilization in the mid-1980s, growth persisted until the end of the decade. The overall increase in alliance activity in the IT sector during the 1980s coincides with a period of structural and technological turbulence in all the IT sectors under study. During this period both production and R&D costs had been rising rapidly whereas ongoing internationalization tendencies had increased the 'global' character of the industry.[4] All these factors seem to have increased the need to establish strategic alliances. The observed pattern of growth closely resembles our expectation that was put forward in *Hypothesis 10*, with the exception that at the end of the decade the growth rate in the number of newly established alliances seems to level off. A closer look at the sectoral data (Figure 7.3) reveals that this pattern of slower growth has alrady started in the mid-1980s in all IT sectors except software.

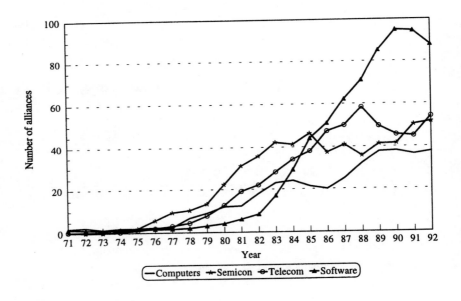

Figure 7.3 Number of newly established strategic technology alliances in various sub-fields (three-year moving averages, 1971–1992)

An explanation for this slower growth rate can be found in difficulties associated with the management and control of strategic alliances. As companies become more aware of the risks and dangers of cooperation, they tend to become more careful in choosing strategic alliances as their most preferred contractual form (Hagedoorn, 1993). Figure 7.3 shows the evolution of the number of newly established strategic technology alliances in the different sub fields of the information technology industry. We can see that despite a decreasing number of alliances during the mid-1980s, the computer industry is characterized by a slow but steady increase in the number of alliances over time. After the mid-1980s, growth in the number of newly established alliances takes off again temporarily during the late 1980s before another slowdown takes place during the early 1990s. The same pattern of slower growth during the mid-1980s is also found in the semiconductor industry. Whereas the computer industry was characterized by an upheaval in the late 1980s, in the semiconductor market the growth in the number of alliances does not take off again until the 1990s. In telecommunications we find a steady increase in the number of alliances until the late 1980s. After 1988 the number of newly established alliances starts to decline until 1992, when the number of telecommunication alliances increases again. The remarkable growth in software alliances during the 1980s can be ascribed to the mediating role of software in the convergence of information technologies. The pervasive and systemic nature of software encourages a large number of hardware producers to establish strategic technology alliances with leading software companies. These results indicate that, despite the pattern of strong growth in the early 1980s that is present in all sectors and a slowdown in the number of alliances during the early 1990s, there are major sectoral differences in terms of the number of alliances as well as in their pattern of evolution over time. Different characteristics of the individual segments seem to have led to different patterns of growth in the number of newly established strategic technology alliances.

7.3.1. Modes of Cooperation

Traditionally joint ventures accounted for the majority of all alliances. In a joint venture[5] partners agree to combine their skills and resources in a company that is characterized by joint equity ownership. Joint ventures used to be established for market-entry reasons. Today, equity participation is often used in an attempt to lower transaction costs between two related companies. Because equity participation creates mutual dependence among the participating companies the chances of cheating on the other partner can be reduced significantly. If one of the partners does not behave responsibly, then the whole venture suffers and equity diminishes for all participants (Buckley and Casson, 1988). Others (Stuckey, 1983; Davies, 1977; Teece, 1981; Hennart, 1988) have argued that equity agreements are particularly suited to transfer 'tacit' knowledge. Tacit knowledge (Polanyi, 1958) refers to knowledge which cannot be transferred in codified form; e.g. country or firm-specific know-how. If knowledge is tacit, transfer of technology is not sufficient. As stated by Hennart (1988: 366), 'Tacit knowledge is difficult to codify, and often non-patentable. Even if patented, the patent will provide only a small part of the information necessary to market the new product or to use the new process. Tacit knowledge will be more efficiently transferred if the transferor and the recipient are linked through common ownership'.

Another type of equity agreement (direct investment) has also been used extensively for the transfer of technological knowledge. In high-technology industries, direct investments are often coupled with technology exchange agreements. In turbulent industries large companies are well known to invest in small high-tech companies in order to acquire promising new technologies. This allows large firms to explore new fields of technology without the need to come up with the full amount of investment that would be needed for internal development. If the technology of the small firm becomes more important to the acquiring firm, a takeover can be considered. Accessing technology by direct investment, however, seems to be very difficult because of the limited influence in the decision-making process of the other company. Therefore other modes of cooperating are often more preferable for companies which wish to acquire technological knowledge.

Whereas equity agreements are often established in order to raise mutual dependence or to transfer tacit knowledge, an increasing number of organizations prefer a more flexible relationship with other organizations. The growing importance of flexibility as an element of the overall corporate strategy is noted, for example, in Schreuder and van Cayseele (1988), who concluded that flexibility contributed more to the long-term success of firms than the existence of economies of scope. In this context we will also stress the importance of 'strategic flexibility' as put forward by Harrigan (1985a). Strategic flexibility refers to the ability of organizations 'to reposition themselves in a market, change their game plans, or dismantle their current strategies when the customers they serve are no longer as attractive as they once were' (Harrigan, 1985a: 1). Especially in high-technology industries which are characterized by ever-shortening technology and product life cycles, firms feel constant pressure to remain flexible in order to respond quickly to changing market needs and to new technological opportunities. In the previous chapters we discussed several examples of companies that lost their dominant position because of their slow reaction to radical technological changes (see also Cooper and Schendel, 1976; Foster, 1986). New groups of firms were often much more able to enter a new market riding the waves of new technologies.

Non-equity agreements are used extensively by large incumbent organizations to raise their ability to switch from research in one technology to another (Obleros and MacDonald, 1988). Withdrawal, or transfer of know-how, personnel and assets is often much easier to accomplish in those more flexible types of agreements than in agreements that involve equity (Kreiken, 1986; Harrigan, 1988a). Therefore, non-equity agreements are often preferred above joint ventures if demand is uncertain or business risks are high (Harrigan, 1988a). Because of the globalization of markets, the increasing complexity of technologies, rapid technological changes and the increasing costs of R&D, firms are no longer able to monitor all the technological developments that are important for their core markets. Cooperation enables companies to monitor several technological developments and at the same time, let them concentrate on a few, most promising, projects internally. If certain technologies turn out to be less successful then cooperative agreements can be terminated with only a relatively small loss. It must be stressed, however, that non-equity agreements lack some of the benefits of joint ventures. As stated by Harrigan (1988a: 142), 'owners rarely pool their resources and efforts in cooperative agreements in the way that they do when using joint ventures'.

Above, we described how shorter technology and product cycles in combination with elevating R&D and capital costs during the 1980s have increased the need for flexibility. We would therefore expect that the boom in the number of alliances during the 1980s is likely to be due to a rise in the number of more flexible forms of cooperation (see *Hypothesis 11*). New, more flexible forms of strategic technology alliances seem to have taken over the dominant role that used to be played by joint ventures and other forms of equity agreements. Figure 7.4 describes the relative distribution of newly established cooperative agreements according to their organizational form. We can see that the number of non-equity agreements grows from 35 per cent of all alliances in 1980 to almost 80 per cent of all alliances in 1992. This pattern of growth clearly confirms our expectation about the rise of more flexible forms of organization during the 1980s and early 1990s (see *Hypothesis 11*).

7.3.2. Rationales for Strategic R&D Partnering

Viewing the upheaval in the absolute number of strategic technology alliances in the past decades, there have to be specific advantages of those agreements over internal development, merger or arm's-length transactions. Although the rationales for cooperation are numerous[6] we will restrict our attention to those rationales that are important for firms in the information technology industry.

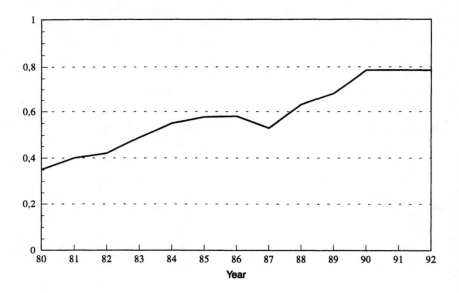

Figure 7.4 Non-equity agreements in information technologies (as a percentage of total agreements, three-year moving averages, 1980–1992)

As we have shown in the previous chapters, fixed costs of R&D have rocketed in virtually all major IT sectors. The costs of developing a new computer, digital switching equipment or microprocessor can be up to billions of dollars. The development of every new generation of products involves a much larger amount of capital, whereas, due to shrinking life cycles, costs are much more difficult to recoup within such a short period. It is obvious that, with the exception of some very large multinational firms (e.g. IBM, Fujitsu, AT&T), it is very difficult to finance such projects by a single organization. Even for the largest companies, the risk of failure involved in those capital-intensive projects becomes too high to be accepted. Therefore sharing capital investments among companies can be a very attractive option to companies. Cooperation, however, can also be used to meet economies of scale in production and R&D. It is often more efficient to use one R&D facility instead of separate facilities. By integrating previously separate activities, cooperative agreements raise the total volume of activities and therefore significant scale advantages can be reaped.

A specific category of costs that can be reduced by cooperative agreements are transaction costs which arise from contractual agreements among interacting organizations. It is often argued that, compared to arm's-length transactions, cooperative agreements ease transactional and contractual difficulties (Williamson, 1979, 1985; Hennart, 1988; Jarillo, 1988). Williamson, the most well-known contributor to transaction-cost economics, argued that mixed modes of governance (cooperative agreements) are preferred if asset specificity is intermediate. The degree of asset specificity is closely linked to the degree in which specific investments have been made. According to Williamson (1985: 54) 'specialized assets cannot be redeployed without sacrifice of productive value if contracts should be interrupted or prematurely terminated'. The degree of redeployment of assets has a strong impact on the choice of contractual modes (Klein and Leffler, 1981; Williamson, 1985; Hennart, 1988). If specialized investments are incurred, companies become increasingly dependent on each other. Standard market contracts could then well lead to very high contractual costs in order to prevent so-called 'hold-up' situations in which one party could threaten to withdraw unless the contract is revised in a profitable way for this party (Groenewegen, 1989; Williamson, 1979, 1985). The threat of 'hold-up' situations becomes higher when transactions are recurrent. Under these conditions, the costs of setting up a bilateral governance structure (cooperative agreement) may well offset the costs involved in spot-market contracting. However, under conditions of very high asset specificity, unified governance structures are often more efficient.

Apart from a reduction in transaction costs, cooperative agreements can also be used to reduce risk. Teaming up with other partners significantly reduces the investments in a specific R&D project. As in the case of stock markets, risk can be reduced by spreading investments over a large portfolio of R&D projects. Teaming up with a competent partner can also be used to reduce the risk of bringing a non-state-of-the-art product on to the market. The likelihood of success for a new innovation can often be enhanced tremendously by reducing the time needed to bring the product on to market. In markets such as semiconductors, where prices sometimes decline by more than 30 per cent a year, it is obvious that a reduction in the lead time of a new product can bring about significant rewards to the companies involved.

In the introduction we described how traditionally cooperative agreements were undertaken to achieve access to foreign markets or to bypass government regulations. Today this rationale still holds for a number of markets such as China, Japan and several less-developed countries (LDCs), as well as in regulated telecommunication markets. Access reasons can also be of importance in another context, in terms of access to the technological competencies of other companies. Because of the globalization of markets, the increasing complexity of technological development, rapid technological changes and the increasing costs of R&D, firms are no longer able to monitor all the technological developments that are important for their core markets. Cooperation enables companies to monitor several technological developments and at the same time let them concentrate internally on a few, most promising, projects. If certain technologies turn out to be less successful, then cooperative agreements can be terminated with only a relatively small loss. Apart from monitoring purposes, the combination of asymmetric skills and knowledge of two different companies can be extremely beneficial to both companies. Synergy effects that arise from technological complementarities among organizations often create win–win situations for all the companies involved.

It is obvious that there are major differences in the relative importance among the various motives. Data from the MERIT-CATI databank enables us to look at the importance of the various motives over time (Figure 7.5). Again all numbers are calculated as three-year moving averages in order to smooth yearly fluctuations which might attract too much attention away from the overall trend. In the first section we argued that although the traditional rationale for the establishment of strategic alliances (market access) is still evident, its importance decreases over the 1980s in favour of other rationales such as a reduction in lead times, technological complementarity and a reduction of the costs of research and development. Figure 7.5 shows that indeed the relative share of the market entry motive has dropped about 10 per cent from 25 per cent in 1980 to about 15 per cent in the late 1980s.

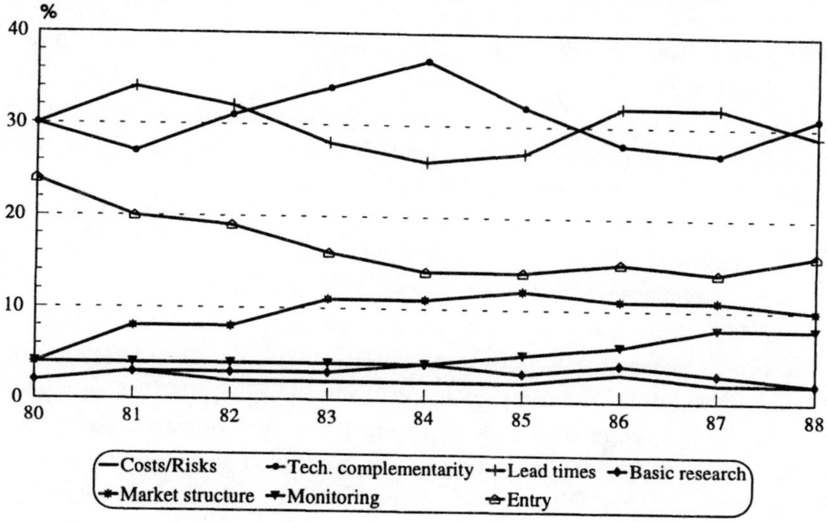

Figure 7.5 Distribution of motives for strategic technology alliances (as a percentage of the total number of motives, three-year moving averages, 1980–1988)

Technological complementarity and the reduction of lead times stand out as the most important motives during the 1980s. The importance of these rationales is not surprising given the increasing complexity of technologies and the importance of steep learning curves in all sectors of the industry. Technological monitoring and the ability to influence market structures seem to have become more important during the 1980s. The monitoring aspect of strategic technology alliances has become more important because declining opportunities in the current paradigm are driving firms to explore new technological opportunities in the market, whereas the rapid maturation of virtually all the major IT sectors has increased the need to influence market structures. The joint undertaking of basic research and the reduction of costs and risks seem to be less important rationales for undertaking strategic technology alliances.

7.3.3. Dangers of Cooperation

Although the description of the various motives might suggest win–win situations for all the companies involved in cooperative agreements, mortality rates of cooperative agreements have always been extremely high (*Business Week*, 1986; Kogut, 1989). Studies by consulting firms such as McKinsey and Coopers and Lybrand have shown a 70 per cent failure rate for joint ventures (*Business Week*, 1986). Reasons for these extremely high failure rates have always remained rather vague. It is often argued that firms enter cooperative agreements with 'hidden agendas' (Hamel et al., 1986; Haklisch, 1989; Hagedoorn, 1990). Firms which enter cooperative agreements with 'hidden agendas' do not participate in the venture for the sake of both partners. Instead they have the incentive to absorb the other partner's knowledge, skills and sometimes even its assets. Once a party is able to absorb the other partner's skills or knowledge, the coalition is likely to fail. From a transaction-cost perspective (Williamson, 1985, 1990) it is argued that the cost of cooperation rises if so-called 'hold-up' situations occur. One partner may be capable of capturing a large proportion of the profits, because it has a superior bargaining position compared to the other partner which has made some irreversible investments in the coalition (Porter, 1986). In that context Porter and Fuller (1986: 329) state that 'coalitions designed to gain the benefits of scale or learning in performing an activity have a more enduring purpose'. Moreover they assert that 'the stability of coalitions rises when partners make balanced or complementary contributions in forms that are not one-time or self-liquidating'. These observations are confirmed by the results of an analysis of the stability of joint ventures by Kogut (1989). Kogut found that when companies were involved in more than one alliance with the same partner, the stability of all those alliances was raised significantly.[7] Another threat to cooperating companies is concerned with the danger of creating a potential competitor, or strengthening an existing competitor through cooperation.

From these examples it might be clear that cooperation cannot be seen as a 'panacea' for all problems (Hagedoorn and Schakenraad, 1990). A firm should therefore always assess the particular advantages of cooperation against the advantages of other forms of organizations. If a company decides that cooperation is the preferred option then it should be careful in choosing its partners and to think about the content of the alliance and the contributions of each partner.[8]

7.4. NETWORKS OF PARTNERSHIPS IN INFORMATION TECHNOLOGIES

After having identified the basic trends in technology partnering, we will now turn to the evolution of cooperative networks. Our main goal in this section is to study the changes in the overall structures of the networks over time and to identify the focal players in the cooperative networks of the various subfields. This enables us to evaluate five hypotheses that are related to the structural differences among the various IT sectors and the possible reflection of these strategies in the networks of alliances.

Today, sophisticated statistical software packages (e.g. UCINET) and powerful micro-computers allow us to reveal particular characteristics of a network which were impossible to detect in the past. Although the basic underpinnings of network analysis have been around ever since the Second World War (see e.g. Bavelas, 1948) recent advances in graph theory and computer technology have brought about major changes in the use of network analysis as an analytic tool. The use of network analysis as a tool to analyse complex social systems was introduced in the 1970s (see e.g. Burt, 1976; Freeman, 1979) and further developed in the 1980s (see e.g. Bonacich, 1987). As argued by Nohria (1992: 2) 'network analysis has grown from the esoteric interest of a few mathematically inclined sociologists to a legitimate mainstream perspective'. Today network analysis can be used to analyse complex flows of information. A simultaneous analysis of all the relationships between individual organizations may result in the description of a social system that closely resembles the structure of a specific organizational field (Barley et al, 1992).

For a graphical representation of networks, we make use of a statistical technique that is known as non-metric multidimensional scaling (MDS). Multidimensional scaling is a data-reduction procedure comparable to principal component analysis and other factor-analytical methods. One of the main advantages of MDS is that usually, but not necessarily, MDS can fit an appropriate model in fewer dimensions than can factor-analytic methods. This increases the possibility of easy interpretable two-dimensional pictures. MDS offers scaling of similarity data into points lying in an X-dimensional space. The purpose of this method is to provide coordinates for these points in such a way that distances between pairs of points fit as closely as possible to the observed similarities. In order to facilitate a better understanding of the graphs we include only the most active cooperating companies in our plots.

MDS plots are presented for the periods, 1970–77, 1978–85, 1986–93. A three-year period perspective allows us to add a dynamic perspective to the analysis of the networks. We focus on the parent company level in the sense that we assign all the agreements of subsidiaries to the parent company. As a representation of the links between the various companies we draw lines between the cooperating companies. We use lines of different styles and thickness in order to account for the number of agreements between the companies. Dotted lines represent one alliance whereas solid lines indicate two or three alliances. Fat solid lines indicate more than four alliances.

7.4.1. Centrality Measures

The importance of particular players in a network can be measured by their degree of centrality. Centrality in a network context refers to the importance of a specific organization for the overall structure of a network. Centrality in information networks was first introduced by Bavelas in 1948 to assess the relationship between centrality and power within networks (Freeman, 1979). Advances in graph theory in later years have significantly broadened the use of centrality measures as a tool to assess the importance of a specific point (or actor) in a network. The basic source of information for all the centrality measures discussed in this chapter is the adjacency matrix, which is a matrix in which the cells contain the number of direct links between the various companies. The cell value a_{ij} is therefore equal to the number of ties between company i and company j. In this chapter we will use three basic measures of centrality as put forward by Freeman (1979): degree centrality (C_D), betweenness centrality (C_B) and closeness centrality (C_C).[9]

The most straightforward measure of centrality is the so-called degree centrality (C_D). Degree centrality is measured by summing the total number of actors to which a specific player is adjacent in the matrix. The degree of an actor is therefore equal to the total number of direct links of a particular actor and all the other actors. Actors that are represented by a high degree of point centrality are said to be in 'the thick of things' (Freeman, 1979: 219). Such companies share the ability to access a large stock of potential information sources. They can be referred to as central sources of information, at least in terms of the number of other players they are in contact with. On the other hand, companies that are characterized by a low degree of point centrality are somewhat restricted in terms of their potential outside sources of information.

$$C_D\ (P_k)=\sum_{i=1}^{n} a\ (P_i,P_k)$$

Equation 7.1   *Freeman's (1979) degree centrality measure.*
$a(P_i,P_K)=1$ if P_i and P_K are connected directly, and 0
otherwise.

The second centrality measure that was put forward by Freeman is the so-called betweenness centrality (C_B). Betweenness refers to the number of times an actor is located on the shortest geodesic path between two other actors. The expression geodesic path is used to denote the shortest path between two points in the network. If a certain actor is directly linked to two other actors who are not directly linked to each other, then the first actor is said to be 'between' the other actors. Freeman (1977) has shown that the maximum value of C_B is achieved by the central player in a star-shaped network, in which all the organizations are linked directly only to the most central player. The central player in a star-shaped network is located on the shortest geodesic path between all the other organizations. In an information network a company which has a high degree of betweenness centrality has a potential to control the flows of information between those other companies (Freeman, 1979; Knoke and Kuklinski, 1982). In this chapter we will therefore use C_B as an indicator of the ability to control flows of information within a network.

$$C_B\ (P_k)=\sum_{1}^{n}\ \sum_{<j}^{n}\ \frac{g_{ij}(P_k)}{g_{ij}}$$

Equation 7.2   *Betweenness centrality.*
N represents the number of points in the graph, g_{ij}
represents the number of geodesic paths linking P_i and P_j
that contain P_k.

Freeman's third conception of centrality is associated with the distance between the location of a certain player and the location of the other players in a graph. If a company is centrally located in the graph, which means that it is close to most of the other players in that same graph, then it is able to avoid the control power of others (Freeman, 1979). A centrally positioned company is not dependent on other companies for its information flow with other companies in the network. The flow of information between such central companies can be direct instead of having to go via an intermediator. The degree to which a company is close to other companies can be measured by means of counting the geodesic distances from the location of that particular company to the location of all the other companies in the graph. Low degrees of closeness centralities are therefore associated with the most central players, whereas high degrees of closeness centralities (larger distances) are associated with more peripheral players.[10]

$$C_C\ (P_k) = (n-1)/\sum_{i=1}^{n} d\ (P_i, P_k)$$

Equation 7.3 Closeness centrality.

In this chapter we will analyse networks of alliances on two distinct levels. The first is concerned with the characteristics of the overall networks whereas the second deals with differences in centralities among the various focal players in the network. First we will describe the basic characteristics of the overall network. We decided to focus on mean centrality and density measures in order to evaluate changes in the intensity of alliances between focal firms and to discuss the average centralities that are associated with those companies. Table 7.1 shows the basic changes in centrality during the evolution of the various networks.

Network densities are calculated by dividing the number of existing alliances among actors in the network by the total number of possible links between those actors. Because network densities and mean centrality measures are greatly influenced by the total number of actors in a network we have normalized the various measures by looking at the alliances of the leading 40 companies in each period.[11] The network densities as displayed in Table 7.1 show that there is a strong increase in network density in all sub-sectors under study. The same data shows that although in the period 1970–77 networks were extremely sparse, the period 1978–85 was characterized by a strong growth in the density of all networks under study. This growth continued during the most recent period.

Table 7.1 Average network densities, degree centrality and betweenness centrality measures (40 leading companies, 1970–93)

	Computers			Semiconductors			Telecom		
	70-77	78–85	86–93	70–77	78–85	86–93	70–77	78–85	86–93
Density	0.003	0.132	0.2	0.002	0.181	0.493	0.002	0.214	0.306
Degree	2	6.3	10.7	1.87	10.7	23.6	3.76	9.3	19.6
Betw.	0.3	3	4.7	0.29	3.1	9	2.48	3.9	10.4

Whereas network density remained rather modest in the computer industry, the semiconductor network has become extremely dense during the last period. The relatively low density that is found in the computer industry can be due to the fact that R&D costs in computers are relatively low compared to the huge outlays that are needed to develop a new generation of micro-chip or digital-switching equipment. The pattern of increased density is confirmed by centrality measures that are related to the number of direct links (degree centrality) and in terms of the control power of the leading companies (nBetween). Both measures have gone up consistently during the past 24 years. In the field of semiconductors the number of alliances of leading companies have gone up from an average of 1.87 in the first period to 23.6 in the last period. In the telecommunications industry the average number of alliances has gone up from 3.76 in the first period to 19.6 in the last. The growth in the computer industry has been somewhat slower. These figures confirm *Hypothesis 13* that the trend in the number of alliances is due not only to the entrance of new firms into the networks but also in large part to the increasing number of alliances that are established by individual firms. The betweenness measure indicates that today firms not only have an increasing number of direct links, but that they also have a vast amount of power to control flows of information between other companies. Again the increase in the computer industry has been relatively modest compared to the increase in the other sectors. Leading companies in the telecommunication industry seem to have the largest ability to control flows of information between other companies.

7.4.2. Networks of Alliances in the Computer Industry

Figure 7.6 provides us with a graphical representation of the strategic technology alliances in the computer industry in the period 1970–77. This period started with the invention of the first microprocessor by Intel in 1971 (see Chapter 5) and would soon be characterized by the emergence of new types of computers such as micro-, mini- and super-computers. At that time the advantages of using strategic alliances were relatively unknown to the business community. The new types of small computers which were brought to the market at that time did not require the amount of extensive investments that were needed to develop new generations of mainframe computers. We would expect to find a relatively sparse network in which traditional mainframe manufacturers are dominant. It is therefore not surprising that the MDS plot (Figure 7.6) shows a relatively sparse network that involves 28 firms of which the vast majority are traditional mainframe suppliers.[12] At the left-hand side we can see one rather dense cluster involving a number of major European and US companies which are all centred around the three focal players ICL, Bull and Siemens. A second mixed cluster of US and Japanese companies is located on the right-hand side. This cluster is basically centred around the Japanese giant Mitsubishi. We also observe a number of one-on-one links between either two Japanese or two US companies. An interesting link is the alliance between IBM and Amdahl. IBM was forced into this agreement by the threat of an antitrust suit. It was forced to cross-license nearly all its patents with its former employee Gene Amdahl. This enabled Amdahl to develop very cheap IBM-compatible mainframe computers which became an instant success. Cross-border alliances are relatively rare at that time. Japanese–European alliances are even completely absent during this time period.

The results of the network analysis (Table 7.2) reveal the dominance of European firms in the early computer industry network. According to the number of alliances, four out of six leading companies are based in Europe. The same centrality measures also show that the companies in the first cluster are more centrally located than other firms in the network. Even Mitsubishi, which is by far the most central player in the second cluster with four alliances, has a closeness value that is well below that of all the firms in the first cluster. It does not even come close to the value of a company like NCR which has only two alliances. Three companies stand out as intermediaries of information flows: ICL, Bull and Mitsubishi. They are found to be particularly active in linking other European companies to their US counterparts. Mitsubishi plays a similar intermediating role between US and Japanese companies.

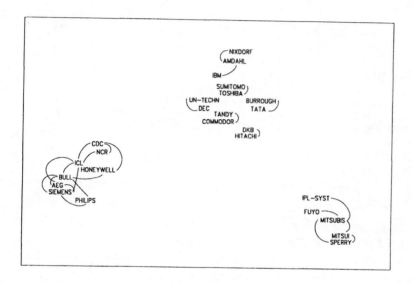

Figure 7.6 Alliances in the computer industry (1970–1977)

Table 7.2 Network centrality measures in the computer industry (1970–1977)

		C_D	C_C	C_B			C_D	C_C	C_B
1	ICL	5	4.9	16	15	OKI	1	4.1	0
2	CII	5	4.9	3	16	IPL–SYST	1	4.1	0
3	SIEMENS	4	4.9	3	17	NIXDORF	1	3.8	0
4	MITSUB.	4	4.1	5	18	HITACHI	1	3.8	0
5	CDC	3	4.9	12	19	IBM	1	3.8	0
6	AEG	3	4.9	0	20	ASAHI	1	3.8	0
7	PHILIPS	2	4.8	0	21	TOSHIBA	1	3.7	0
8	AMDAHL	2	3.8	1	22	RADIO–S	1	3.7	0
9	FUJITSU	2	3.8	1	23	UN–TECH	1	3.7	0
10	SPERRY	2	4.1	0	24	COMMOD	1	3.7	0
11	HONEYW	2	4.9	7	25	DEC	1	3.7	0
12	NCR	2	4.9	0	26	BURROU	1	3.7	0
13	MITSUI	2	4.1	0	27	TATA	1	3.7	0
14	BULL	1	4.8	0	28	NEC	1	3.7	0

Turning to the next period (1978–85) we find a somewhat different pattern (see Figure 7.7). The multitude of lines that connect virtually all the companies in the network illustrate the increased density of the computer network in the period 1978–85 as compared to the previous period. Network density increased from 0.003 in the first period to 0.132 in the second (see Table 7.3). One-on-one links became very rare in this time period. Almost all the major firms are connected to at least two other partners. This is illustrative for the growth in the number of alliances during that time period. In such a closed system where virtually all the players are connected to each other, differences in centrality among the various companies are relatively low. There is only a 0.13 difference in the degree of closeness among the forty leading companies. Very remarkable in that respect is the relatively low closeness degree of industry leader IBM. Of the leading forty companies only Xerox has a lower closeness degree. This means that in spite of its dominant market position, IBM can still be regarded as a peripheral firm in terms of its degree of closeness centrality. Although the early domination of European firms in the network decreased rapidly, a European company (Olivetti) still remains the most active networking company in terms of the number of alliances (see Table 7.3). Olivetti has a degree centrality that is more than 9 points above the degree of the second most cooperating company (DKB). Olivetti is not only the most important player in terms of the total number of links but also in terms of closeness centrality and information betweenness. Only two firms (Sumitomo and Hitachi) have a similar degree of centrality. In terms of information betweenness, other firms such as CDC and the Japanese firms DKB, Sumitomo and Hitachi play an important role.

Japanese firms which played a relatively modest role in the first period have taken 7 out of 15 leading positions in the second period. This increase is due especially to a rapid growth in the number of US–Japanese alliances. The increased Japanese involvement in the network coincides with the Japanese invasion of the world markets during the late 1970s and early 1980s (see *Hypothesis 14*). At that time Japanese companies primarily entered into alliances with technological competent partners in the US in order to absorb their technological knowledge and for market-entry reasons. European firms seem to be less attractive to Japanese companies, probably because of their relatively low degree of technological sophistication. In spite of the still relatively low number of Japanese–European alliances, we find a rapid increase in the number of international alliances. In the first period the alliances between organizations from different Triad regions accounted for a mere 23.6 per cent of all alliances. In the second period their number had increased to 53.1 per cent. This means that more than half of all alliances in the computer industry in the period 1978–85 were undertaken between companies from different Triad regions. This illustrates very clearly the internationalization tendencies during the early 1980s and the use of alliances as a tool to deal with the internationalization phenomenon (see also Chapter 8).

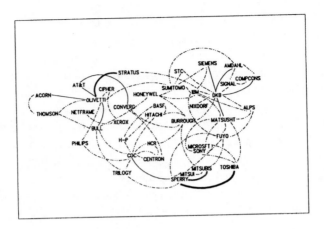

Figure 7.7 Alliances in the computer industry (1978–85)

Table 7.3 Network centrality measures in the computer industry, (1978–1985)

		C_D	C_C	C_B			C_D	C_C	C_B
1	OLIVETTI	28	3.24	1314	21	CONVERG	4	3.18	19
2	DKB	18	3.23	699	22	ALPS	4	3.18	0
3	CDC	15	3.21	530	23	TRILOGY	4	3.17	50
4	SUMITOM	13	3.23	763	24	AT&T	4	3.17	25
5	SPERRY	13	3.18	214	25	NIXDORF	4	3.16	231
6	IBM	11	3.13	285	26	COMPCO	4	3.16	0
7	BURROU	10	3.22	359	27	STC	3	3.19	82
8	MATSUSH	10	3.21	221	28	H–P	3	3.19	20
9	FUYO	8	3.22	206	29	NETFRAM	3	3.18	111
10	BULL	8	3.20	233	30	THOMSON	3	3.18	5
11	HITACHI	7	3.24	557	31	CIPHER	3	3.17	84
12	MITSUBIS	7	3.18	104	32	CENTRON	3	3.16	16
13	TOSHIBA	7	3.16	33	33	ACORN	3	3.16	0
14	HONEYW	5	3.21	100	34	SIGNAL	3	3.16	0
15	SIEMENS	5	3.20	158	35	MITSUI	3	3.15	0
16	BASF	5	3.19	169	36	SONY	3	3.15	0
17	AMDAHL	5	3.19	39	37	MICROSFT	3	3.15	0
18	STRATUS	4	3.20	39	38	XEROX	3	3.11	80
19	PHILIPS	4	3.19	115	39	CORONA	2	3.17	0
20	NCR	4	3.18	38	40	APOLLO	2	3.13	78

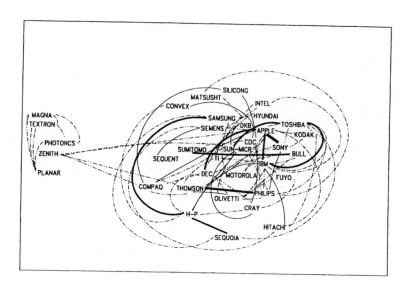

Figure 7.8 Alliances in the computer industry (1986–1993)

Figure 7.8 shows the network of strategic technology alliances in the most recent period (1986–93). The increase in network density as observed in the second period continues in the most recent period (1986–93). Network density increased from 0.132 in the second period to 0.200 in the last period. The network in this period is dominated by four major US companies: Sun Microsystems, Apple, IBM and Digital Equipment (DEC). This is consistent with the market dominance of US companies in the computer industry. The US domination of the network becomes evident from the finding that US firms are involved in more than 80 per cent of all the alliances during the period 1986–93. The expected domination of the network by Japanese firms (see *Hypothesis 14*) can therefore not be found in this industry. Shifts in the leading positions since the previous period were very high (see Table 7.4). Only two companies (Bull and IBM) which were among the leading companies in the second period managed to remain in the top ten of the leading companies in the computer industry network in the third period. Bull even managed to remain in the top ten for three periods in a row, which indicates a remarkable stability in its alliance strategy. Besides a peripheral cluster that involves Magna, Textronics, Photonics, Zenith Data Systems and Planar, centrality among participants is equally distributed. Differences in the normalized degree centralities have also been reduced since the previous period. This means that unlike our assumption in *Hypothesis 15*, networks of strategic partnering cannot be seen as oligopolistic networks in which a select group of firms sign cartel-like agreements among each other. In terms of the mediation of information flows super-computer producer Cray plays a highly influential role. Other important mediators include Apple, Sony and again Groupe Bull.

Table 7.4 Network centrality measures in the computer industry (1986–1993)

		C_D	C_C	C_B			C_D	C_C	C_B
1	SUN–MICR	29	1.39	96	21	CRAY	8	1.38	3411
2	APPLE	28	1.39	2257	22	MICROSFT	8	1.38	985
3	IBM	25	1.39	232	23	SEQUENT	7	1.38	386
4	DEC	21	1.39	527	24	HITACHI	7	1.37	0
5	PHILIPS	20	1.37	0	25	TI	7	1.37	0
6	SONY	17	1.38	2072	26	MATSUSHT	6	1.38	1100
7	H–P	17	1.38	0	27	OIS	6	0.46	0
8	THOMSO	16	1.38	0	28	MAGNA	6	0.46	0
9	TOSHIBA	15	1.39	0	29	TEXTRON	6	0.46	0
10	INTEL	14	1.38	0	30	PHOTONIC	6	0.46	0
11	OLIVETTI	13	1.39	0	31	PLANAR	6	0.46	0
12	BULL	13	1.38	2170	32	ELEC–PLA	6	0.46	0
13	COMPAQ	12	1.39	0	33	CONVEX	5	1.38	1271
14	SUMITOM	12	1.37	0	34	SILICONG	5	1.38	118
15	SIEMENS	11	1.38	591	35	HYUNDAI	5	1.37	0
16	DKB	11	1.37	0	36	MOTOROL	5	1.37	0
17	KODAK	10	1.38	1260	37	SEQUOIA	5	1.37	0
18	CDC	9	1.38	796	38	ZENITH	5	0.45	0
19	SAMSUNG	9	1.38	72	39	NOVELL	4	1.37	385
20	TEKTRON	9	0.46	0	40	UNSISYS	4	1.36	0

7.4.3. Networks of Alliances in Semiconductors

Figure 7.9 shows the network of alliances in the period 1970–77 in the semiconductor industry. Whereas the first period of the computer industry was characterized by a large number of one-on-one links and three clusters, the network in the semiconductor industry can be described as a chain-linked network. In this network almost all firms are linked to each other in a direct or indirect way. There is only one one-on-one link (between Allied Corporation and the Radio Corporation of America). Schlumberger seems to play a central role both in terms of its direct links (C_D), and its closeness centrality (C_C), and as a mediator of information flows (see Table 7.5). There are large differences between companies in terms of degree centrality, closeness and betweenness during this period (Table 7.5). As we focus on the distribution of alliances among countries we can find only two types of alliances: US–European and intra-US alliances. As described in Chapter 5 the Japanese involvement in the global semiconductor market-place started in the mid-1970s. It is therefore not surprising that in the period 1970–77 not a single Japanese firm is involved in the network (see *Hypothesis 14*). Of all the European members of the network not a single European firm is directly linked to another European company. As discussed in Chapter 5, European firms are very similar to each other in terms of their technological skills and resources. It seems therefore likely that European firms seek other technological competencies and technological complementarities from their US competitors instead of turning to other European companies.

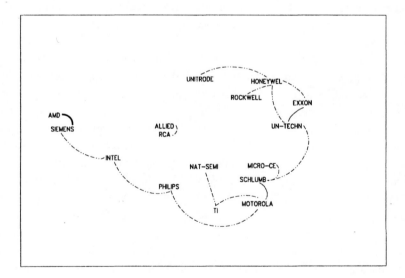

Figure 7.9 Alliances in the semiconductor industry (1970–1977)

Table 7.5 Network centrality measures in the semiconductor industry (1970—1977)

		C_D	C_C	C_B			C_D	C_C	C_B
1	SCHLUM	5	20.2	59	9	INTEL	2	17.2	22
2	UN–TECH	4	19.2	36	10	TI	2	16.4	12
3	HONEYW	4	17.7	23	11	MICRO–CE	1	17.5	0
4	SIEMENS	4	15.5	12	12	ROCKWEL	1	15.6	0
5	MOTOROL	3	18.3	22	13	UNITROD	1	15.6	0
6	EXXON	3	17.3	0	14	NAT–SEMI	1	14.6	0
7	AMD	3	13.9	0	15	RCA	1	6.2	0
8	PHILIPS	2	18.8	30	16	ALLIED	1	6.2	0

Figure 7.10 reveals a closely interlinked dense network of alliances in the semiconductor industry during the period 1978–85. The network density increased from 0.002 in the first period to 0.181 in the second.[13] In spite of their market dominance in the semiconductor market, US companies have shown a relatively low interest in strategic partnering during this period. Japanese companies, on the other hand, were completely absent in the first period but are now represented by four companies in the top ten leading networking companies: i.e. Somitomo, DKB, Toshiba and Mitsubishi. The Japanese involvement in the network again clearly reflects the growing importance of Japanese firms in the world markets at that time (see *Hypothesis 14*). In spite of their relatively high number of alliances (C_D) Japanese firms can be found somewhat in the periphery of the network but with strong links to technologically leading US companies. European firms are represented in the top ten by German Siemens, Dutch Philips and Thomson from France. The US is represented in the top ten by its two leading microprocessor companies, Intel and Motorola. More noticeable is the presence of Exxon in the top ten of most cooperating companies in the field of semiconductors. It is, however, not as remarkable as it seems given that Exxon was active in the IT market through Exxon office systems and through its subsidiary Zilog.[14] There are no major differences in degree centralities among the 40 most cooperating companies. Less central firms are located in the left-hand-side cluster involving Telfin, CTNE, Advent, Brown Bovery, Saabscan and Olivetti or in the periphery; i.e. Exxon, Schlumberger, Lucky

Goldstar, NCR, Gould and Ferranti.

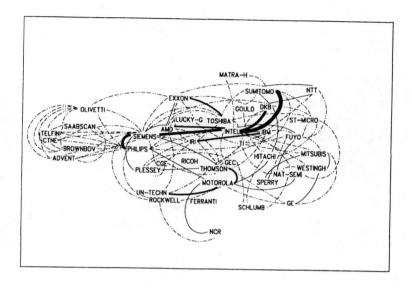

Figure 7.10 Alliances in the semiconductor industry (1978–1985)

Figure 7.11 shows the network of alliances in the semiconductor industry during the period 1986–93. It is evident from the multitude of lines in the network that this industry features the most dense network of all industries under study. The network density has grown from 0.181 in the second period to an impressive 0.493 in the most recent period. The top five firms are all major American companies that seem eager to regain their technological and market leadership over the Japanese. Remarkable in this respect is that precompetitive cooperation projects such as Sematech and US Memories have not led to an increased percentage of intra-US cooperations compared to other alliances. Intra-US cooperation even declined from 65 per cent in the first period to 19.3 per cent in the most recent period. Although they are still active in the alliance network, Japanese firms have not been able to move out of their peripheral positions into more central positions during the last period (see *Hypothesis 14*). Large differences in network density during this period do not allow us to validate *Hypothesis 16*, which assumed that the alliances would be evenly distributed among the various companies.

Table 7.6 Network centrality measures in the semiconductor industry (78-85)

		C_D	C_C	C_B			C_D	C_C	C_B
1	INTEL	33	2.4	1725	21 ROCKWEL		7	2.4	231
2	SIEMENS	29	2.4	1366	22 SCHLUMB		7	2.4	370
3	PHILIPS	23	2.4	948	23 ST–MICRO		7	2.4	231
4	MOTOROL	23	2.4	811	24 ADVENT		7	2.4	0
5	THOMSON	21	2.4	693	25 TELFIN		7	2.4	0
6	SUMITOM	20	2.4	733	26 BROWNB		7	2.4	0
7	DKB	18	2.4	1178	27 SAABSCA		7	2.4	0
8	TOSHIBA	18	2.4	472	28 CGE		6	2.4	227
9	MITSUBIS	14	2.4	490	29 GE		6	2.4	174
10	EXXON	14	2.4	349	30 LUCKY–G		6	2.4	64
11	NAT–SEMI	13	2.4	750	31 WESTINGH		6	2.4	37
12	AMD	12	2.4	99	32 NTT		6	2.4	23
13	IRI	11	2.4	317	33 MATRA–H		5	2.4	309
14	TI	10	2.4	702	34 GOULD		5	2.4	166
15	OLIVETTI	10	2.4	248	35 FERRANTI		5	2.3	450
16	HITACHI	9	2.4	427	36 NCR		5	2.3	132
17	PLESSEY	9	2.4	143	37 SPERRY		5	2.3	18
18	IBM	9	2.4	62	38 RICOH		5	0.6	5
19	UN–TECH	8	2.4	59	39 HONEYW		4	2.4	239
20	CTNE	8	2.4	56	40 VLSI		4	2.3	114

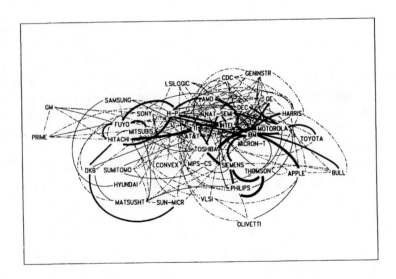

Figure 7.11 Alliances in the semiconductor industry (1986–1993)

Table 7.7 Network centrality measures in the semiconductor industry (1986–1993)

		C_D	C_C	C_B			C_D	C_C	C_B
1	IBM	62	3.5	2219	21	SUMITOM	18	3.5	509
2	TI	61	3.5	3598	22	AMD	17	3.5	548
3	MOTORO	58	3.5	2616	23	GE	17	3.5	53
4	INTEL	56	3.5	3089	24	SUN–MICR	15	3.5	1149
5	H–P	45	3.5	1423	25	SAMSUNG	14	3.5	670
6	THOMSON	40	3.5	2265	26	CDC	14	3.5	82
7	TOSHIBA	40	3.5	1160	27	SONY	13	3.5	232
8	NAT–SEMI	36	3.5	692	28	GENINST	13	3.5	0
9	SIEMENS	35	3.5	1360	29	OLIVETTI	12	3.5	1382
10	FUYO	32	3.5	1329	30	LSILOGIC	12	3.5	445
11	AT&T	30	3.5	1860	31	MIPS–CS	12	3.4	436
12	DEC	29	3.5	884	32	MICRON–T	11	3.5	118
13	HITACHI	29	3.5	201	33	BULL	10	3.5	65
14	PHILIPS	27	3.5	1816	34	VLSI	8	3.5	536
15	AMD	27	3.5	423	35	TOYOTA	8	3.5	8
16	MITSUBIS	25	3.5	1080	36	HYUNDAI	8	3.4	601
17	DKB	23	3.5	1001	37	PRIME	8	3.4	187
18	HARRIS	21	3.5	362	38	GM	7	3.4	0
19	APPLE	19	3.5	671	39	CONVEX	7	3.4	0
20	MATSUSH	18	3.5	852	40	TADPOLE	6	3.5	0

7.4.4. Networks of Alliances in Telecommunications

Figure 7.12 illustrates the network of alliances in the telecommunications sector during the period 1970–77. In this network we can find three major clusters. The first cluster on the left-hand-side is a very dense European-dominated cluster which is centred around Plessey, GEC, BT and STC. The second is a purely US cluster involving a number of non-telecommunications companies, i.e. Xerox, DEC and Intel. The last is a mixed cluster in terms of home countries, involving DKB, American Telecom and Telephone.

The results of the network analysis that are presented in Table 7.8 reveal that the leading four companies in terms of their number of alliances are all European companies. Again we note the relative absence of Japanese companies in the first period. The only Japanese firm that was involved in the telecommunications network at that time was DKB. The closeness centrality indicator reveals that there are major differences in centrality among the organizations. The firms that can be found in the first European-dominated cluster are the most central companies in the network, whereas the one-on-one linked firms, Pirelli, IRI, Turktel and NT, are the least central players. In terms of betweenness centrality two firms stand out: i.e. GEC, which connects African Telephone Cables to BT, STC and Plessey, and American Telephony which performs a bridge function between DKB and Telephonay.

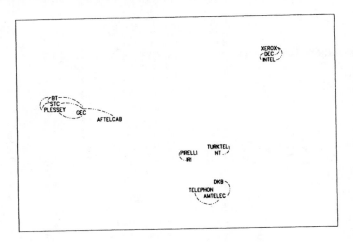

Figure 7.12 Alliances in the telecommunications industry (1970–1977)

Table 7.8 Network centrality measures in the telecommunications industry (1970–77)

	C_D	C_C	C_B		C_D	C_C	C_B
1 GEC	4	9	3	9 AFTELCA	1	8.9	0
2 BT	3	9	0	10 TELEPHO	1	7.6	0
3 STC	3	9	0	11 DKB	1	7.6	0
4 PLESSEY	3	9	0	12 NT	1	7.1	0
5 AMTELEC	2	7.6	1	13 PIRELLI	1	7.1	0
6 XEROX	2	7.6	0	14 IRI	1	7.1	0
7 DEC	2	7.6	0	15 TURKTEL	1	7.1	0
8 INTEL	2	7.6	0				

As in the other sectors we are witnessing the entrance of Japanese companies into the telecommunications network during the second period (1977–85). Again we can find basically three clusters (Figure 7.13). The first cluster on the left-hand-side is dominated by the so-called 'baby Bells', which were eager to gain more independence from AT&T by linking up with other partners. The second cluster, on the upper right of the figure, is dominated by Japanese firms which are centred around major industry giants such as Sumitomo, Fuyo, DKB and Hitachi. The third broad cluster features AT&T, Philips and GE as their most important players. In this cluster we can find all the European firms and all the major US manufacturing companies except for IBM, which is located in the Japanese cluster. AT&T, the world market leader, dominates the network in all respects.

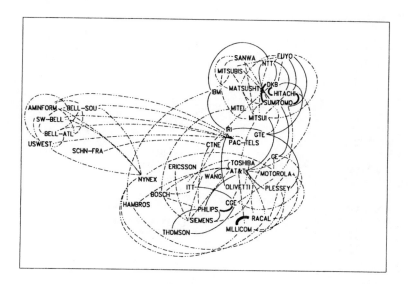

Figure 7.13 Alliances in the telecommunications industry (1978–1985)

Except for the cluster that is centred around the baby Bells there is not much difference in terms of closeness centrality among the various companies (Table 7.9). Two firms stand out in terms of their mediating role in information transfer: i.e. AT&T and Siemens.

In the third period (1986–93) AT&T was able to retain its dominance in the network (see Table 7.10). Another industry giant, IBM, even managed to penetrate the top five of most active networking companies in all three sectors in the period 1986–93. This might be seen as an attempt to deal with the ongoing convergence of information technologies (see Chapter 6). In the most recent period network density increased from 0.214 in the second period to 0.306. Although this growth is considerable it still lags behind the growth in density that was experienced in the semiconductor industry. Therefore *Hypothesis 17* cannot be confirmed in this respect.

Table 7.9 Network centrality measures in the telecommunications industry (1978–1985)

		C_D	C_C	C_B			C_D	C_C	C_B
1	AT&T	25	3.3	1788	21	ERICSSON	7	3.2	945
2	SUMITOM	22	3.2	739	22	PAC–TELS	7	3.2	648
3	PHILIPS	15	3.2	921	23	BOSCH	7	3.2	638
4	IBM	15	3.2	872	24	THOMSON	7	3.2	335
5	FUYO	15	3.2	378	25	GE	7	3.2	285
6	CGE	14	3.2	626	26	SANWA	7	3.2	33
7	ITT	13	3.2	830	27	MITSUBIS	6	3.2	117
8	DKB	13	3.2	429	28	BELL–SOU	6	3.1	0
9	HITACHI	13	3.2	115	29	BELL–ATL	6	3.1	0
10	NTT	12	3.2	397	30	NYNEX	6	3.1	0
11	PLESSEY	12	3.2	324	31	AMINFOR	6	3.1	0
12	SIEMENS	11	3.2	1530	32	USWEST	6	3.1	0
13	MITSUI	11	3.2	1530	33	SW–BELL	6	3.1	0
14	RACAL	11	3.2	213	34	CTNE	5	3.2	901
15	GTE	10	3.2	271	35	MITEL	5	3.2	228
16	OLIVETTI	9	3.2	418	36	TOSHIBA	5	3.2	191
17	MILLICON	9	3.2	50	37	MATSUSH	5	3.2	0
18	WANG	8	3.2	535	38	HAMBROS	5	3.2	0
19	IRI	8	3.2	398	39	NT	4	3.2	138
20	MOTOROL	8	3.2	212	40	FERRANTI	4	3.2	65

Figure 7.14 reveals a very similar structure to the one we found in the previous period. Japanese companies are once again clustered in a separate cluster at the left-hand-side of the figure whereas on the upper right-hand-side we find a cluster of Telecom operators now featuring PTT–Telecom of the Netherlands, France Telecom, Deutsche Bundespost and British Telecom. All the major European and US manufacturing companies are located in the

centre of the figure. Together these firms form the core of the network. The top ten of most cooperating companies is still clearly dominated by European companies. Five out of the first ten companies are based in Europe; AT&T is the only telecommunications company from the US that is represented in the top ten. This is not remarkable if one considers AT&T's dominant position in the US market. BT seems to play a role in linking the operators to the equipment manufacturers. Motorola can be seen to play a similar role in terms of linking Japanese companies to the more centrally located European and US companies. In contrast to the expected dominant positions of Japanese firms in the network (*Hypothesis 14*) Japanese companies still form a very homogenous group, in which they are primarily cooperating with each other. The expected growth in the number of international alliances in the most recent period (*Hypothesis 17*) also did not take place. There even appears to be a relative decrease in the number of international alliances since the second period. Whereas international alliances accounted for 37.7 per cent of all alliances in the second period, their share gradually decreased to 30.8 per cent in the most recent period.

Table 7.10 Network centrality measures in the telecommunications industry (1986–1993)

		C_D	C_C	C_B			C_D	C_C	C_B
1	AT&T	54	7.4	7130	21	MITSUI	17	7	334
2	ERICSSON	43	7.3	4244	22	NOVELL	16	7.1	1320
3	SIEMENS	41	7.3	5034	23	TANDEM	15	7.2	2002
4	IBM	35	7.3	2999	24	TELECOM	14	7	233
5	SUMITOM	31	7.1	793	25	TOYOTA	14	6.9	520
6	CGE	30	7.2	3477	26	NYNEX	13	7.2	858
7	DKB	30	7.2	2492	27	C&W	13	7.1	1299
8	MITSUBIS	29	7.1	927	28	DBP	13	7	93
9	BT	28	7.3	2536	29	SANWA	13	7	9
10	PTT–TEL	24	7.1	1763	30	RACAL	12	7.2	1134
11	PHILIPS	21	7.3	2383	31	NOKIA	12	7.1	1352
12	NTT	21	7.2	1258	32	MATRA	12	7.1	933
13	CTNE	20	7.1	1301	33	BOSCH	12	7	1192
14	MOTOROL	19	7.2	2843	34	SUN–MICR	11	6.9	1555
15	DEC	19	7.2	1786	35	MICROSFT	10	7.2	410
16	FUYO	19	7.2	1019	36	INTEL	10	7.2	340
17	FRTELEC	19	7.2	521	37	IRI	10	7.1	165
18	NT	19	7.1	2014	38	SCANTEL	10	7	0
19	H–P	18	7.3	1941	39	SOCGEN	9	7	82
20	STC	17	7.2	1579	40	COMPUS	9	7	0

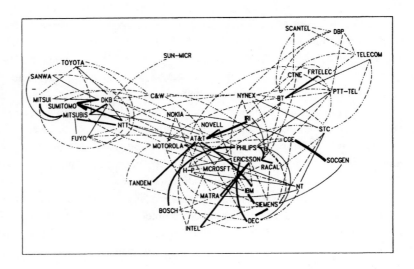

Figure 7.14 Alliances in the telecommunciations industry (1986–1993).

7.5. SUMMARY AND DISCUSSION

This chapter aimed to describe the growing importance of strategic technology alliances in three major IT sectors. Our main goal was to broaden our basic understanding of the patterns of evolution of strategic alliances and their related networks. Empirically we tried to validate or reject eight hypotheses that were put forward in the first section. Our first hypothesis in this chapter was concerned with the expected growth in the number of alliances during the 1980s and early 1990s. An empirical analysis which was based on the MERIT–CATI database reveals that ever since the 1970s the number of strategic technology alliances in the field of information technology has gone up dramatically. Before the 1970s, strategic technology alliances were virtually unknown. In the following years as companies were slowly becoming more aware of the advantages that were associated with such alliances, the number of newly established alliances started to grow steadily. During the 1980s we witness an explosive growth in the number of strategic technology alliances. This high growth rate was due to various technological and non-technological factors such as the globalization of markets, the convergence of IT technologies and rapidly rising R&D costs in combination with shorter technology and product cycles. Together these and other factors seem to have accelerated the pace with which new cooperative agreements were established. At the end of the decade the growth in the number of newly established strategic technology alliances remains very high but seems to level off. In spite of the observed stabilization of the number of newly established alliances in the late 1980s and early 1990s this pattern closely resembles our expectations as put forward in *Hypothesis 10*. Growth rates in the individual IT sectors reveal that, apart from the pattern of strong growth in the early 1980s that is found in all sectors and the slowdown in the number of alliances during the early 1990s, there are major sectoral differences in both the number and evolution of newly established alliances. Market structural and technological differences among the various industry sectors seem to be reflected in different trends in the number of alliances in each sector.

After we assessed the overall growth of newly established alliances we focused on the forms of cooperation. Although the joint venture has received by far the most attention in the literature, other forms of cooperation, such as research corporations, joint development agreements, one-directional technology flows and technology exchange agreements, seem to play an increasingly important role. We divided the various modes of cooperation into two broad categories: equity and non-equity agreements. Equity agreements are known for raising the mutual dependence among companies, whereas non-equity agreements are often used to increase the flexibility of the participating firms. An assessment of the evolution of equity versus non-equity agreements over time has shown that the relative importance of non-equity agreements has increased considerably as compared to equity agreements. This is consistent with the often noted drive towards flexibility which was put forward in *Hypothesis 11*.

In the next section we describe some of the basic rationales for strategic partnering in IT technologies. Firms in virtually all IT sectors have made use of strategic alliances to cope with escalating R&D costs, the globalization of markets and the need to monitor a broad range of technologies. In line with *Hypothesis 12* we found that the traditional rationale for the establishment of strategic alliances (market access) has made way for new rationales such as a reduction in lead times and technological complementarity. In spite of what was expected in this hypothesis we did not find a significant increase in the relative importance of cost sharing as a rationale for the creation of strategic technology alliances. It is also stressed, however, that cooperative agreements do not bring about win–win situations for all the companies involved. Failure rates of over 70 per cent have been reported in the literature. To raise the stability of its agreements companies should be extremely cautious in partner selection and in deciding upon the content of the alliance.

After having identified the basic trends in strategic technology partnering we described the evolution of the cooperative networks by means of a statistical tool that is appropriately known as 'network analysis'. We made use of multi-dimensional scaling plots to display the networks graphically and employed various centrality measures to assess the importance of the individual actors in the network. An analysis of the overall network shows a strong increase in network density in all IT subsectors under study. In line with *Hypothesis 13* we found that sparse networks in the early 1970s seem to have evolved into extremely dense networks in the late 1980s and early 1990s. The semiconductor network stands out in that respect, whereas the computer industry shows only a relatively modest network density in the last period. The same pattern of increased alliance activity is found in the centrality measures that are related to the number of direct links (degree centrality) and in the power to control flows of information between other companies in the network (betweenness centrality).

In the last section we focused on the roles of the individual players in the network. We tried to find out whether market structural changes are reflected in changing positions in the networks of strategic technology alliances. One of the major observations in this chapter was the absence of Japanese companies in the first period and their massive entrance during the second period. This is in line with *Hypothesis 14*, which argues that Japanese firms become apparent in cooperative networks during the second period. However, the expectation that they have moved into central positions by the end of the third period could not be validated by our data. Japanese firms can still be found in the periphery of the networks whereas US firms have been able to capture dominant positions in all sectors except telecommunications. For the computer industry we expected to find a structure that resembled the market structure in that industry: an oligopolistic network which was dominated by IBM (Hypothesis 15). Although IBM managed to gain a dominant position in the most recent period the small differences in centrality values indicate that the number of links are equally distributed among the various companies. Therefore *Hypothesis 15* cannot not be validated by our findings. *Hypothesis 16* was concerned with the cooperative network of the semiconductor industry and assumes that our analysis reveals a dense network in which virtually all firms are connected by more or less equally distributed links. As described above the cooperative network of the semiconductor industry stands out in terms of density but the expected equal distribution of alliances over participating companies cannot be found. Therefore *Hypothesis 16* also can not be validated by our empirical analysis. The last hypothesis that was put forward in this chapter (*Hypothesis 17*) argues that cooperative networks in the telecommunications sector will be very sparse during the first and second period. The most recent period would, however, be characterized by a dense network in terms of the number of alliances as well as in their international orientation. In spite of the observed growth in network density from 0.214 in the second period to 0.306 in the most recent period, this growth still lags behind the growth in density that was found in the semiconductor industry. Also the expected internationalization in terms of strategic alliances did not take place. There even appears to be a relative decrease in the number of alliances since the second period. Therefore *Hypothesis 17* can not be validated on the basis of our analysis.

In this chapter we were able to validate our first four hypotheses (10 to 13) but we were not able to confirm hypotheses 14 to 17. All the hypotheses that could not be validated were based on the assumption that there was a strong relationship between technological and market structural developments and the networks of strategic technology alliances (Casson, 1987; Chesnais, 1988; Mytelka, 1991). The involvement of leading companies in the networks do not confirm Porter's (1990) assumption that networking companies are basically non-leading companies that try to catch up with the leaders. However, despite the involvement of leading companies in the network our results indicate no clear linear relationship between market positions and positions in the network. This is in line with the findings of Hagedoorn (1995: 10), who argued that 'a possible interpretation of hierarchies of strategic technology partnering as a reproduction of existing international market hierarchies has to be rejected as too mechanistic and simplistic'. Therefore we assume that although there are a large number of indirect relationships between industry development and networks of strategic technology alliances, our results do not indicate a linear relationship between them.

NOTES

1. For a detailed discussion of this relationship, see Hagedoorn (1995).
2. Because of our focus on the 'core' sectors of the Information Technology industry we did not include industrial automation in our study.
3. This so-called 'imitation effect' is dealt with more extensively in Hagedoorn (1992).
4. See Chapter 8 for a more detailed analysis of the globalization process.
5. R&D ventures undertaken with distinctive research programmes are labelled research corporations (Hagedoorn, 1990).
6. See Hagedoorn (1993) for a complete overview of motives for strategic R&D alliances.
7. Kogut (1989) also found that R&D ventures were significantly more stable than other ventures.
8. Partner selection seems crucial for the stability of new ventures (see e.g. Geringer, 1991; Hamel, 1991).
9. We decided to focus on three centrality measures instead of one because each measure provides us with additional (complementary) information.
10. Because we make use of a relative closeness centrality measure, the most central players have the highest closeness degrees.
11. It is well known that the density of a network decreases exponentially by an increasing number of nodes (Barley et al. 1992).
12. The only links that can be associated with micro- or mini-computers are the alliances between United Technologies and DEC and between Tandy and Commodore.
13. This degree of network density can be compared to the density in the computer industry during the last period.
14. Zilog became independent again in 1989.

8 Internationalization of Corporate Technological Activity[1]

The previous chapters of this book have shown that globalization is an important and critical feature of today's IT markets. The telecommunications industry as well as the semiconductor and computer sectors seem to have in common that an increasing amount of boundary-spanning competition between major multinational, or even globally operating companies is going on. Internationalization is, however, not restricted to the largest companies but affects virtually all the companies in these sectors. Because of the noted importance of internationalization it seems interesting to study this phenomenon in more detail.

The so-called 'globalization' of the world economy has received widespread interest from scholars in business as well as in economics (see e.g. Vernon, 1966, 1979; Hirschey and Caves, 1981; Pearce, 1989; Bartlett et al., 1990). The expression 'globalization' is extensively used to describe the increase in the degree of which companies establish value-added activities outside their national boundaries (Dunning, 1988; Cantwell, 1991; OECD, 1992a). Globalization is often described as a process that will eventually lead to a single global world market in which companies have become 'footloose' with no particular relationship to any specific country. In such a global market, large companies would have a global presence in virtually all countries (Reich, 1991).[2] The globalization tendencies which are widely portrayed and heralded in the literature (see e.g. Dunning, 1988, 1993; Reich, 1991) have, however, been questioned by others (see e.g. Porter, 1986, 1990; Patel and Pavitt, 1991; Hu, 1992). The debate among scholars about the degree of globalization and the character of the companies involved has become known as the 'Who is US?' debate. Reich (1990, 1991) started the debate by questioning the importance of national backgrounds for US companies. He described a process of continuing globalization in which 'national champions everywhere are becoming global webs with no particular connection to any single nation' (Reich, 1991: 131). Hu (1992) responded to

187

Reich's statements about 'stateless' companies by arguing that although companies have internationalized parts of their corporate activities over a large number of countries, these organizations can still be regarded as national companies with some international operations.

Because the evolution of high-technology markets is central to our book we will pay particular attention to the internationalization of corporate technological activity. Our contribution to the 'Who is US' debate can be found in an empirical analysis of the importance of national backgrounds for a number of large multinational enterprises (MNEs) in the IT sector. In the first part of this chapter we will analyse the internationalization of R&D from a dynamic perspective of industrial change. The main question that will be answered in this part is whether companies are gradually becoming more international in terms of their internal and external technology flows and the location of their R&D facilities. The second part of this chapter addresses the question whether the internationalization process has led to convergence among the structures and strategies of companies from various home regions.

8.1. THE INTERNATIONALIZATION OF CORPORATE TECHNOLOGICAL ACTIVITY

Several empirical studies have pointed out that companies are increasingly engaged in foreign production activities (see e.g. Dunning, 1988, 1993). Internationalization of R&D has received considerably less attention but is expected to follow behind the establishment of production activities with a certain time-lag (Pearce, 1989; Cantwell, 1991). In the literature on multinational enterprises, several advantages of an international dispersed network of R&D facilities have been reported (Granstrand et al., 1992; Miller, 1994; Pearce and Singh, 1992). The traditional rationale for the creation of foreign R&D facilities was to adapt products to the local market or to satisfy host country government regulations. By creating local R&D facilities firms can be in close contact with their customers and major local suppliers. This enables them to respond quickly to differences in demand among the various countries and allows them to interact with their major local suppliers. Sometimes local R&D is a necessity to gain government contracts in telecommunications or military equipment or to facilitate local clinical testing as in pharmaceuticals (Granstrand et al., 1992). However, there are also a number of factors that favour the geographical centralization of R&D

facilities in the home country. The main reason to centralize R&D within the home country is the existence of economies of scale and scope in R&D. If economies of scale and scope exist, then one R&D facility is often more efficient than several smaller facilities. The establishment of centralized R&D facilities near the major production centres can also be used to improve the interaction between the production, marketing and R&D departments. It has also been noted that centralization of R&D aids the protection of firm-specific technologies (Rugman, 1981). In the case of centralized R&D there seems to be less danger of knowledge 'leaking' to competitors (Granstrand et al., 1992).

In this chapter we will try to identify the major trends in the internationalization of corporate technological activities over a certain time period. Because the developments in the information technology industry are our main research issue in this book we will study three major subfields of this industry in more detail: i.e. telecommunications, computers and semiconductors. As described in the previous chapters, all these IT sectors are characterized by international competition among a number of large multinational companies. It is even claimed that IT-producing companies (in particular IBM) are leading the internationalization process (OECD, 1992a). Therefore we might argue that if patterns of internationalization can be found at all, they should become apparent in a study of the IT industry.

8.2. INTERNATIONALIZATION OF R&D: SOME EMPIRICAL TRENDS

A number of recent studies suggest that multinational companies have gradually increased their foreign R&D activities. An increase of overseas R&D has been reported by, among others, Lee and Reid (1991), Reich (1991), Graves (1991) and Miller (1994). These studies suggest that foreign R&D has grown much more rapidly than domestic R&D expenditures. Others have reported a strong increase in the number of overseas R&D facilities of major multinational companies (Peters, 1992; Pearce and Singh, 1992). In addition to innovation input statistics, measures of innovation output have also been subject to a number of studies (Cantwell and Hodson, 1991; Patel and Pavitt, 1991). Patel and Pavitt (1991) made use of US patent statistics to analyse international patenting activities of large multinational corporations. In their study they distinguished between patents taken out in the US by 'national' companies in each country from those taken out by foreign subsidiaries of those same companies. Their study confirmed that although foreign subsidiaries of multinational companies do indeed contribute significantly to world innovative activities, this contribution was less than 10 per cent of world patenting during the first half of the eighties.[3] Other authors (Cantwell and Hodson, 1991) found somewhat higher shares of international patenting. They estimate the share of US patents attributable to research in foreign locations for the world's largest firms during the first half of the eighties at about 10 per cent. These differences are partly due to the fact that whereas Patel and Pavitt include small and medium-sized companies, universities and government laboratories, Cantwell and Hodson include only the largest companies. However, their research also indicates 'that the world's largest firms witnessed a mild trend towards the internationalization of technological activity over the 1969–86 period' (Cantwell and Hodson, 1991: 137).

Following Patel and Pavitt (1991) and Cantwell and Hodson (1991) we performed a somewhat similar analysis to detect a possible continuation of trends in the internationalization of innovative output, measured by patents. In our analysis we compare patenting activity in two periods, i.e. 1980–85 and 1986–91. Instead of using data from the US Patent Office, as done in the studies of Patel and Pavitt and Cantwell and Hodson, we compiled our data from the European Patent Office (EPO). We choose to focus on EPO patents because it seemed interesting to evaluate the internationalization tendencies from a different (European) perspective. The EPO data set enables us to compare and extend the findings of Patel and Pavitt and Cantwell and Hodson on US patenting activity to our findings based on patenting activity in Europe. As with US patent data, the EPO data allows us to differentiate between the applicant and the inventor. In our analysis we discriminate between the total number of patents that were filed by institutions from a specific region and the percentage of those patents that was based on inventions from outside this specific region. We calculated the percentages for the whole population irrespective of size and institutional form. Using the whole population of patenting organizations implies that we can expect a lower degree of internationalization, as in the case of Patel and Pavitt (1991) and Cantwell and Hodson (1991) who focused exclusively on large organizations.[4]

In our analysis we compare internationalization patterns for three major regions: Europe, Japan and the US. Our findings on the internationalization of R&D in information technologies, see Table 8.1, show that the US is leading the internationalization process in all segments but suffered a severe drop from 8.0 per cent in the first period to 6.0 per cent in the second period. Although for the US the percentage of international patents fell in all information technology segments, this decrease can be attributed primarily to a decrease of 5.6 per cent in the telecommunications industry.[5] International technological activity of European institutions outside Europe remains at 2.0 per cent of total patents. Europe's percentage seems to rise in telecommunications and semiconductors but decreases in dataprocessing. Japan, on the other hand, shows an increase in all three segments. The major differences between our findings and those of the other contributors can be attributed to the fact that we aggregated our data at a European level. This implies that the internationalization patterns for European firms found by Patel and Pavitt and Cantwell and Hodson probably refer to intra-European internationalization. It seems that extra-European internationalization of technological activity of European firms is found only in a relatively small number of cases.

Table 8.1 Foreign subsidiary patenting (as a percentage of total EPO patents, 1980–1985 and 1986–1991)

	IT total		Computers		Micro		Telecom	
	80-85	86-91	80-85	86-91	80-85	86-91	80-85	86-91
Europe	2.0	2.0	3.2	2.3	1.3	1.6	1.5	2.0
US	8.0	6.0	7.2	6.4	6.4	5.1	11.7	6.1
Japan	0.4	1.4	1.0	2.1	0.1	1.3	0.5	0.8

Source: European Patent Office.

8.3. INTERNATIONAL STRATEGIC TECHNOLOGY ALLIANCES

In the literature on internationalization it is sometimes suggested that strategic alliances are essential to international corporate strategies (Ohmae, 1990; de Woot, 1990; OECD, 1992a). It seems therefore interesting to consider whether the increase in cooperative activity as reported in Chapter 7 has been of a primarily international character or whether companies are predominantly searching for partnerships with companies from the same economic region. Table 8.2 shows the distribution of strategic technology alliances within and between economic blocs in two time periods (1978–85 and 1986–93). For the total number of IT alliances the relative importance of inter-region alliances shows a decrease from 46.2 per cent in the first period to 34.7 per cent in the second period. The largest drop in inter-regional alliances is found in the computer industry. In this industry international alliances accounted for more than half (53.1 per cent) of the total number of alliances in the first period but showed a decrease to 39.8 per cent in the second period. The decreases in the relative importance of inter-regional alliances were significantly lower in other IT sectors. Decreases in the other sectors range from 7 per cent in telecommunications to 4 per cent for semiconductors. Although these decreases are significantly smaller than the decrease in the computer industry they confirm that alliances are not the vehicles for internationalization they were thought to be.

Table 8.2 Distribution of strategic technology alliances within and between economic blocs (percentages, 1978-1985 and 1986-1993)

	Total 78–85	86–93	Computers 78–85	86–93	Telecom 78–85	86–93	Semicond. 78–85	86–93
US–EU	21.2	18.0	24.2	16.1	20.5	22.6	20.7	16.4
US–JAP	21.5	13.5	21.9	19.7	14.6	5.2	32.9	30.5
JAP–EU	3.5	3.2	7.0	4.0	2.6	3.0	3.2	6.1
EUR–EU	21.0	14.9	14.8	7.2	26.5	22.6	13.1	13.8
US–US	27.3	42.4	25.8	45.8	28.5	35.1	25.7	19.3
JAP–JAP	5.5	7.9	6.3	7.2	7.3	11.7	4.5	13.8
Total	100.0	100.0	100.0	100.0	100.0	100.0	100.0	100.0

Most of the arguments pro or contra the internationalization of corporate R&D also bear relevance to the international partial externalization of innovative activities through inter-firm partnerships. The bottom line of the argument would be that there is a clear tension between international partnering benefiting from 'foreign' capabilities and a larger degree of control through alliances that are closer to the 'domestic' span of control. We assume that joint R&D is closer to the corporate core of most companies than is the sharing of certain production facilities or the joint entry of uncontrolled foreign markets. Therefore we can expect that the internationalization of R&D through international strategic technology alliances will still be at a moderate level compared to partnerships which are more directly related to market-entry arrangements and joint production. We therefore expect strongly international-oriented inter-firm alliances to be more concentrated on commercial and production activities, whereas R&D-focused alliances are probably of a less international character.

The data from the MERIT–CATI database until 1989 enables us to differentiate between strategic technology alliances which are primarily related to R&D and alliances which, despite their technology content, are also undertaken to access markets or to produce- or market-specific products. This distinction enables us to assess whether R&D-inclined alliances are undertaken by companies within a certain region and whether market-oriented technology alliances have a more international character. In order to reveal patterns of internationalization we will introduce a new measure of relative internationalization which we calculated by setting the ratio of intra-regional partnering against the ratio for inter-regional partnering for each sector[6] (see Table 8.3). This index confirms our expectation that market-oriented alliances are more international than more R&D-focused alliances. All the sectors, with the exception of telecommunications, show a strong decrease in the degree of internationalization during the second half of the 1980s. The overall pattern therefore suggests that, despite some sector-specific and/or international irregularities, strategic partnering has become relatively more concentrated within major regions of the Triad instead of becoming overwhelmingly international.

Table 8.3 Relative internationalization index of strategic technology partnering in overall information technology[7] (computers, semiconductors and telecommunications, 1980–1984 and 1985–1989)

	R&D		Market	
	80–84	*85–89*	*80–84*	*85–89*
Total	0.88	0.66	2.49	1.69
Computers	1.35	0.69	2.45	1.52
Semiconductors	1.07	0.7	3.87	1.75
Telecom	0.93	0.85	1.4	1.42

8.4. CONVERGENCE OF GLOBALLY OPERATING COMPANIES

After having assessed the degree of internationalization of corporate technological activities we will proceed with another indicator of internationalization that is related to the structure and strategies of major IT-producing companies. In the past decades many previously domestic companies have evolved into so-called multinational enterprises (MNEs). These multinational enterprises increasingly directed their attention away from their home markets towards more internationally oriented activities. In this section we will consider how the assumed internationalization process has affected the companies involved. In the 'Who is US' debate as described in the introduction, Reich (1990, 1991) argued that firms which are operating in a global economy would have no particular relationship to any single country. If internationalization has indeed taken place on a large scale it can be assumed that multinational companies are all facing the same homogeneous competitive environment irrespective of their home countries. Many authors (Hawley, 1968; Meyer and Rowan, 1977; Hannan and Freeman, 1977; Dimaggio and Powell, 1983) have argued that such a homogeneous competitive environment creates a group of homogeneous companies. Those authors stress a process of isomorphism among companies that face the same environmental conditions. Following the lead of Hawley (1950, 1968) they contend that 'units subjected to the same environmental conditions, or to environmental conditions as mediated by a given key unit, acquire a similar form of organization' (Hawley, 1968: 334).

In organizational theory the issue of isomorphism is discussed in terms of two fundamental forces: adaptation and selection. Adaptation takes place as firms try to increase their fit with the environment (Burns and Stalker, 1961; Lawrence and Lorsch, 1967); selection takes place if firms are unable to obtain the required degree of adaptation. A better fit increases the profitability of companies and enhances their survival chances in the long run. Less successful firms often try to increase their fit with the environment by mimicking the structures and strategies of their more successful competitors. Adaptation to changes is, however, not always possible. It is often noted that adaptation to changing environmental circumstances is generally low, as compared to the speed of change. Under such conditions, selection is given the time to take place. In organizational literature this relatively slow process of adaptation is referred to as 'relative inertia', i.e. relative in comparison to fast environmental changes.[8] Inspired by the Darwinian conception of 'natural selection' many authors in the population ecology tradition (Aldrich, 1979; Carroll, 1987, 1988; Hannan and Freeman, 1977, 1989; Singh and Lumsden, 1990) contend that organizations that are best adapted to a specific environment survive while other less well-adapted organizations die. In such a framework isomorphism among organizations will take place because only those organizations that have a good 'fit' with their environment will survive. The same deterministic relationship between the environment and the organization can be found in the so-called institutional school of thought. From an institutional perspective isomorphism does not take place as a result of competitive pressures but rather as a result of interactions between organizations. Institutionalists have argued that isomorphism occurs either through coercive, mimetic or normative mechanisms (Dimaggio and Powell, 1983). Coercive isomorphism is associated with legitimation and political pressures. Organizations are expected to behave according to cultural and political standards and according to pressures from other organizations with which they interact. Mimetic behaviour stems from standardized reactions to challenges from an uncertain environment. In order to reduce risk, firms tend to mimic structures and strategies of successful organizations. Normative pressures result from an increasing professionalism within organizations. All three forms of isomorphism are linked to the institutional structure in which firms are embedded.

The concept of isomorphism assumes a rather deterministic relationship between the environment and the individual organization in the sense that organizations are strictly contingent on their environment. Although this might hold for a number of small organizations, advocates of resource dependence and strategic choice (Child, 1972; Pfeffer, 1972; Pfeffer and Salancik, 1978) have, in our opinion, appropriately argued that it would be very unrealistic to view powerful multinational enterprises as such. In line with, for instance, oligopoly theory in economics, large multinational enterprises do not have to be considered as merely passive recipients of environmental pressures, but they are primarily seen as active organizations that are well capable of influencing their own environment (Pfeffer and Salancik, 1978). Under these conditions, variations among organizations occur partly as a result of strategic decision making within organizations. Strategic-choice theorists argued that companies can change their structures and strategies according to their own perception of the environment. Child (1972), for example, raised three arguments against the environmental deterministic view of ecological and institutional theorists. First, he argued that top management has a considerable autonomy in the organizational decision-making process. They can choose from a large number of options regarding their response to environmental pressures. The second argument claims that organizations are often able to influence or modify their environment. The third argument stresses that environmental demands are not always very clear and that organizational decision makers often interpret these demands differently. This may lead to different reactions to the same environmental demands. It is clear that strategic-choice theorists have a completely different view of the relationship between organizations and their environments from their more deterministic counterparts.

In this chapter we contend that multinational enterprises are neither perfect adapters nor completely contingent on their environment. The attention paid in this book to the international context of the competitive environment of firms not only reflects the growing importance of the internationalization of firms itself, but also it contributes to the 'imprintment' line of theory. Stinchcombe (1965) argued that social, cultural, technological and competitive conditions under which a company is established will have a continuing effect on an organization's strategy and structure. Although the imprintment hypothesis is discussed at length in the literature (see e.g. Aldrich, 1979; Hannan and Freeman, 1977, 1984 and 1989; Tolbert and Zucker, 1983) there is, to the best of our knowledge, no empirical research on, for instance, the continuing effects of the domestic background of companies on their behaviour and organization in an international competitive environment.

The main goal of the second part of this chapter is to assess whether we are still able to distinguish among companies according to their region of origin despite the reported internationalization of the world economy. We will try to establish whether and to what degree companies from each of the major economic regions have converged or diverged in terms of their strategies and structures. The IT markets that are studied in this book are generally referred to as 'global' markets in which companies compete on a world-scale level. According to Porter (1986), such global markets are characterized by similar demand structures and similar product specifications. If isomorphism takes place then we would expect that such a homogeneous market would lead to an increasing number of similar organizations. Two factors in particular are able to influence our findings. The first factor could be the lack of a sufficient scale of internationalization. If the degree of internationalization is too low, then the condition of a homogeneous environment is not met. In that case we would expect to find companies that can still be distinguished in terms of their country of origin. The second factor is the degree of relative inertia that is faced by the major companies. If inertial forces are very strong as suggested by Stinchcombe's (1965) 'imprintment' line of theory, then firms are still basically influenced by the social, cultural, technological and competitive conditions under which a company is established, i.e. these conditions have become imprinted in their organizational structure (Boeker, 1988).[9]

Patterns of isomorphism are analysed in the same three sectors of the information technology industry that are studied in the previous chapters. In this chapter we will study the structures and strategies of the leading companies of each particular sector. Forty multinational enterprises are analysed in the computer industry. Of these 40 companies, 22 are based in the US, 6 are European, 11 are Japanese and 1 falls in the category 'others'. The population of the telecommunications industry consists of 5 US companies, 12 European companies, 7 Japanese-based companies and 1 'miscellaneous' company. Our last sector, the semiconductor industry, has a population of 20 companies of which 1 falls in the category 'others', 6 are based in the US, 3 are based in Europe and 10 are Japanese (Table 8.4). For the analysis of differences or similarities among companies from different home regions we applied a number of statistical techniques such as discriminant function analysis and analysis of variance (ANOVA). Discriminant function analysis is used to find out which set of predictors can most clearly distinguish between groups of companies that are combined in terms of their region of origin. In contrast to regression analysis where the dependent variable is continuous, discriminant function analysis can be used to deal with categorical dependent variables. This allows us to differentiate among the various regions by means of a discriminant function which derives the maximum discrimination among the various regions using the country of origin of firms (COUNTRY) as a categorical, dependent variable.[10] ANOVA is used to generate additional information that can be used to determine which regions differ significantly on the various structural and strategic variables.

For our analysis we make use of a broad set of structural and strategic variables. Measures of size and diversification are used as indicators of the structure of organizations whereas three basic technology indicators are used to measure the technology strategies of organizations.[11] Size of companies is measured by taking the average of the corporate revenues that companies realized during the period 1986–90. We have chosen revenues as an indicator instead of the more frequently applied employment indicator to account for quasi-integration. It is well known that Japanese companies have fewer employees than their US and European competitors on account of the Japanese lean production practice and sophisticated customer–supplier networks. However, their size in terms of revenues, which roughly equals turnover, is in our opinion a better indicator of their economic magnitude in comparison with companies from other regions. Differences in size between European, Japanese and US companies are analyzed by means of two specific indicators. The first indicator consists of the average total revenues of companies for the yearly average of the period 1986–90 (SIZE). The second indicator of size (DPSIZE) is related to the dataprocessing activities of these companies, i.e. their average dataprocessing revenues during the same period.

Diversification is first measured as the average number of information technology segments from a total of twenty segments in which companies were engaged during 1989. The degree of specialization is a different measure, indicating the share of dataprocessing sales in total corporate sales during the period 1986–89. These two variables suggest an inverse relation which, although plausible, is not logically binding because the statistical basis of both measures is quite different. We have combined our findings on diversification and specialization in one measure, i.e. the overall degree of diversification.

Table 8.4 *Companies in the population of dataprocessing, telecommunications and semiconductor industries*

	Dataprocessing	Telecom	Semiconductors
US	Apple AT&T CDC Compaq Data General DEC H–P IBM Memorext Motorola NCR Prime Seagate Storage Sun–Micr. Tandem Tandy TI Unisys Wang Xerox	AT&T GTE IBM Motorola Rockwell TI	AMD AT&T Intel Motorola Nat.Sem.
Europe	Bull Mannesmann Nokia Olivetti Philips Siemens	Alcatel Ascom Bosch Ericsson GEC Matra Nokia Philips Racal Sagem Siemens STC	Philips Siemens SGS–Thomson
Japan	Amdahl Canon Fujitsu Hitachi Matsushita Mitsubishi NEC NTT OKI Ricoh Toshiba	Fujitsu Hitachi Matsushita Mitsubishi NEC OKI Ricoh Toshiba	Fujitsu Hitachi Masushita Mitsubishi NEC OKI Sanyo Sharp Sony Toshiba
Others	NT	NT	Samsung

Factor analysis, in particular principal component analysis, is applied to reduce our data set to arrive at one composite variable (DIV). Principal component analysis provides us with a tool to generate a single composite variable from several variables by reducing the data by means of the factor scores that are produced in the initial analysis, see Hagedoorn (1989).

The technology strategy variable (TECH) is based on a number of innovation- and technology-related indicators. The absolute innovative strength of companies is indicated by their number of sector-relevant US patents, granted in the period 1980–88. We have taken US patents because we expect the US market to be the most advanced in terms of the combination of competition, openness and technological sophistication, in particular in information technology. The absolute number of patents granted was taken to have at least one indicator of absolute strength next to a number of more relative indicators. Also, we found that the correlation between R&D intensity, alliance-related variables and patenting intensity is extremely weak, whereas the correlation with the absolute number of patents is significant. The other, more relative, indicator of innovative capabilities that we apply is the R&D intensity of firms, i.e. their total R&D expenditures as a percentage of total corporate sales during the period 1986–90.

Apart from these two 'standard' innovation-strategy indicators we will also look at two measures that are related to strategic technology partnering behaviour of firms during the eighties. One of these indicators is the so-called T–M ratio, which indicates if the strategic technology alliances of companies made in the period 1980–89 are primarily related to R&D or whether these alliances are more closely related to marketing and market-entry activities. We have included this indicator because Hagedoorn and Schakenraad (1994) found that in information technology in particular, R&D-inclined strategic linkages are associated with improved economic performance. The other partnering-related indicator is the generation–attraction ratio which indicates the degree to which the strategic partnerships of companies generate technology to their partners or absorb technology from them. We assume that the more a company generates technology to its partners the stronger the technological position of this company. We have standardized both these ratios at a $\log_{10}$ scale. Technology–market ratios between 0 and +1 indicate an R&D inclination of the alliances of companies; scores between 0 and −1 refer to a stronger market orientation of the alliances made by companies. Generation–attraction ratios between 0 and +1 indicate a technology-generating effect through the alliances of companies; scores between 0 and −1 show an absorption tendency in the alliances of companies. In order to construct a combined indicator of strategic technology-partnering behaviour of companies we applied principal component analysis in a similar way as for the measure of overall diversification.

The overall indicator of technology strategy (TECH) consists of the combined variables for patenting, R&D intensity and technology partnering by means of factor analysis.

8.5 EMPIRICAL PATTERNS OF CONVERGENCE IN INFORMATION TECHNOLOGIES

As described in the previous section, the variables for the characteristics of companies operating in the three subfields of information technology are: diversification patterns (DIV), technology strategy (TECH), overall size (SIZE) and size in the subfield of information technology (DPSIZE, TELSIZE, SEMSIZE). To determine the most distinguishing variables, we start our examination of companies in the dataprocessing industry with an evaluation of the Wilks' Lambda and F-values of the various variables (see Table 8.5). The Wilks' Lambda statistic is concerned with the ratio between the within group variance and the total variance. A ratio close to 1 points to an equality of group means, whereas lower values are associated with large differences between the various group means. For each variable the F-ratios are calculated in order to test the hypothesis that all group means are equal. The results for the dataprocessing industry indicate a strong rejection of this hypothesis in the case of the diversification (sign. 0.0006) and size (sign. 0.0085) variables. The remaining two variables, TECH and DPSIZE, show relatively high Wilks' Lambda values and low significance levels; therefore, we cannot reject the hypothesis that the group means for these two variables are equal.

In order to achieve a better understanding of the two variables that most clearly distinguish between the major regions, we performed a 'one-way' ANOVA to measure whether group means differ significantly from each other. As our study refers to three groups (regions) a 'normal' T-test study, which is only capable of dealing with two groups, could not be performed. In addition to the ANOVA we apply the so-called Scheffe test because the size of groups is not equal. The Scheffe test makes use of the differences between means to calculate an F-ratio. This enables us to calculate which groups differ significantly from each other with respect to a particular variable.

Table 8.5 Wilks' Lambda (U-statistic) and univariate F-ratio (with 2 and 36 degrees of freedom), dataprocessing

Variable	Wilks' Lambda	F	Significance
DIV	0.66225	9.180	0.0006
TECH	0.94071	1.134	0.3328
SIZE	0.76746	5.454	0.0085
DPSIZE	0.99175	0.1498	0.8614

The first ANOVA table (Table 8.6) shows that the mean values of the variables measuring diversification for US dataprocessing companies differ significantly from European companies, as well as from Japanese companies. The second ANOVA table (Table 8.7) clearly indicates that US firms differ significantly from their Japanese competitors with respect to their overall size.

After we evaluated the discriminatory power of separate variables we continue with the assessment of the overall discriminatory power of the total set of variables. We will consider the 'goodness' of the discriminant functions as is reflected in various indicators presented in Table 8.8. The first indicator is the eigenvalue which represents the relationship of the between group and the within group sum of squares. Higher eigenvalues can be associated with more discriminating functions. In this case the functions seem to have considerable discriminating power. Other important statistics include Corr (canonical correlation), which represents the proportion of total variance which is accounted for by differences among regions. A chi-square value of 19.621 and a corresponding significance of 0.0119 implies that the hypothesis that the mean scores on the various variables for different regions are equal, can be rejected.

Table 8.6 One-way analysis of variance in diversification, dataprocessing

		U S	E u r	J a p
Mean	Group			
- 0.5079	US			
0.4915	Europe		*	
0.7414	Japan		*	

* Denotes pairs of groups significantly different at the 0.05 level.

Table 8.7 One-way analysis of variance in overall size, dataprocessing

		U S	E u r	J a p
Mean	Group			
15.1958	US			
16.2576	Europe			
16.4720	Japan		*	

* Denotes pairs of groups significantly different at the 0.05 level.

Table 8.8 Canonical discriminant functions, dataprocessing

Fcn	Eigenvalue	Pct of Variance	Cum Pct	Canonical Corr	After Fcn	Wilks' Lambda	Chi-square	DF	Sig
					0	0.5662	19.621	8	0.0119
1*	0.5539	80.23	80.23	0.5970	1	0.8799	4.415	3	0.2200
2*	0.1365	19.77	100.00	0.3466					

* Mark the 2 canonical discriminant functions remaining in the analysis.

The effectiveness of the discriminant functions is measured by classifying all cases according to their scores on the combined discriminant functions. Whereas the prior probability of classification is 33.33 per cent, the actual classification procedure results in a correct classification of 58.97 per cent of the cases (see Table 8.9). This points to a relatively large degree of divergence among companies from various home regions. Japanese firms seem to form the most homogeneous group with a correct classification result of 63.6 per cent. They are, however, closely followed by US and European firms, respectively.

Table 8.9 Results of the discriminant analysis, dataprocessing

Actual Group	No. of Cases	Predicted Group Membership		
		US	Europe	Japan
US	22	13 59.1%	3 13.6%	6 27.3%
Europe	6	1 16.7%	3 50.0%	2 33.3%
Japan	11	1 9.1%	3 27.3%	7 63.6%
Ungrouped	1	1 100.0%	0 0%	0 0%

We will follow similar statistical procedures for the international telecommunications industry. The evaluation of the Wilks' Lambda and F-values of the various variables in Table 8.10 leads to the rejection of the hypothesis that all group means are equal in the case of total size (sign. 0.0534). All the other variables show relatively high Wilks' Lambda values and low significance levels. Additional ANOVA indicates that no groups were found to be significantly different from each other in terms of their size.

The 'goodness' of the discriminant functions which is reflected in the canonical discriminant functions is not very satisfying. A chi-square value of

9.876 which corresponds with a significance of 0.2739 indicates that the hypothesis that the mean scores on the various variables for different regions are equal cannot be rejected, see Table 8.11.

Table 8.10 Wilks' Lambda (U-statistic) and univariate F-ratio (with 2 and 21 degrees of freedom), telecommunications

Variable	Wilks' Lambda	F	Significance
DIV	0.86703	1.610	0.2235
TECH	0.87885	1.447	0.2577
SIZE	0.75645	3.381	0.0534
TELSIZE	0.93246	0.761	0.4799

Table 8.11 Canonical discriminant functions, telecommunications

Fcn	Eigenvalue	Pct of Var	Cum Pct	Canonical Corr	After Fcn	Wilks' Lambda	Chi-square	DF	Sig
					0	0.6026	9.876	8	0.2739
1*	0.4610	77.24	77.24	0.5617	1	0.8804	2.483	3	0.4783
2*	0.1358	22.76	100.00	0.3458					

* mark the 2 canonical discriminant functions remaining in the analysis

Table 8.12 gives the results of the discriminant analysis for telecommunications companies for which, somewhat surprisingly, 62.5 per cent of the cases are correctly classified. This percentage of correctly categorized firms indicates that the classification results are better than expected on the basis of the canonical discriminant functions. The classification procedure even managed to classify 75 per cent of the European companies correctly. This result points to a relatively homogeneous group of European companies. The results for the Japanese firms, on the other hand, indicate a relatively large degree of heterogeneity among Japanese telecommunication equipment manufacturers.

Table 8.12 Results of the discriminant analysis, telecommunications

Actual Group	No. of Cases	Predicted Group Membership		
		US	Europe	Japan
US	5	3 60.0%	1 20.0%	1 20.0%
Europe	12	1 8.3%	9 75.0%	2 16.7%
Japan	7	1 14.3%	3 42.9%	3 42.9%
Ungrouped	1	1 100.0%	0 0%	0 0%

Finally in the following tables we present the analysis of the situation in the population of semiconductor firms. Table 8.13 indicates that for two variables related to the semiconductor companies we can reject the hypothesis that all their group means are equal. These variables are diversification (sign. 0.0107) and technological strength (sign. 0.0120), others show higher Wilks' Lambda values and lower significance levels.

Table 8.13 Wilks' Lambda (U-statistic) and univariate F-ratio (with 2 and 16 degrees of freedom), semiconductors

Variable	Wilks' Lambda	F	Significance
DIV	0.56722	6.104	0.0107
TECH	0.57537	5.904	0.0120
SIZE	0.76751	2.423	0.1204
SEMSIZE	0.90796	0.811	0.4619

Analyses of variance, see Tables 8.14 and 8.15, indicate some major differences between Japanese firms and other groups of companies. Table 8.14 shows that with respect to the variable diversification Japan differs significantly from the US. In Table 8.15 we see that European companies differ from both their Japanese and US competitors on technological strength.

Table 8.14 One-way analysis of variance in diversification, semiconductors

		U S	E u r	J a p
Mean	**Group**			
-0.9822	US			*
0.1764	Europe			
0.4563	Japan			

* Denotes pairs of groups significantly different at the 0.05 level

Table 8.15 One-way analysis of variance in technological strength, semiconductors

		U S	E u r	J a p
Mean	**Group**			
-0.5909	USA		*	
0.9492	Europe			
-0.5241	Japan		*	

* Denotes pairs of groups significantly different at the .05 level.

The 'goodness' of the discriminant functions is reflected in Table 8.16. A chi-square value of 27.064 which corresponds with a significance of 0.0007 for the first function and a chi-square value of 7.029 with a corresponding significance level of 0.0710 for the second function indicate that the

The Dynamics of Technical Innovation

hypothesis of the uniformity of mean scores on the various variables between different regions can be strongly rejected.

Table 8.16 Canonical discriminant functions, semiconductors

Fcn	Eigenval	Pct of Var	Cum Pct	Canonical Corr	After Fcn	Wilks' Lambda	Chi-square	DF	Sig
					0	0.1547	27.064	8	0.0007
1*	2.9818	82.70	82.70	0.8654	1	0.6158	7.029	3	0.0710
2*	0.6238	17.30	100.0	0.6198					

* Marks the 2 canonical discriminant functions remaining in the analysis.

The, by now familiar, classification procedure, see Table 8.17, demonstrates that a total number of 89.47 per cent of cases are correctly classified. This clearly indicates that in the international semiconductor industry a substantial amount of inter-regional discriminating power of the variables exists. Especially striking is the result for Japanese companies where all the companies were classified correctly.

Table 8.17 Results of the discriminant analysis, semiconductors

Actual	Group	No. of Cases	Predicted Group Membership		
			USA	Europe	Japan
US		6	5 83.3%	1 16.7%	0 0%
Europe		3	1 33.3%	2 66.7%	0 0%
Japan		10	0 0%	0 0%	10 100.0%
Ungrouped		1	0 0%	0 0%	1 100.0%

8.6. DISCUSSION AND CONCLUSIONS

In this chapter we discussed the internationalization of corporate technological activities and the possible convergence of globally operating companies. The first part of this chapter explored the empirical question of whether we can find increasing patterns of internationalization of corporate technological activity in the IT industry. In the second part, which can be seen as a contribution to the so-called 'Who is US?' debate, we discussed the importance of national backgrounds for major internationally operating companies.

Our analysis of the internationalization trends in the IT industry reveals that there seems to be no sudden explosion of globalization in terms of innovative activity. Our findings suggest that if internationalization takes place at all we can detect only a moderate trend towards internationalization of technology during the 1980s and early 1990s. The majority of the companies in the IT sector appear to rely extensively on their home country with respect to their innovative activities. EPO patent statistics have shown that only a small degree of corporate technological activity takes place outside the home country. Additional research on strategic alliances shows that despite a rapid increase in the total number of strategic technology alliances during the 1980s, those alliances have become relatively more concentrated within major economic regions instead of becoming overwhelmingly global. A related analysis shows that there are major differences between alliances that are undertaken for market-related purposes and those that have a more technological-oriented content. Market-related alliances seem to be much more international in focus than R&D-oriented alliances. All these results indicate that apparently the IT industry, which is often referred to as being 'globalized', is found to be not very internationalized in terms of its technological activities.

After having assessed the degree of internationalization of corporate technological activity, we considered the impact of a possible internationalization on the strategies and structures of the companies involved. Our findings suggest that patterns of isomorphism have not yet become apparent in the sense that they have led companies to acquire one identical or largely identical form of organization. Despite their international orientation, companies in all three sectors can still be recognized in terms of their region of origin if one considers their strategies and structures.

In the statistical analysis of major differences between companies from each of the three economic regions we found that only two factors have a significant effect on the international differentiation of the dataprocessing industry. These factors are the degree of corporate diversification and the size of companies. In particular, US companies are significantly smaller than their Japanese competitors, and they are also less diversified than both European and Japanese dataprocessing firms. In other words, at the level of multivariate analysis European, Japanese and US companies are not significantly different if we consider their technological capabilities and their size in dataprocessing. Our results also suggest that although there is some convergence, the majority of firms still have a number of characteristics that put them in certain 'national' groups. This holds in particular for Japanese and US companies. Half of the European dataprocessing companies, on the other hand, are clearly less identifiable as such. Turning to the telecommunications industry we found that size is the only factor differentiating between companies from each of the three regions, although the effect is not significant for national groups as a whole. The degree of diversification, the technological capabilities and the size of companies' activities in telecommunications do not differentiate between firms from Europe, Japan, or the US. However, the combined effect of some characteristics shows that there is still some divergence in the international telecommunications industry, in particular with respect to the differences between US and European companies, whereas the Japanese telecommunications manufacturers appear to be quite diverse.

The third subsector of information technology, i.e. the international semiconductor industry, generates somewhat different results. It is shown that Japanese firms differ significantly from their US competitors in terms of diversification and from both European and US firms in terms of their technology strategies. The classification procedure demonstrates that almost 90 per cent of the cases are correctly classified. This indicates that in the international semiconductor industry a substantial amount of inter-regional discriminating power of the variables exists. Japanese companies, especially, seem to form a very homogeneous group of companies. For dataprocessing and telecommunications we found a larger percentage of companies that are not clearly identifiable as belonging to one particular region. Although this indicates less divergence as in the case of semiconductors in these two sectors the distribution is also skewed, and therefore convergence remains rather small.

Our results therefore suggest that either internationalization tendencies have not been strong enough to generate clear patterns of isomorphism or that imprintment forces have restricted companies from taking on 'global' structures and strategies. Firms seem to be still basically influenced by the social, cultural, technological and competitive conditions under which they are established. The main conclusion of this contribution therefore seems to be that, despite all the attention given to the subject, internationalization of innovation, although by no means insignificant, still appears less important than expected both in terms of actual internationalization trends as well as in terms of the globalization of companies themselves.

NOTES

1. This chapter is partly based on Duysters and Hagedoorn, 1995, 1996.
2. The foreign subsidiaries of these multinational enterprises (MNEs) would then be linked through major information networks that enable the corporate headquarters to communicate with their subsidiaries and to maintain control at relatively low cost.
3. Only in the case of Dutch and Swiss companies does the number of patents from subsidiaries rise to a very high proportion. This is mainly due to the existence of a few very large Dutch and Swiss companies which have strong manufacturing and R&D assets outside their small domestic base.
4. We are aware of the fact that our findings are somewhat biased because we are not consolidating the data to the mother firm. Research on a relatively large data set (50 companies) has, however, indicated that in virtually all cases mother firms applied for the patents that were invented by their subsidiaries. An exception seems to be Philips, where its US subsidiary tends to apply for patents independent from its mother company. Other examples include subsidiaries that are acquired over time. It might be argued that these companies are still operating as separate companies, at least in terms of their R&D strategy. For a comparison of countries and changes over time consolidation seems to affect our results only marginally.
5. This drop could well be the result of the divesture of large parts of ITT's an telecom subsidiary to Alcatel in 1986.
6. This relative internationalization index (*RII*) is calculated per sector as the relative distribution of the inter-regional alliances (*IA_i*) set against the number of intra-regional alliances (*RA_i*) :

$$RII_i = \frac{IA_i}{RA_i}$$

7. The index for the overall information technology includes software and industrial automation.
8. Sometimes changes in the environment are so radical that adaptation to these changes is impossible (see Hannan and Freeman, 1977).

9. These arguments are in line with the ideas of Hu (1992) and Porter (1986, 1990) who argue that in spite of their international activities, multinational enterprises can often still be identified by their national backgrounds.
10. The weights of the discriminant function are estimated in order to obtain the largest discriminating power between the various countries.
11. All the data that is used in this chapter is based on the MERIT–CATI database (see Appendix I).

9. Summary and Conclusions

This book explores the evolution of complex industrial systems over time, more in particular it focuses on the development of three major information technology sectors: i.e. computers, telecommunications and semiconductors. Whereas traditional theories of organization and economics are often concerned with static, cross-sectional analyses, we put forward an integrated evolutionary framework which is inherently dynamic. We argue that the use of such a framework considerably improves our understanding of the evolution of complex industrial systems. Our integrated framework is based on two distinct but related biology-inspired schools of thought. For the study of the evolution of market structures and the importance of particular organizational types under different environmental circumstances we make use of ideas derived from organizational ecology theories, whereas for the study of technological change we build on the elaborated framework developed by evolutionary economists. Although ecological and evolutionary approaches form the core of our framework we combine biology-inspired concepts with ideas from strategic management, organization theory, industrial economics, new institutionalism and international business studies.

Following evolutionary theorists, we argue that technological change is gradual and that superior firms and technologies are rewarded by the 'selection' environment. In the initial phase of the industry life cycle, technological change is expected to be radical and uncertainty is high. Over time a product or technology is likely to arise which stands out above all other products or technologies. These so-called 'basic designs' serve as sorts of 'technological guideposts' for further developments in the technology. Once a basic design is established, technological progress tends to follow consistent paths or trajectories. The cumulative character of technological progress facilitates a rapid expansion of the boundaries of the technology until the natural limits of the technology are approached and technological progress slows down. At that time decreasing returns from investment in research and development induce firms to redirect their focus towards other technological paths.

Supply-side developments in the industry are described on the basis of five different organizational types. In the early stages of a high-technology industry when both market and technological uncertainty are high, first-mover firms are said to have a considerable advantage in the preemption of new market opportunities. These so-called r-type firms are generally characterized by small and fast-to-build organizational structures which enable them to move quickly into new resource spaces. After some time, the establishment of a technological regime initiates a period of more stable technological development. Efficiency then replaces innovativeness as the most important element in a firm's competitive strategy. At that time so-called K-generalists enter the market. K-generalists rely on efficient rigid organizational structures and tend to emphasize efficiency and accountability. When the natural limits of the current paradigm are approached and a stabilization of the industry takes place, another type of firm, so-called K-specialists start to outcompete their generalist rivals. Ultimately the market growth starts to decline and new opportunities in other technological directions are likely to emerge. At that time a new life cycle might be initiated and r-type firms are once again expected to be the first to invade the new market.

On the basis of this pattern of market and technological evolution we came up with seven basic hypotheses. These hypotheses are empirically evaluated under three completely different industry settings. First we studied one of the most dynamic industry sectors of all times, namely the international computer industry. We examined the history of the computer industry ever since its creation up to recent developments in the market. The computer industry has always been characterized by intense international competition and rapid technological progress. Then we proceeded with a market which, in contrast to the computer industry, has for a long time been characterized by the absence of competition in its market, namely the telecommunications industry. The telecommunications industry has always been characterized by domestic internally directed markets in which one main supplier occupied a monopolistic position. At first this monopolistic market structure was due to the dominance of a single patent, later regulatory forces reinforced the monopoly position of the dominant firm. Only recently have liberalization and deregulatory actions paved the way for more (international) competition in the market. After we evaluated our framework under such diverse industry conditions we focused on the semiconductor industry. We choose to study this industry because it is characterized by strong forces of creative destruction that take place after the establishment of a new technological regime. Therefore, market structures have changed substantially over time. In the most recent period a battle for market dominance takes place between Japanese firms that dominate the memory market and US companies that occupy superior positions in the important semiconductor market. Given the large differences among the various sectors it is very interesting to compare the effectiveness of our integrated framework under such diverse conditions. Table 9.1 shows the findings of our evaluation of the seven basic hypotheses as put forward in the second chapter.

Table 9.1 Confirmation or rejection of seven basic hypotheses for three different industry settings

Hypotheses

Indus try	1	2	3	4	5	6	7
Comp uters	√	√	√	√	√	√	*
Telec om	–	√	√	√	√	√	√
Semic ondu ctors	–	–	√	√	√	√	√

√   hypothesis confirmed.
–   hypothesis not confirmed.
*   hypothesis not evaluated.

Our first hypothesis was based on the assumption that new markets are created by radical technological innovations. At the time of founding, a new market is often characterized by substantial uncertainty about the technological feasibility of the innovation and its potential market size. Therefore commercial firms and potential investors are often very sceptical about entering the newly born market. Because of the absence of a commercial market and because technological developments are often dependent on the underlying scientific knowledge base, we hypothesize that universities and government institutions are the main incubators of radically new technologies. Our analyses show that this hypothesis can only be confirmed in the computer industry. In the United States universities carried out large government-sponsored projects, whereas in Germany and Britain a large number of government institutions were trying to develop computers for wartime applications. In the telecommunications industry government institutions and universities played a more modest role. In particular, Schumpeterian entrepreneurs, such as Cooke and Wheatherstone, and Samuel Morse in the telegraph market, and Graham Bell and Elisha Gray in the telephone market, played a much more important role. The importance of these entrepreneurs in the first stage of the telecommunications industry was possible because their early devices were relatively simple and easy to build. Neither sophisticated materials, expensive equipment nor thorough scientific knowledge was needed to build the early telecommunication devices. In the semiconductor industry, government purchasement and support played a vital role in the establishment of the early market but universities and government institutions played only a minor role. The great majority of developments in the early semiconductor market came from the efforts of a single firm: American Telephone and Telegraph (AT&T). AT&T was extremely interested in the development of semiconductor devices for use in its switching and transmission equipment. Our analysis therefore indicates that the role of incubators can be played by a variety of organizations, depending on the complexity of the early devices, the role of scientific knowledge and the potential value of a new device for commercial organizations.

Our second hypothesis argues that a newly emerging high-technology market is likely to be explored by r-specialist organizations which pursue offensive innovation strategies. This hypothesis is, among others, based on the classic argument given by Arrow (1962a) that a new entrant benefits more from a new innovation than incumbent organizations, because for incumbent organizations innovations may cannibalize profits from other products. Therefore, the impetus to move into a new market is correspondingly higher for new organizations. Because innovative features are often more important than price during this stage of development, firms are expected to focus on technological leadership in the market. Our second hypothesis was confirmed in all sectors but the semiconductor industry, where it could be confirmed only for the US market and not for Europe and Japan. In the computer industry the major university institutes spun off a large number of new enterprises which used offensive innovative strategies in order to satisfice military demand for highly innovative products. In the telecommunications industry early customers consisted primarily of stockbrokers, newspaper agencies, railroad owners and the state. This group of customers was well prepared to pay premium prices for increased quality of the services and for a larger distance that could be achieved by the telecommunication services. In the early telecommunications industry, new organizations did not spin off from the major universities but were created by the same entrepreneurs who invented the first telecommunication devices. The importance of innovative new companies was also found in the early US semiconductor industry where small new organizations managed to drive all the major vacuum-tube-producing companies out of the market. A somewhat different pattern was found in the case of Europe and Japan where the low mobility of engineers and the lack of sufficient venture capital inhibited the entrance of small organizations into the market. Therefore *Hypothesis 2* could only partly be confirmed in the semiconductor industry.

Our third hypothesis was concerned with the cumulative nature of technological developments after the establishment of a technological regime. It is argued that the market and technological uncertainty that characterizes newly born markets gradually decreases. Through selection processes it becomes clear which technology stands out above all other technologies. A product or technology which is able to accumulate a critical mass of consensus may then be able to become a 'basic design' on which future research will be based. The search for radical new technological changes is then substituted by cumulative improvements along a specific path or trajectory (*Hypothesis 3*). This hypothesis is confirmed in all sectors under study. Basic designs, such as the von Neumann architecture (computer industry), Morse's telegraph device, Bell's telephone (telecommunications industry) and Texas Instrument's silicon transistor, have all served as a 'technological guidepost' for many decades.

The standardized character of technological change induces firms to redirect their focus away from technological performance and design towards price. Under circumstances of fierce competition large efficient organizations are often much better placed to serve the, now price-sensitive, market than their smaller competitors. Their advantages in terms of static economies of scope and scale enable these firms to set prices well below those of their smaller competitors. We therefore expect that after the establishment of a new technological regime, K-generalists and polymorphists start to outcompete r-specialists (*Hypothesis 4*). This hypothesis is confirmed in all three industries under study. In the computer industry this so-called r to K transition was started by a wave of acquisitions in which major r-type organizations were taken over by larger K-type organizations. In the telecommunications industry the r to K transition started by the gradual transformation of the two most important r-type organizations (American Bell and Western Union) into large K-type organizations. By taking advantage of their patents and rights of way, American Bell and Western Union were able to complete their transformation into large well-established companies. Only a few years after the establishment of every new technological regime in the semiconductor industry, large organizations proved to be more successful in commercializing the newly established products than smaller organizations. It must, however, be stressed that, in addition to static economies of scale and scope, dynamic economies of scale such as learning-curve advantages also played a very important role in this industry. Therefore large organizations need to combine their efficient production structures with a high-tech orientation. Our evaluation of the evolution of the three distinct industrial systems therefore confirms that after the establishment of a new technological regime, K-generalists tend to outcompete r-specialists.

Although the pattern of r to K transition at first may take place very slowly the rate of r- to K transition increases enormously when competitive pressures intensify (*Hypothesis 5*). This hypothesis is based on the assumption that the degree of selection is positively related to the degree of competition in the market. From an organizational ecology point of view, the degree of competition is above all dependent on the carrying capacity of a specific organizational field. As the carrying capacity is approached and competitive forces intensify, r-type organizations will increasingly be replaced by their K-type competitors, at least under conditions of price-based competition. In all three studies we were able to confirm this hypothesis. Increased competition in the computer industry enabled the leading K-type organizations to reinforce their dominant position in the market. In the telecommunications industry, increased competition that was due to the deregulation of the telecommunications markets has led to oligopolistic rivalry among a small number of very large K-type organizations. In the semiconductor industry the early dominance of r-type organizations was soon replaced by a concentrated market structure that was dominated by only five large organizations.

Our sixth hypothesis is based on the concept of 'niche-elaboration' (Pianka, 1978) which argues that the sophistication of users and the preoccupation of large firms with serving the overall market opens up a number of niches in which specialized firms can gain high rewards by focusing on the specific needs of a sophisticated customer group. We argue that whereas initially the market was not large enough to support multiple niches, the emergence of a mass market makes a strategy of segmentation viable (Popper and Buskirk, 1992). Once again this hypothesis was confirmed in all sectors. In the computer industry, IBM's power to dominate the market, high entry barriers and the emphasis on price competition gave smaller firms not a single opportunity to compete effectively in the mainframe market. Therefore, small specialist firms started to focus on specific market niches. Small specialist organizations were responsible for opening up three very important market niches. DEC opened up the mini-computer market, whereas Amdahl and Apple opened up the markets for super-computers and micro-computers respectively. In the telecommunications industry the efforts of small specialist firms were at first not very successful. Strong government regulation prohibited other organizations from entering AT&T's markets. The persistent actions of small organizations would, however, eventually open up markets for Customer Premises Equipment (CPE) and the microwave services market for new competition. Although new firms were not able to attack AT&T's dominant position in its core markets (transmission and switching), swarms of new organizations have successfully entered specific market niches. In the semiconductor industry, specialist organizations opened up market niches for application-specific memory devices, custom chips and RISC microprocessors.

In analogy with the 'success breeds failure syndrome' that was described by Starbuck et al. (1978) we argue that large K-type organizations would have severe difficulties in dealing with a paradigmatic technology shift (*Hypothesis 7*). The elaborated structure of K-strategists and their capital intensive production system enables them to withstand competition for a long time, but also prevents them from moving swiftly into new resource spaces. Therefore, if new technological opportunities arise and the opportunities in the 'old' paradigm decrease, r-strategists will be able to take advantage of the new opportunities much more quickly than their established competitors. This so-called K to r transition was found in all markets except for the computer market where a paradigmatic technology shift has not (yet) occurred. A typical example of a K to r transition took place in the telecommunications industry where Bell managed to establish a dominant position in the telephone market because its much larger K-type competitor (Western Union) failed to recognize the opportunities in this market. In the semiconductor industry a paradigmatic shift in the early 1970s weakened the positions of large well-established K-type organizations in favour of small new innovative companies. From the established companies only Motorola managed to gain a dominant position in the new paradigm.

To summarize, our integrated framework as presented in the second chapter was able to predict fairly accurately the technological and market developments in all industries that were studied. Despite the important differences in industrial conditions which characterize the three markets there is a remarkable resemblance in their evolution over time. This gives strong support for a further development of an integrated evolutionary framework.[1] All aspects considered we might conclude that both biology-inspired theories, although in their infancy, seem to be very promising in handling dynamic phenomena. However, much effort is needed for the construction of a mature framework. According to Kuhn (1970) 'the success of a paradigm ... is at the start largely a promise of success discoverable in selected and still incomplete examples. Normal science consists in the actualization of that promise, an actualization achieved by extending the knowledge of those facts that the paradigm displays as particularly revealing, by increasing the extent of the match between those facts and the paradigm's predictions, and by further articulation of the paradigm itself' (Kuhn, 1970: 23–4). Thus, if 'normal science' is able to enhance the ecological and evolutionary paradigm sufficiently, it may eventually replace the prevailing economic paradigms. Cross-fertilization between the evolutionary and ecological theories seems to be an extremely important tool in achieving maturity of both the ecological and evolutionary economic theories (see also Andersen, 1994). Opportunities for cross-fertilization are, however, not restricted to biology-inspired theories. In the literature the integration of biology-inspired theories with theories of industrial organization (Boone and van Witteloostuijn, 1995), new institutionalism (Tucker et al., 1990) and even with strategic management theories (Carroll, 1990) have been proposed. Therefore we will argue that 'local search' on a specific scientific trajectory should be replaced by broader search patterns into new trajectories and scientific paradigms. This might eventually lead to the convergence of previously distinct scientific paradigms.

The second part of this book is concerned with an in-depth empirical analysis of three major forces which have jointly determined a considerable part of the development of the IT sector during the past decade: technological convergence, strategic technology partnering and globalization tendencies.

Table 9.2 shows the findings of our evaluation of ten hypotheses as put forward in the second part of our book.

Table 9.2 Confirmation or rejection of ten basic hypotheses

Hypoth.	8	9	10	11	12	13	14	15	16	17
	√	–	√	√	√	√	–	–	–	–

√ hypothesis confirmed.
– hypothesis not confirmed.

Chapter 6 was concerned primarily with an empirical analysis of the technological convergence process. Technological convergence can be described as the growing similarity among the technological foundations of the different IT segments. The pervasive effect of semiconductors and software has blurred the traditional boundaries between the various IT markets. An empirical analysis is used to examine whether the convergence of information technologies has led to a growing similarity of companies that are active in different IT markets. More in particular we tried to find out whether ongoing patterns of technological and product market convergence have affected the technological cores of leading companies in the computer, telecommunications and semiconductor industries. Following evolutionary and ecological theorists we argue that a firm's reliance on basic routines severely reduces its speed of adaptation. In spite of the technological convergence that is found in technologies and products, we therefore expected to find companies that are still basically focused on their traditional core technologies. The second major research issue that is addressed in Chapter 6 is concerned with the use of strategic alliances as a means to monitor several technological developments. We therefore argued that firms would tend to converge through means of strategic technology alliances. Our empirical analysis was based on two types of data: patent data and data on strategic technology alliances. A simple linear regression is used to measure the relationship between time and the relative importance of patents and alliances in a particular industry sector. The results of the regression analysis showed a confirmation of *Hypothesis 8*, which asserted that firms are still doing more of the same instead of being involved in a process of redefining their 'core' business. *Hypothesis 9*, which argued that firms converge through means of strategic alliances, could, however, not be confirmed by our empirical analysis. In spite of an overall growth in the number of strategic technology alliances over time, cooperative agreements have not been used extensively to deal with the forces of technological convergence. A possible explanation for this finding is that the use of cooperative agreements for technology acquisition is effective only if those agreements are combined with a comparable degree of internal development. Overall our findings indicate that in spite of the observed growth in technological convergence the technological structures of firms have not been significantly affected, at least not in terms of their patents and strategic technology alliancing behaviour.

Chapter 7 has been concerned with the rapid increase in the number of strategic technology alliances in the IT sector. Traditionally cooperative agreements used to be undertaken between enterprises in order to gain access to foreign markets or to bypass government regulations. Today cooperative agreements are undertaken for a much wider range of strategic reasons. The scope of these alliances is usually global, and cooperative companies are often more or less comparable in size. Because firms are now often engaged in multiple alliances with different partners at the same time it has become necessary to abandon the traditional focus on the alliances of one specific organization. Instead a 'network' perspective is proposed. From a network perspective the number of alliances is only one of several important variables. It is argued that the assessment of the power of organizations in a network requires a more extensive analysis of the position of that particular organization in the network and its connection to other players, as well as its ability to control flows of information. Our main goal of Chapter 7 is to evaluate eight basic hypotheses about the use of strategic technology alliances. The first part of Chapter 7 is concerned with the identification of the basic trends in strategic technology partnering. We expected that the number of alliances would increase considerably over time (*Hypothesis 10*). An empirical analysis of the growth of the number of strategic technology alliances in the field of information technology shows that the number of such alliances has gone up dramatically. Before the 1970s, strategic technology alliances were virtually unknown. A steady growth in the number of newly established alliances in the 1970s was replaced by escalating growth during the 1980s. In the early 1990s the growth in the number of newly established strategic technology alliances remains very high but seems to level off. This pattern of growth clearly confirms *Hypothesis 10*.

A detailed analysis of sectoral data on the establishment of strategic technology alliances showed that there were major differences in both the number and evolution of newly established alliances among the various industry sectors. We assumed that the rapid increase in the number of alliances over time was for a large part due to the need for more flexibility in the market. The increasing importance of flexibility in today's market was said to drive firms to choose more flexible forms of organization. Therefore we expected that the equity/non-equity ratio of strategic technology alliances would decrease significantly over time (*Hypothesis 11*). A critical assessment of the number of equity versus non-equity agreements confirmed this hypothesis by showing that this ratio has indeed increased considerably over time. A related analysis was concerned with the evolution of the basic rationales for strategic partnering in information technologies. A critical evaluation of the relative distribution of various rationales over time showed that new rationales such as a reduction in lead times and technological complementarity have taken over the role of market access as the predominant reason to establish strategic technology alliances. This confirms *Hypothesis 12*, which argues that traditional (access) reasons have been replaced by other reasons that are related to recent changes in the international environment.

After we evaluated the trends in the number of newly established strategic technology alliances we focused on the evolution of cooperative networks. An analysis of the overall network structure of the various sectors showed that sparse networks in the early 1970s have evolved into extremely dense networks in the late 1980s and early 1990s. In particular, the semiconductor network stands out in this respect, whereas the computer industry shows only a relatively modest rise in network density in the last period under study. This confirms our expectation (*Hypothesis 13*) that the trend in the number of alliances is due not only to the entrance of new firms into the network but also for a considerable part to the increasing number of alliances that are established by individual firms. The same pattern of increased alliance activity was found in the centrality measures that were related to the number of direct links (degree centrality) and in the power to control flows of information between other companies in the network (betweenness centrality). After having focused on the overall network structures we directed our attention to the positions of the individual players in the network. Our main expectation was that there would be a strong relationship between technological and market structural developments and the evolution of networks of strategic technology alliances (*Hypotheses 14–17*). The results of our analysis on the evolution of networks in the various industry sectors, however, show that although there are a large number of indirect relationships between industry development and networks of strategic alliances there appears to be no linear relationship between them.

Chapter 8 addresses one of the most important and critical features of today's economy: internationalization. This process of internationalization has received widespread interest in the literature. Most authors have argued that patterns of internationalization would lead to a single global world market in which companies have no particular relationship to any specific country. In the first part of the chapter we analyse patterns of internationalization of corporate technological activity in the, by now familiar, three industry sectors: computers, telecommunications and semiconductors. The main question that is addressed in this part is whether companies are gradually becoming more international in terms of their internal and external technology flows and the location of their R&D facilities. Data from the European Patent Office (EPO) enabled us to analyse patterns of international patenting behaviour. The results of the analysis indicate that only a small degree of corporate technological activity takes place abroad. Additional research on strategic alliances shows that in spite of becoming more international in focus, alliances have become increasingly concentrated within major economic regions. Therefore our analysis suggests that if internationalization takes place at all it is found only in a number of exceptional cases.

After we assessed trends in the degree of internationalization of corporate technological activity we focused on the nature of globally operating companies. The question was raised whether large multinational firms are gradually losing their national characteristics and becoming truly globalized companies. In the literature it is often argued that firms that face the same homogeneous environment will take on similar structures and strategies. The results of an empirical analysis on the structures and strategies of companies from various different home countries revealed that despite their international orientation, companies in all three sectors can still be recognized in terms of their region of origin. Our results, therefore, suggest that either internationalization tendencies have not been strong enough to generate clear patterns of isomorphism or that imprintment forces have restricted companies from taking on 'global' strategies and structures. Firms are found to be still basically influenced by the social, cultural, technological and competitive conditions under which they were established. The main conclusion, therefore, is that internationalization of innovation appears to be still less important than expected both in terms of actual internationalization trends as well as in terms of the globalization of companies themselves.

The empirical analyses in the second part of this book seem to confirm our basic assumption that companies seem to be characterized by strong inertia. Whereas firms seem to make increasing use of strategic alliances as a means of dealing with changing environmental conditions, they do not seem to be able (or willing) to change their 'core' structures according to the demands of the environment. Although pressures for internationalization and convergence seem to be very high, companies seem to have retained their traditional structures and strategies. This gives strong support for the further development of theories that do not assume rapid adaptive change within organizations. Inertia seems to be an essential characteristic of organizations and should therefore be a core concern of every theory of organization.

NOTE

1. Given the observed importance of the policy framework in the telecommunications sector, in particular, an extension of the framework to treat the policy environment might be needed to grasp the full dynamics of these sectors.

Appendix I

TIMETABLE

	1850	1900	1920	1950	1960	1970	1980	1990	2000
semi-conductors		valve		transistor	IC	LSI	VLSI	ULSI	
Computers				special-purpose vacuum-tube computer	multipurpose transistorized computer	solid state computer; multi-processing computer; mini-computer	micro-computer	distributed comp.	
Software				machine language	higher-level languages	modular programs; end-user languages	CASE tools; very high level lang.	artif. intelligence; automated software generation	
Telecommunications.									
Customer Premises Equipment	telegraph	telephone	telex; photo-facsimile	data-transmission	facsimile; PBX	LANs; WANs; PABX	teletex; videotext; mobile telecom.	video-confer.; col-fax	
Transmission	copper cables	wireless			coaxial cables	fibre-optics; microwave; satellite			
Switches			electro-mechanical : strowger/rotary crossbar		semi-electronic; space-division with SPC		full electronic; time-division	optical	

227

Appendix II

THE COOPERATIVE AGREEMENTS AND TECHNOLOGY INDICATORS (CATI) INFORMATION SYSTEM

The CATI databank is a relational database which contains separate data files that can be linked to each other and provide (dis)aggregate and combined information from several files. The CATI database contains three major entities. The first entity includes information on over 10,000 cooperative agreements involving some 4,000 different parent companies. The databank contains information on each agreement and some information on companies participating in these agreements. We define cooperative agreements as common interests between independent (industrial) partners which are not connected through (majority) ownership. In the CATI database only those inter-firm agreements are being collected that contain some arrangements for transferring technology or joint research. Joint research pacts, second-sourcing and licensing agreements are clear-cut examples. We also collect information on joint ventures in which new technology is received from at least one of the partners, or joint ventures having some R&D programme. Mere production or marketing joint ventures are excluded. In other words, our analysis is primarily related to technology cooperation. We are discussing those forms of cooperation and agreements for which a combined innovative activity or an exchange of technology is at least part of the agreement. Consequently, partnerships are omitted that regulate no more than the sharing of production facilities, the setting of standards, collusive behaviour in price-setting and raising entry barriers – although all of these may be side effects of inter-firm cooperation as we define it.

We regard as a relevant input of information for each alliance: the number of companies involved; names of companies (or important subsidiaries); year of establishment, time-horizon, duration and year of dissolution; capital investments and involvement of banks and research institutes or universities; field(s) of technology[1]; modes[2] of cooperation; and some comment or

229

available information about progress. Depending on the very form of cooperation we collect information on the operational context; the name of the agreement or project; equity sharing; the direction of capital or technology flows; the degree of participation in the case of minority holdings; some information about motives underlying the alliance; the character of cooperation, such as basic research, applied research, or product development possibly associated with production and/or marketing arrangements. In some cases we also indicate who has benefited most.

The second major entity is the individual subsidiary or parent company involved in one (registered) alliance at least. In the first place we assess the company's cooperative strategy by adding its alliances and computing its network centrality. Second, we ascertain its nationality, its possible (majority) owner in case this is an industrial firm, too. Changes in (majority) ownership in the eighties were also registered. Next, we determine the main branch in which it is operating and classify its number of employees. In addition, for three separate subsets of firms time-series for employment, turnover, net income, R&D expenditures and numbers of assigned US patents have been stored. The first subset is based on the *Business Week* R&D scoreboard, the second on *Fortune*'s International 500, and the third group was retrieved from the US Department of Commerce's patent tapes. From the *Business Week* R&D scoreboard we took R&D expenditure, net income, sales and number of employees. In 1980 some 750 companies were filed; during the next years this number gradually increased to 900 companies in 1988, which were spread among 40 industry groups. The *Fortune*'s International 500 of the largest corporations outside the US provides, among others, information about sales (upon which the rankings are based), net income and number of employees. A third entity was recently added in order to perform more in-depth research in the information technology field. For this purpose, detailed information on leading companies in the three major segments of the information technology industry were included in the database. These major segments comprise the dataprocessing, telecommunications and micro-electronics industry. For all three industries information on the direction of technology flows and on technology to market ratios of major players in these industries were processed from the CATI alliance database and stored in a separate entity. Information on technology flows is used to measure the degree to which the strategic partnerships of companies generate technology to their partners or absorb technology from them. Technology to market ratios are created in order to measure whether a company's alliances are primarily focused on research or used for market-entry purposes. This information was subsequently complemented by information technology diversification patterns of the same firms which we were able to obtain from Elsevier's World Electronics Company File. In order to measure the research activities of these firms detailed patenting behaviour information was processed from the US Department of Commerce patent tapes. In addition we included complementary data from various sources. The Gartner Group provided us with a comprehensive data set which comprised information on corporate sales, data-processing sales, R&D expenditures and operating income of the 100 largest world-wide data-processing companies. Data on the telecommunications industry was gathered from various sources. Publications of telecommunications sales of major telecommunications firms were found in specialized journals and newspapers, books and annual reports. Sources include IDATE, DATAQUEST and BIPE. R&D expenditures were already available from the CATI database, or taken from annual reports or Elsevier's World Electronics Company File. Micro-electronics sales data were also obtained from various specialized journals and from newspapers. All journals and newspapers we used for our sample made use of Dataquest data. Once again R&D expenditure data as well as total sales data were obtained from the CATI database as well as from annual reports and Elsevier's World Electronics Company File.

NOTES

1. The most important fields in terms of frequency are information technology (computers, industrial automation, telecommunications, software, micro-electronics), biotechnology (with fields such as pharmaceuticals and agro-biotechnology), new materials technology, chemicals, automotive, defence, consumer electronics, heavy electrical equipment, food and beverages, etc. All fields have important subfields.
2. Principal modes of cooperation are equity joint ventures, joint R&D projects, technology exchange agreements, minority and cross-holdings, particular customer–supplier relations and one-directional technology flows. Each mode of cooperation has a number of particular categories.

Appendix III

LEADING COMPANIES

Computers	Telecommunications	Micro-electronics
Amdahl	Alcatel	AMD
Apple	Ascom	AT&T
AT&T	AT&T	Fujitsu
Bull	Bosch	Hitachi
Canon	Ericsson	Intel
CDC	Fujitsu	Matsushita
Compaq	GEC	Mitsubishi
Dec	GTE	Motorola
Fujitsu	Hitachi	National Semicon.
H-P	IBM	NEC
Hitachi	Matra	OKI
IBM	Matsushita	Philips
Matushita	Motorola	Samsung
Mitsubishi	NEC	Sanyo
NCR	Nokia	SGS Thomson
Nec	Northern Telecom	Sharp
NTT	OKI	Siemens
Olivetti	Philips	Sony
Philips	Racal	Texas Instruments
Seagate	Ricoh	Toshiba
Siemens	Sagem	
Toshiba	Siemens	
Unisys	STC	
Wang	Toshiba	
Xerox		

References

Abernathy, W.J. and J.M. Utterback (1978), 'Patterns of Industrial Innovation', *Technology Review*, 80: 41–47.

Acs, Z.J. and D.B. Audretsch (1989), 'Patents as a Measure of Innovative Activity', *Kyklos*, 4: 171–80.

Alchian, A. (1950), 'Uncertainty, Evolution, and Economic Theory', *Journal of Political Economy*, 58: 211–21.

Aldrich, H.E. (1979), *Organizations and Environments*, Prentice-Hall, Englewood Cliffs.

Aldrich, H. and E.R. Auster (1986), 'Even Dwarfs Started Small: Liabilities of Age, Size and their Strategic Implications', in B. Staw and L.L. Cummings, *Research in Organizational Behavior*, JAI Press, Greenwich, 8: 165–98.

Aldrich, H.E. and J. Pfeffer (1976), 'Environments of Organizations', *Annual Review of Sociology*, 2: 79–105.

Aldrich, H.E. and G. Wiedenmayer (1990), 'From Traits to Rates: An Ecological Perspective on Organizational Foundings', Paper presented at the 1989 Gateway Conference on Entrepreneurship, St Louis University, St Louis.

Andersen, E.S. (1994), *Evolutionary Economics: Post Schumpeterian Contributions*, Pinter Publishers, London.

Archibugi, D. (1992), 'Patenting as an Indicator of Technological Innovation: A Review', *Science and Public Policy*, 6: 357–8.

Arrow, K.J. (1962a), 'Economic Welfare and the Allocation of Resources for Invention', in National Bureau of Economic Research, *The Rate and Direction of Inventive Activity: Economic and Social Factors*, Princeton University Press, Princeton.

Arrow, K.J. (1962b), 'The Economic Implications of Learning-by-Doing', *Review of Economic Studies*, 29: 155–73.

235

Astley, W.G. (1985), 'The Two Ecologies: Population and Community Perspectives on Organizational Evolution', *Administrative Science Quarterly*, 30: 224–41.

Averch, H. and L. Johnson (1962), 'Behavior of the Firm Under Regulatory Constraint', *American Economic Review*, 52: 1053–69.

Barley, S.R., J. Freeman and R.C. Hybels (1992), 'Strategic Alliances in Commercial Biotechnology', in N. Nohria, and R.G. Eccles (eds), *Networks and Organizations: Structure, Form and Action*, Harvard Business School Press, Boston, Mass.

Barnett, W.P. and T.L. Amburgey (1990), 'Do Large Organizations Generate Stronger Competition', in J.V. Singh (ed.), *Organizational Evolution: New Directions*, Sage Publications, Newbury Park, London.

Bartlett, C.A., Y. Doz and G. Hedlund (1990), *Managing the Global Firm*, Routledge, London.

Baum, J.A.C. and J.V. Singh (1994), *Evolutionary Dynamics of Organizations*, Oxford University Press, New York.

Baum, J.A.C. and R.J. House (1990), 'On the Maturing and Aging of Organizational Populations', in J.V. Singh (ed.), *Organizational Evolution: New Directions*, Sage Publications, Newbury Park, London.

Baumol, W., J. Panzar and R. Willig (1982), *Contestable Markets and the Theory of Industry Structure*, Harcourt, Brace, Jovanovich, San Diego.

Bavelas, A. (1948), 'A mathematical model for group structures', *Human Organization*, 7: 16–30. Op. Cit. L.C. Freeman, 'Centrality in Social Networks: Conceptual Clarification', *Social Networks*, 1: 215–39.

Bedian, A.C. (1984), *Organizations Theory and Analysis*, The Dryden Press, Hinsdale.

Belitsos, B. and J. Misra (1986), *Business Telematics: Corporate Networks for the Information Age*, Dow Jones-Irwin, Homewood.

Berg, S., J. Duncan and P. Friedman (1982), *Joint Venture Strategies and Corporate Innovation*, Oelgeschlager, Gunn & Hain, Cambridge.

Blair, J.A. (1991), *Proprietary Technology and Industrial Structure: The Semiconductor, Computer and Consumer Electronics Industries*, Stanford University Press, Stanford.

Boeker, W.P. (1988), 'Organizational Origins: Entrepreneurial and Environmental Imprinting at the Time of Founding', in G.R. Carroll (ed.), *Ecological Models of Organizations*, Ballinger, Cambridge, Mass.

Bonacich, P. (1987), 'Power and Centrality: A Family of Measures', *American Journal of Sociology*, 92: 1170–82.

Boone, C. and A. van Witteloostuijn (1995), 'Industrial Organization and Organizational Ecology: The Potentials for Cross-Fertilization', *Organization Studies*, forthcoming.

Bornholz, R. and D.S. Evans (1983), 'The Early History of Competition in the Telephone Industry', in D.S. Evans (ed.), *Breaking Up Bell, Essays on Industrial Organization and Regulation*, North Holland, New York.

Braun, E. and S. MacDonald (1982), *Revolution in Miniature*, Second Edition, Cambridge University Press, Cambridge.

Breyer, S. (1982), *Regulation and Its Reform*, Harvard University Press, Cambridge, Mass.

Brittain, J. and J. Freeman (1980), 'Organizational Proliferation and Density-Dependence Selection', in J.R. Kimberley and R.H. Miles (eds), *Organizational Life Cycles*, Jossey-Bass, San Francisco.

Brock, G.W. (1975), *The U.S. Computer Industry; A Study of Market Power*, Ballinger, Cambridge, Mass.

Brock, G.W. (1981), *The Telecommunications Industry; The Dynamics of Market Structure*, Harvard University Press, Cambridge, Mass.

Brock, G.W. and D.S. Evans (1983), 'Creamskimming', in D.S. Evans (ed.), *Breaking Up Bell, Essays on Industrial Organization and Regulation*, North Holland, New York.

Bruce, R., J. Cunard and M. Director (1986), *From Telecommunications to Electronics Services: A Global Spectrum of Definitions, Boundary Lines and Structures*, Butterworths, Austin.

Buckley, P.J. and M. Casson (1988), 'A Theory of Cooperation in International Business', in F.J. Contractor and P. Lorange (eds), *Cooperative Strategies in International Business*, D.C. Heath & Company, Lexington, Mass.

Burns, T. and G.M. Stalker (1961), *The Management of Innovation*, Tavistock, London.

Burt, R.S. (1976), 'Positions in Networks', *Social Forces*, 55: 93–122.

Business Week (1986), 'Corporate Odd Couples: Beware of the Wrong Partner', 21 July.

Campbell, D.T. (1969), 'Variation and Selective Retention in Socio-Cultural Evolution', *General Systems*, 16: 69–85.

Cantwell, J. (1990), 'The Technological Competence Theory of International Production and its Implications', Mimeo.

Cantwell, J. (1991), 'The International Agglomeration of R&D', in M. Casson (ed.), *Global Research Strategy and International Competitiveness*, Blackwell, Oxford.

Cantwell, J. and C. Hodson (1991), 'Global R&D and UK competitiveness', in M. Casson (ed.), *Global Research Strategy and International Competitiveness*, Blackwell, Oxford.

Carroll, G.R. (1984), 'Organizational Ecology', *Annual Review of Sociology*, 10: 71–93.

Carroll, G.R. (1985), 'Concentration and Specialization: Dynamics of Niche Width in Populations of Organizations', *American Journal of Sociology*, 90: 1262–83.

Carroll, G.R. (1987), *Publish and Perish: The Organizational Ecology of Newspaper Industries*, JAI Press, Greenwich.

Carroll, G.R. (1988), *Ecological Models of Organizations*, Ballinger, Cambridge, Mass.

Carroll, G.R. (1990), 'On the Organizational Ecology of Chester I. Barnard', in O.E. Williamson (ed.), *Organization Theory: From Chester Barnard to the Present and Beyond*, Oxford University Press, New York.

Carroll, G.R. and M.T. Hannan (1990), 'Density Delay in the Evolution of Organizational Populations: A Model and Five Empirical Tests', in J.V. Singh (ed.), *Organizational Evolution: New Directions*, Sage Publications, Newbury Park, London.

Casson, M. (1987), *The Firm and the Market*, Blackwell, Oxford.

Chandler, A. (1977), *The Visible Hand: The Managerial Revolution in American Business*, Belknap Press, Harvard University Press, Cambridge, Mass.

Charles, D., P. Monk and E. Sciberras (1989), *Technology and Competition in the International Telecommunications Industry*, Pinter Publishers, London.

Chesnais, F. (1988), 'Multinational Enterprises and the International Diffusion of Technology', in G. Dosi, C. Freeman, R. Nelson, G. Silverberg and L. Soete (eds), *Technical Change and Economic Theory*, Pinter Publishers, London.

Child, J. (1972), 'Organizational Structure, Environment and Performance: The Role of Strategic Choice', *Sociology*, 6: 1–22.

Clark, M.P. (1991), *Networks and Telecommunications: Design and Operation*, John Wiley & Sons, Chichester.

Clark, N. and C. Juma (1991), *Long-Run Economics, An Evolutionary Approach to Economic Growth*, Pinter Publishers, London.

Cohen, W.M and R.C. Levin (1989), 'Empirical Studies of Innovation and Market Structure', in R. Schmalensee and R.D. Willig, *Handbook of Industrial Organization*, Volume II, Elsevier Science Publishers, New York.

Cohen, W.M and D.A. Levinthal (1990), 'Absorptive Capacity: A New Perspective on Learning and Innovation', *Administrative Science Quarterly*, 35: 128–52.

Contractor, F.J. and P. Lorange (1988), *Cooperative Strategies in International Business*, D.C. Heath & Company, Lexington, Mass.

Cooper, A.C. and D.E. Schendel (1976), 'Strategic Responses to Technological Threats', *Business Horizons*, 19: 61–9.

Craig, S.R. (1986), 'Seeking Strategic Advantage with Technology? – Focus on Customer Value!', *Long Range Planning*, 19: 50–56.

Crandall, R.W. (1989), 'The Role of US Local Operating Companies', in R.W. Crandall and K. Flamm (eds), *Changing the Rules: Technological Change, International Competition and Regulation in Communications*, The Brookings Institute, Washington.

Cutaia, A. (1990), *Technology Projection Modelling of Future Computer Systems*, Prentice Hall, Englewood Cliffs.

Cyert, R.M. and J.G. March (1963), *A Behavioral Theory of the Firm*, Prentice-Hall, Englewood Cliffs.

David, P. (1985), 'CLIO and the Economics of QWERTY', *American Economic Review*, 75: 332–7.

Davies, A.C. (1991), 'The Digital Divide: A Political Economy of the Restructuring of Telecommunications', unpublished D.Phil. thesis, University of Sussex, Brighton.

Davies, H. (1977), 'Technology Transfer through Commercial Transactions', *Journal of Industrial Economics*, 26: 161–75.

Day, G.S. (1986), *Analysis for Strategic Market Decisions*, West Publishing Company, St. Paul.

Day, G.S. (1981), 'The Product Life Cycle: Analysis and Application Issues', *Journal of Marketing*, 45: 60–67.

De Bresson, C. (1987), 'The Evolutionary Paradigm and The Economics of Technological Change', *Journal of Economic Issues*, 21: 751–62.

de Jonquières G. (1989), 'The Deadly Mirage of Convergent Technology', *Financial Times*, 24 July.

de Woot, P. (1990), *High Technology Europe: Strategic Issues for Global Competitiveness*, Blackwell, Oxford.

Dimaggio, P.J. and W.W. Powell (1983), 'The Iron Cage Revisited: Institutional Isomorphism and Collective Rationality in Organizational Fields', *American Sociological Review*, 48: 147–60.

Dodgson, M. (1989), *Technology Strategy and the Firm, Management and Public Policy*, Longman, London.

Dorfman, N.S. (1987), *Innovation and Market Structure : Lessons from the Computer and Semiconductor Industries*, Ballinger, Cambridge, Mass.

Dosi, G. (1980), *Structural Adjustment and Public Policy under Conditions of Rapid Technical Change: The Semiconductor Industry in Western Europe*, Working Paper, Sussex European Research Centre, Brighton.

Dosi, G. (1981), *Technical Change and Survival: Europe's Semiconductor Industry*, Sussex European Papers, University of Sussex, Brighton.

Dosi, G. (1983), 'Technological Paradigms and Technological Trajectories', in C. Freeman, *Long Waves in the World Economy*, Pinter Publishers, London.

Dosi, G. (1984), *Technical Change and Industrial Transformation*, Macmillan Press, London.

Dosi, G. (1988), 'Sources, Procedures, and Microeconomic Effects of Innovation', *Journal of Economic Literature*, 26: 1120–71.

Dosi, G. and L. Orsenigo (1988), 'Coordination and Transformation: An Overview of Structures, Behaviours and Change in Evolutionary Environments', in Dosi et al. (eds), *Technical Change and Economic Theory*, Pinter Publishers, London.

Dunning, J.H. (1988), *Multi-Nationals, Technology and Competitiveness*, Unwin Hyman, London.

Dunning, J.H. (1993), *Multinational Enterprises and the Global Economy*, Addison-Wesley Publishing Company, Wokingham.

Duysters, G. and W. Vanhaverbeke (1996), 'Strategic interactions in DRAM and RISC Technology: A network approach', *Scandinavian Journal of Management*, Forthcoming.

Duysters, G. and J. Hagedoorn (1994), 'Convergence and Divergence in the International Information Technology Industry', in Hagedoorn (ed.), *Technical Change and the World Economy*, Edward Elgar Publishers, Cheltenham.

Duysters, G. and J. Hagedoorn (1996), 'Internationalization of Corporate Technology through Strategic Partnering: An Empirical Investigation', *Research Policy*, forthcoming.

Economic Commission for Europe (1987), *The Telecommunication Industry: Growth and Structural Change*, United Nations, New York.

Ergas, H. (1988), 'Regulation, Monopoly and Competitition in the Telecommunications Infrastructure', in OECD, *Trends of Change in Telecommunications Policy*, OECD, Paris.

Ernst, D. (1983), *The Global Race in Micro-Electronics*, Campus Verlag, Frankfurt.

Evan, W.M. (1966), 'The Organization-set: Toward a Theory of Interorganizational Relations', in J.D. Thompson (ed.), *Approaches to Organizational Design*, University of Pittsburgh Press, Pittsburgh.

Evans, D.S. and S.J. Grossman (1983), 'Integration', in D.S. Evans (ed.), *Breaking Up Bell, Essays on Industrial Organization and Regulation*, North Holland, New York.

Ferguson, C.H. and C.R. Morris (1994), *Computer Wars: The Fall of IBM and the Future of Global Technology*, Times Books, New York.

Flamm, K. (1988), *Creating the Computer: Government, Industry, and High Technology*, The Brookings Institute, Washington.

Flamm, K. (1989), 'Technological Advance and Costs: Computers versus Communications', in R.W. Crandall and K. Flamm (eds), *Changing the Rules: Technological Change, International Competition and Regulation in Communications*, The Brookings Institute, Washington.

Forester, T. (1993), *Silicon Samurai: How Japan Conquered the World's IT Industry*, Blackwell Publishers, Cambridge.

Fortune (1966), 'IBM's $5,000,000,000 Gamble', No. 118, September.

Foster, R.N. (1986), *Innovation: The Attacker's Advantage*, Summit Books, New York.

Freeman, C. (1982), *The Economics of Industrial Innovation*, Pinter Publishers, London.

Freeman, C. (1991), 'The nature of techno-economic paradigm and biological analogies in economics', *Revue Economique*, 42: 211–31.

Freeman, J. (1990), 'Ecological Analysis of Semiconductor Firm Mortality', in J.V. Singh (ed.), *Organizational Evolution: New Directions*, Sage Publications, Newbury Park, London.

Freeman, J., C. Carroll and M.T. Hannan (1983), 'The Liability of Newness: Age Dependence in Organizational Death Rates', *American Sociological Review*, 48: 692–710.

Freeman, L.C. (1977), 'A Set of Measures of Centrality Based on Betweenness', *Sociometry*, 40: 35–41.

Freeman, L.C. (1979), 'Centrality in Social Networks: Conceptual Clarification', *Social Networks*, 1: 215–39.

Friedman, P., S.V. Berg and J. Duncan (1979), 'External vs. Internal Knowledge Acquisition: Joint Venture Activity and R&D Intensity', *Journal of Economics and Business*, 32: 103–10.

Fusfeld, H.I. and C.S. Haklisch (1985), 'Cooperative R&D for Competitors', *Harvard Business Review*, 85: 60–76.

Galambos, L. (1988), 'Looking for the Boundaries of Technological Determinism: A Brief History of the U.S. Telephone System', in R. Mayntz and T.P. Hughes (eds), *The Development of Large Technical Systems*, Campus Verlag, Frankfurt am Main.

Georghiou, L., J.S. Metcalfe, M. Gibbons, T. Ray and J. Evans (1986), *Post-Innovation Performance: Technological Development and Competition*, Macmillan, New York.

Geringer, J.M. (1991), 'Strategic Determinants of Partner Selection Criteria in International Joint Ventures', *Journal of International Business Studies*, 22: 41–62.

Gerybadze, A. (1984), 'International Competition in High-Technology Industries', in K.P. Friebe and A. Gerybadze, *Microelectronics in Western Europe*, Erich Schmidt Verlag GmbH, Berlin.

Gill, J. (1990), *The Speed of Technology Change and the Development of Market Structure: 3: Memory Chips*, CRICT Discussion Paper, Brunel University, Uxbridge.

Goldhar, J. and M. Jelinek (1983), 'Plan for Economies of Scope', *Harvard Business Review*, 61: 141–8.

Gomulka, S. (1990), *The Theory of Technological Change and Economic Growth*, Routledge, London.

Gould, R.V. (1987), 'Measures of Betweenness in Non-Symmetric Networks', *Social Networks*, 9: 277–82.

Gowdy, J.M. (1992), 'Higher Selection Processes in Evolutionary Economic Change', *Journal of Evolutionary Economics*, 2: 1–16.

Granstrand, O., L. Hakanson and S. Sjolander (1992), *Technology Management and International Business: Internationalization of R&D and Technology*, John Wiley & Sons, Chichester.

Graves, A. (1991), 'International Competitiveness and Technological Development in the World Automobile Industry', D.Phil. thesis, University of Sussex, Brighton.

Greenstein, S.M. (1991), *Lock-In and the Costs of Switching Mainframe Computer Vendors: What Do Buyers See?*, Working paper, College of Commerce and Business Administration, University of Illinois at Urbana-Champaign.

Griliches, Z. (1990), 'Patent Statistics as Economic Indicators: A Survey', *Journal of Economic Literature*, 28: 1661–797.

Groenewegen, J. (1989), 'De transaktiekostentheorie nader bezien', *Tijdschrift voor Politieke Economie*, 12: 50–76.

Guy, K. (1985), 'Communications', in L. Soete (ed.), *Electronics and Communications*, Gower Publishing Company, Brookfield, Vermont.

Hagedoorn, J. (1984), *Some Recent Contributions in Neo-Schumpeterian Economic Theory*, STB-TNO paper, Apeldoorn.

Hagedoorn, J. (1989), *The Dynamic Analysis of Innovation and Diffusion*, Pinter Publishers, London.

Hagedoorn, J. (1990), 'Organizational Modes of Inter-firm Cooperation and Technology Transfer', *Technovation*, 10: 17–30.

Hagedoorn, J. (1992), 'Strategic Alliances in Information Technology among Firms in Western Industrialized Nations', in L.S. Peters (ed.), *International Issues in the Management of Technology*, Vol. 10, JAI Series on International Business and Finance, Greenwich, Conn.

Hagedoorn, J. (1993), 'Understanding the Rationale of Strategic Technology Partnering: Interorganizational Modes of Cooperation and Sectoral Differences', *Strategic Management Journal*, 14: 371–85.

Hagedoorn, J. (1995), 'A Note on International Market Leaders and Networks of Strategic Partnering', *Strategic Management Journal*, 16:241–50.

Hagedoorn, J. and J. Schakenraad (1990), 'Inter-firm Partnerships and Cooperative Strategies in Core Technologies', in C. Freeman and L. Soete (eds), *New Explorations in the Economics of Technological Change*, Pinter Publishers, London.

Hagedoorn, J. and J. Schakenraad (1991), 'Interfirm Partnerships for Generic Technologies – The Case of New Materials', *Technovation*, 11: 429–44.

Hagedoorn, J. and J. Schakenraad (1992), 'Leading Companies and Networks of Strategic Alliances in Information Technologies', *Research Policy*, 21: 163–90.

Hagedoorn J. and J. Schakenraad (1993), 'Strategic Technology Partnering and International Corporate Strategies', in K. Hughes (ed.), *European Competitiveness*, Cambridge University Press, Cambridge.

Hagedoorn, J. and J. Schakenraad (1994), 'The Effect of Strategic Technology Alliances on Company Performance', *Strategic Management Journal*, 15: 291–309.

Haklisch, C.S. (1986), 'Technical Alliances in the Semiconductor Industry', unpublished manuscript, New York University.

Haklisch, C.S. (1989), 'Technical Alliances in the Semiconductor Industry: Effects on Corporate Strategy and R&D', in Background Papers for Conference on Changing Global Patterns of Industrial Research and Development, Stockholm, 20–22 June.

Hamel, G. (1991), 'Competition for Competence and Inter-partner Learning within International Strategic Alliances', *Strategic Management Journal*, 12: 83–103.

Hamel., G., Y. Doz and C.K. Prahalad (1986), 'Strategic Partnerships: Success or Surrender?', Paper presented at the Rutgers/Wharton Colloquium on Cooperative Strategies in International Business, New Brunswick, NJ, October 1986.

Hannan, M.T. and G.R. Carroll (1992), *Dynamics of Organizational Populations: Density, Legitimation, and Competition*, Oxford University Press, New York.

Hannan, M.T. and J. Freeman (1977), 'The Population Ecology of Organizations', *American Journal of Sociology*, 82: 929–64.

Hannan, M.T. and J. Freeman (1984), 'Structural Inertia and Organizational Change', *American Sociological Review*, 49: 149–64.

Hannan, M.T. and J. Freeman (1988), 'Density Dependence in the Growth of Organizational Populations', in G.R. Carroll (ed.), *Ecological Models of Organization*, Ballinger Publishing Company, Cambridge, Mass.

Hannan, M.T. and J. Freeman (1989), *Organizational Ecology*, Harvard University Press, Cambridge, Mass.

Hannan, M.T., J. Ranger-Moore and J. Banaszak-Holl (1990), 'Competition and the Evolution of Organizational Size Distribution', in J.V. Singh (ed.), *Organizational Evolution: New Directions*, Sage Publications, Newbury Park, London.

Harper, J.M. (1986), *Telecommunications and Computing: The Uncompleted Revolution*, Communications Educational Services, London.

Harrigan, K.R. (1985a), *Strategic Flexibility: A Management Guide for Changing Times*, Lexington Books, Lexington, Mass.

Harrigan, K.R. (1985b), *Strategies for Joint Ventures*, Lexington Books, Lexington, Mass.

Harrigan, K.R. (1988a), 'Joint Ventures and Competitive Strategy', *Strategic Management Journal*, 9: 141–58.

Harrigan, K.R. (1988b), *Managing Mature Businesses*, Lexington, Mass.

Hawley, A. (1950), *Human Ecology*, Macmillan, New York.

Hawley, A. (1968), 'Human Ecology', in D.L. Sills (ed.), *International Encyclopedia of the Social Sciences*, Macmillan, New York.

Hazewindus, N. (1982), *The U.S. Microelectronics Industry: Technical Change, Industry Growth and Social Impact*, Pergamon Press, New York.

Hennart, J.F. (1988), 'A Transaction Costs Theory of Equity Joint Ventures', *Strategic Management Journal*, 9: 361–74.

Hergert, M. and D. Morris (1988), 'Trends in International Collaborative Agreements', in F.J. Contractor and P. Lorange (eds), *Cooperative Strategies in International Business*, D.C. Heath & Company, Lexington, Mass.

Hills, J. (1986), *Deregulating Telecoms: Competition and Control in the United States, Japan and Britain*, Pinter Publishers, London.

Hirschey, R.C. and R.E. Caves (1981), 'Internationalisation of Research and Transfer of Technology by Multinational Enterprises', *Oxford Bulletin of Economics and Statistics*, 42: 115–30.

Hladik, K.J. (1985), *International Joint Ventures: An Economic Analysis of U.S.–Foreign Business Partnerships*, Lexington Books, Lexington, Mass.

Hobday, M. (1989), 'The European Semiconductor Industry: Resurgence and Rationalization', *Journal of Common Market Studies*, 28: 155–86.

Hobday, M. (1990), 'The World Semiconductor Industry: Industrial Organisation, Technological Change and Prospects for Developing Countries', Paper prepared for the United Nations Development Programme in Brazil.

Hu, Y.S. (1992), 'Global or Transnational Corporations and National Firms with International Operations', *California Management Review*, 34: 107–27.

Hutchinson, G.E. (1959), 'Homage to Santa Rosalia, or Why Are There So Many Kinds of Animals?', *American Naturalist*, 93: 145–59.

Jarillo, J.C. (1988), 'On Strategic Networks', *Strategic Management Journal*, 9: 31–41.

Jelinek, M. and C.B. Schoonhoven (1990), *The Innovation Marathon: Lessons from High Technology Firms*, Basil Blackwell, Oxford.

Jewett, F.B. (1928), 'The Telephone Switchboard – Fifty Years of History, Bell Telephone Quarterly', Vol. VII, New York, republished in G. Shiers (1977), *The Telephone – an Historical Anthology*, Arno Press, New York.

Kay, N. (1986), *The Emergent Firm*, Macmillan, London.

Klein, B. and K.B. Leffler (1981), 'The Role of Market Forces in Assuring Contractual Performance', *Journal of Political Economy*, 89: 615–41.

Knoke, D. and J.H. Kuklinski (1982), *Network Analysis*, Sage Publications, Newbury Park, London.

Kogut, B. (1989), 'The Stability of Joint Ventures: Reciprocity and Competitive Rivalry', *The Journal of Industrial Economics*, 38: 183–98.

Korzeniowski, P. (1988), 'Partners to be Part of IBM's Future', *Communications Week*, 28 March.

Kreiken, E.J. (1986), 'De coalitiestrategie: creatieve cooperative competitie', in J. Bilderbeek, J.M.L. Jansen and G.W.A. Vijge (eds), *Ondernemingsstrategie; theorie en praktijk*, H.E. Stenfert Kroese, Leiden.

Krepps, D.M. (1990), *Course in Microeconomic Theory*, Princeton University Press, Princeton.

Kuhn, T.S. (1970), *The Structure of Scientific Revolutions*, University of Chicago Press, Chicago.

Lambkin, M. (1988), 'Order of Entry and Performance in New Markets', *Strategic Management Journal*, 9: 127–40.

Lambkin, M. and G.S. Day (1989), 'Evolutionary Processes in Competitive Markets: Beyond the Product Life Cycle', *Journal of Marketing*, 53: 4–20.

Lant, T.K. and S.J. Mezias (1992), 'An Organizational Learning Model of Convergence and Reorientation', *Organization Science*, 3: 47–71.

Lawrence, P.R. and J.W. Lorsch (1967), *Organization and Environment*, Harvard Business School Press, Boston, Mass.

Leban, R., J. Lesourne, K. Oshima and T. Yakushiji (1989), *Europe and Japan Facing High Technologies*, Economica, Paris.

Lee, T. and P. Reid (1991), *National Interests in an Age of Global Technology*, NAP, Washington.

Levinthal, D.A. (1990), 'Organizational Adaptation, Environmental Selection, and Random Walks', in J.V. Singh (ed.), *Organizational Evolution: New Directions*, Sage Publications, Newbury Park, London.

Levinthal, D.A. (1994), 'Surviving Schumpeterian Environments: An Evolutionary Perspective', in J.A.C. Baum and J.V. Singh (eds), *Evolutionary Dynamics of Organizations*, Oxford University Press, New York.

Malerba, F. (1985), *The Semiconductor Business: The Economics of Rapid Growth and Decline*, Pinter Publishers, London.

Malerba, F., S. Torrisi and N. von Tunzelmann (1991), 'Electronic Computers', in C. Freeman, M. Sharp and W. Walker (eds) , *Technology and the Future of Europe: Global Competition and the Environment in the 1990s*, Pinter Publishers, London.

Mansell, R. (1993), *The New Telecommunications: A Political Economy of Network Evolution*, Sage Publications, Newbury Park, London.

Marshall, A. (1948), *Principles of Economics*, Macmillan, New York.

Martin, J. (1977), *Future Developments in Tele-Communications*, Prentice-Hall, Englewood Cliffs.

Martin, M.J.C. (1984), *Managing Technological Innovation and Entrepreneurship*, Reston Publishing Company, Reston.

Mason, E.C. (1939), 'Price and Production Policies of Large Scale Enterprise', *American Economic Review*, 29: 61–74.

McKelvey, B. (1982), *Organizational Systematics*, University of California Press, Berkeley.

McKelvey, B. and H.E. Aldrich (1983), 'Populations, Natural Selection and Applied Organizational Science', *Administrative Science Quarterly*, 28: 101–28.

Meyer, M.W. (1990), 'Notes of a Skeptic: From Organizational Ecology to Organizational Evolution', in J.V. Singh (ed.), *Organizational Evolution: New Directions*, Sage Publications, Newbury Park, London.

Meyer, M.W. and B. Rowan (1977), 'Institutionalized Organizations: Formal Structure as Myth and Ceremony', *American Journal of Sociology*, 83: 340–63.

Meyer, M.W. and L.G. Zucker (1989), *Permanently Failing Organizations*, Sage Publications, Newbury Park, London.

Miller, R. (1994), 'Global R&D Networks and Large-scale Innovations: The Case of the Automobile Industry', *Research Policy*, 23: 27–46.

248   *The Dynamics of Technical Innovation*

Molina, A.H. (1991), *Pressures for Change in the Global Distribution of the Microprocessor Industry: Is U.S. Domination about to come to an end?*, PICT Working Paper No. 36, Edinburgh.

Molina, A.H. (1992), *Current Trends, Issues and Strategies in the Development of the Microprocessor Industry*, PICT Working Paper No. 42, Edinburgh.

Morgan, K. and A. Sayer (1988), *Microcircuits of Capital*, Polity Press.

Morris, P.R. (1990), *A History of the World Semiconductor Industry*, Peter Peregrinus, London.

Mowery, D.C. (1988), *International Collaborative Ventures in U.S. Manufacturing*, Ballinger, Cambridge, Mass.

Mueller, D.C. and J.E. Tilton (1969), 'Research and Development Costs as a Barrier to Entry', *Canadian Journal of Economics*, 2: 570–79.

Mueller, M. (1989), 'The Switchboard Problem: Scale, Signalling, and Organization in Manual Telephone Switching', *Technology and Culture*, 30: 534–60.

Mytelka, L. (1991), *Strategic Partnerships and the World Economy*, Pinter Publishers, London.

Nelson, R.R. (1987), *Understanding Technical Change as an Evolutionary Process*, Elsevier Science Publishers, New York.

Nelson, R.R. and S.G. Winter (1982), *An Evolutionary Theory of Economic Change*, Belknap Press, Cambridge, Mass.

Nguyen, G.D. (1985), 'Telecommunications: a Challenge to the Older Order', in M. Sharp (ed.), *Europe and the New Technologies*, Pinter Publishers, London.

Nohria, N. (1992), 'Introduction: Is a Network Perspective a Useful Way of Studying Organizations?', in N. Nohria and R.G. Eccles (eds), *Networks and Organizations: Structure, Form and Action*, Harvard Business School Press, Boston, Mass.

Nohria, N. and R.G. Eccles (1992), *Networks and Organizations : Structure, Form and Action*, Harvard Business School Press, Boston, Mass.

Nohria, N. and C. Garcia-Pont (1991), 'Global Strategic Linkages and Industry Structure', *Strategic Management Journal*, 12: 105–24.

Nystrom, H. and B. Edvardsson (1980), 'Research and Development Strategies for Swedish Companies in the Farm Machinery Industry', in D. Sahal, *Research, Development, and Technological Innovation*, Lexington Books, Lexington, Mass.

Obleros, F.J. and R.J. MacDonald (1988), 'Strategic Alliances: Managing Complementarity to Capitalize on Emerging Technologies', *Technovation*, 7: 155–76.

Office of Technology Assessment Congress of the United States (1985), *Information Technology Research and Development: Critical Trends and Issues*, OTA, Washington.

Ohmae, K. (1990), *The Borderless World*, Harper, New York.

Okimoto, D.I., S.M. Tatsuno, E.F. Kvamme, Y. Nishi and E.J. DeWath (1984), *U.S.–Japan Strategic Alliances in the Semiconductor Industry: Technology Transfer, Competition and Public Policy*, Office of Japan Affairs.

Organisation for Economic Co-operation and Development (1992a), *Technology and the Economy: The Key Relationships*, OECD, Paris.

Organisation for Economic Co-operation and Development (1992b), *Telecommunications and Broadcasting: Convergence or Collision ?*, OECD, Paris.

Osborn, R.N. and C.C. Baughn (1990), 'Forms of Interorganizational Governance for Multinational Alliances', *Academy of Management Journal*, 33: 503–19.

Parker, J.E.S. (1978), *The Economics of Innovation: The National and Multinational Enterprise in Technological Change*, second edition, Longman Group Ltd., London.

Patel, P. and K. Pavitt (1991), 'Large Firms in the Production of the World Technology: An Important Case of Non-globalisation', Journal of International Business Studies, 22: 1–21.

Pavitt, K. (1988), 'Uses and Abuses of Patent Statistics', in A.F.J. van Raan, *Handbook of Quantitative Studies of Science and Technology*, Elsevier, Amsterdam.

Pearce, R.D. (1989), *The Internationalisation of Research and Development by Multinational Enterprises*, Macmillan, London.

Pearce, R. and S. Singh (1992), *Internationalization of R and D Among the World's Leading Enterprises*, Macmillan, London.

Perrow, C. (1986), *Complex Organizations: A Critical Essay*, Scott Foresman, Glencoe.

Peters L.S. (1992), *Technology Management and the R&D Activities of Multinational Enterprises*, CSTP–RPI paper.

Pfeffer, J. (1972), 'Size and Composition of Corporate Boards of Directors: The Organization and its Environment', *Administrative Science Quarterly*, 17: 218–28.

Pfeffer, J. and G. Salancik (1978), *The External Control of Organizations: A Resource Dependence Perspective*, Harper & Row, New York.

Pianka, E. (1978), *Evolutionary Ecology*, Harper & Row, New York.

Polanyi, M. (1958), *Personal Knowledge: Towards a Post Critical Philosophy*, University of Chicago Press, Chicago.

Pool, Ithiel and De Sola (1977), 'The Social Impact of the Telephone', MIT Press, Cambridge, Mass, Cited in B. Belitsos and J. Misra (1986), *Business Telematics: Corporate Networks for the Information Age*, Dow Jones-Irwin, Homewood.

Popper, E.T. and B.D. Buskirk (1992), 'Technology Life Cycles in Industrial Markets', *Industrial Marketing Management*, 21: 23–31.

Porter, M.E (1980), *Competitive Strategy*, The Free Press, New York.

Porter, M.E. (1985), *Competitive Advantage*, The Free Press, New York.

Porter, M.E. (1986), *Competition in Global Industries*, Harvard Business School Press, Boston, Mass.

Porter, M.E. (1990). *The Competitive Advantage of Nations*, The Free Press, New York.

Porter, M.E. and M.B. Fuller (1986), 'Coalitions and Global Strategies', in M.E. Porter (ed.), *Competition in Global Industries*, Harvard Business School Press, Boston, Mass.

Raphael, D.E. (1989), *The Changing Structure of the Global Information Industry*, SRI International, Report No. 807.

Rappaport, A.S. and S. Halevi (1991), 'The Computerless Computer Company', *Harvard Business Review*, 69: 69–80.

Reich, R.B. (1990), 'Who is US?', *Harvard Business Review*, 68: 53–64.

Reich, R.B. (1991), *The Work of Nations*, Vintage Books, New York.

Rhodes, F.L., (1929), 'Beginnings of Telephony', New York, cited in J. Bruggeman, J.H. Schulenga, J.D. Tours and J.G. Visser, *Honderd jaar telefoon*, 's-Gravenhage (1981).

Roman, D.D. and J.F. Puett (1983), *International Business and Technological Innovation*, Elsevier Science Publishing Co., Inc., New York.

Rosenberg, N. (1976), *Perspectives on Technology*, Cambridge University Press, Cambridge.

Rosenberg, N. (1982), *Inside the Black Box: Technology and Economics*, Cambridge University Press, Cambridge.

Rugman. A.M. (1981), Cited in O. Granstrand, L. Hakanson, and S. Sjolander (eds). (1992), *Technology Management and International Business: Internationalization of R&D and Technology*, John Wiley & Sons, Chichester.

Sahal, D. (1981), *Patterns of Technological Innovation*, Addison-Wesley, Mass.

Saviotti, P.P. and J.S. Metcalfe (1984), 'A Theoretical Approach to the Construction of Technological Output Indicators', *Research Policy*, 13: 41–151, North Holland.

Schreuder H. and P. van Cayseele (1988), 'Strategiebepaling door ondernemingen: een overzicht', *Economisch Statische Berichten*, Vol. 73, 7 December.

Schreuder, H. and A. van Witteloostuijn (1990), 'The Ecology of Organizations and the Economics of Firms', Research Memorandum, University of Limburg, Maastricht.

Schumpeter, J.A. (1934: 1980), *The Theory of Economic Development*, Oxford University Press, London.

Schumpeter, J.A. (1942: 1987), *Capitalism, Socialism and Democracy*, Unwin, London.

Scott, W.R. (1987), *Organizations: Rational, Natural, and Open Systems*, Prentice-Hall, Englewood Cliffs.

Sharp, M. (1985), *Europe and the New Technologies*, Pinter Publishers, London.

Sherwin, C. and R. Isenson (1967), 'Project Hindsight', *Science*, 156: 1571–7.

Simon, H.A. (1955), 'A Behavioral Model of Rational Choice', *Quarterly Journal of Economics*, 69: 99–118.

Simon, H.A. (1959), 'Theories of Decision Making in Economics', *American Economic Review*, 49: 253–83.

Simon, S. (1985), *After Divestiture: What the AT&T Settlement Means for Business and Residential Telephone Service*, Knowledge Industry, New York.

Singh, J.V. (1986), 'Performance, Slack, and Risk-taking in Organizational Decision Making', *Academy of Management Journal*, 29: 562–85.

Singh, J.V., R.J. House and D.J. Tucker (1986), 'Organizational Change and Organizational Mortality', *Administrative Science Quarterly*, 31: 587–611.

Singh, J.V. and C.J. Lumsden (1990), 'Theory and Research in Organizational Ecology', *Annual Review of Sociology*, 16: 161–95.

Soma, J.T. (1976), *The Computer Industry*, Lexington Books, Lexington, Mass.

Stankiewicz, R. (1990), 'Basic Technologies and the Innovation Process', in J. Sigurdson (ed.), *Measuring the Dynamics of Technological Change*, Pinter Publishers, London, New York.

Starbuck, W.H., A. Greve and B.L.T. Hedberg (1978), 'Responding to Crisis', *Journal of Business Administration*, 9: 111–37.

Steinmueller, W.E. (1987), 'Microeconomics and Microelectronics: Economic Studies of Integrated Circuit Technology', Unpublished Ph.D. thesis, Stanford University.

Steinmueller, W.E. (1994), 'The US Software Industry: An Analysis and Interpretive History', in D.C. Mowery (ed.), *The International Computer Software Industry*, Oxford University Press, Oxford.

Steinmueller, W.E. and P.A. David (1994), 'Economics of Compatibility Standards and Competition in Telecommunication Networks', *Information and Economic Policy*.

Steutzer, O.M. (1952), *Proceedings of the IRE*, 40: 1529–36.

Stinchcombe, A.L. (1965), 'Social Structure and Organizations', in J.G. March (ed.), *Handbook of Organizations*, Rand McNally, Chicago.

Stopford, J.J. and L.T. Wells (1972), *Managing the Multinational Enterprise: Organization of the Firm and Overlap of Subsidiaries*, Basic Books, New York.

Stuckey, J. (1983), *Vertical Integration and Joint Ventures in the Aluminium Industry*, Harvard University Press, Cambridge, Mass.

Swann, G.M.P. (1986), *Quality Innovation, an Economic Analysis of Rapid Improvements in Microelectronic Components*, Pinter Publishers, London.

Swann, G.M.P. (1990), *The Speed of Technology Change and Development of Market Structure: 2: Microprocessors*, CRICT Discussion Paper, Brunel University, Uxbridge.

Teece, D., (1981), 'The Market of Know-how and the Efficient International Transfer of Technology', *Annals of the American Academy of Political and Social Science*, pp. 81–96.

Temin, P. (1987), *The Fall of the Bell System: A Study in Prices and Politics*, Cambridge University Press, Cambridge.

Teubal, M. and W.E. Steinmueller (1986), 'Government Policy, Innovation, and Economic Growth: A Study of Satellite Communications', in M. Teubal (ed.), *Innovation Performance, Learning, and Government Policy: Selected Essays*, University of Wisconsin Press, Wisconsin.

Thomas, M.D. (1988), 'Innovation and Technology Strategy: Competitive New-Technology Firms and Industries', in M. Giaoutzi, P. Nijkamp and D.J. Storey (eds), *Small and Medium Size Enterprises and Regional Development*, Routledge, London.

Tilton, J.E. (1971), *International Diffusion of Technology: The Case of Semiconductors*, The Brookings Institute, Washington.

Todd, D. (1990), *The World Electronics Industry*, Routledge, London.

Tolbert, P and L.G. Zucker (1983), 'Institutional Sources of Change in the Formal Structures of Organizations: The Diffusion of Civil Service Reform', *Administrative Science Quarterly*, 29: 22–39.

Train, K.E. (1991), *Optimal Regulation: The Economic Theory of Natural Monopol*, The MIT Press, Cambridge, Mass.

Tucker, D.J., J.V. Singh and A.G. Meinhard (1990), 'Founding Characteristics, Imprinting and Organizational Change', in J.V. Singh (ed.), *Organizational Evolution: New Directions*, Sage Publications, Newbury Park, London.

Tunstall, J. (1986), *Communications Deregulation: The Unleashing of America's Communications Industry*, Basic Blackwell, Oxford.

Tushman, M.L. and P. Anderson (1986), 'Technological Discontinuities and Organizational Environments', *Administrative Science Quarterly*, 31: 439–65.

Uenohara, M., T. Sugano, J.G. Linvill and F.B. Weinstein (1984), in D.I. Okimoto, T. Sugano and F.B. Weinstein (eds), *Competitive Edge: The Semiconductor Industry in the U.S. and Japan*, Stanford University Press, Stanford.

UNIDO (1981), *Restructuring World Industry in a Period of Crisis – the Role of Innovation*, UNIDO Working Paper on Structural Changes.

Utterback, J.M. (1974), 'Innovation in Industry and the Diffusion of Technology', *Science*, 198: 620–26.

van Tulder, R. and G. Junne (1988), *European Multinationals in Core Technologies*, John Wiley & Sons, Chichester.

van Wegberg, M. (1994), 'Multi-market competition theory: A conceptual framework', Ph.D. thesis, State University of Limburg, Maastricht.

van Zand, P. (1990), *Microchip Fabrication: A Practical Guide to Semiconductor Processing*, McGraw Hill, New York.

Veblen, T. (1898), 'Why is Economics Not an Evolutionary Science?', *Quarterly Journal of Economics*, 13: 374–97.

Vernon, R. (1966), 'International Investment and International Trade in the Product Cycle', *Quarterly Journal of Economics*, 88: 190–207.

Vernon, R. (1979), 'The Product Cycle Hypothesis in a New International Environment', *Oxford Bulletin of Economics and Statistics*, 41: 255–67.

von Tunzelmann, N. (1988), 'Convergence of Firms in Information and Communication: A Test using Patents Data', Mimeo, Science Policy Research Unit, Brighton.

von Tunzelmann, N. and L. Soete, (1987), *Diffusion and Market Structure with Converging Technologies*, Research Memorandum, University of Limburg, Maastricht.

Vonortas, N.S. (1989), *The Changing Economic Context: Strategic Alliances among Multinationals*, Mimeo, Center for Science and Technology Policy, New York.

Warrant, F. (1991), *Développement mondiale de la R&D industrielle*, FAST, CEC Research Paper, Brussels.

Warren, R.L. (1967), 'The Interorganizational Field as a Focus for Investigation', *Administrative Science Quarterly*, 30: 103–30.

Wasserman, N.H. (1985), *From Invention to Innovation: Long-Distance Telephone Transmission at the Turn of the Century*, Johns Hopkins University Press, Baltimore.

Webbink, D.W. (1977), *The Semiconductor Industry: A Survey of Structure, Conduct, and Performance*, Staff report to the Federal Trade Commission.

Weinstein, F.B., M. Uenohara and J.G. Linvill (1984), 'Technological Resources', in D.I. Okimoto, T. Sugano and F.B. Weinstein (eds), *Competitive Edge: The Semiconductor Industry in the U.S. and Japan*, Stanford University Press, Stanford.

Williamson, O.E. (1975), *Markets and Hierarchies*, Free Press, New York.

Williamson, O.E. (1979), 'Transaction Cost Economics: The Governance of Contractual Relations', *Journal of Law and Economics*, 22: 233–61.

Williamson, O.E. (1985), *The Economic Institutions of Capitalism, Firms, Markets, Relational Contracting*, The Free Press, New York.

Wilson, R.W., P.K. Ashton and T.P. Egan (1980), *Innovation, Competition, and Government Policy in the Semiconductor Industry*, Lexington Books, Lexington, Mass.

Wind, Y.J. (1982), *Product Policy: Concepts, Methods, and Strategy*, Addison-Wesley, Reading.

Winter, S.G. (1964), 'Economic Natural Selection and the Theory of the Firm', *Yale Economic Essays*, 4: 225–72.

Winter, S.G. (1971), 'Satisficing, Selection and the Innovating Remnant', *Quarterly Journal of Economics*, 85: 237–61.

Winter, S.G. (1975), 'Optimization and Evolution in the Theory of the Firm', in R.H. Day and T.Grovers (eds), *Adaptive Economic Models*, New York.

Winter, S.G. (1990), 'Survival, Selection, and Inheritance in Evolutionary Theories of Organization', in J.V. Singh (ed.), *Organizational Evolution: New Directions*, Sage Publications, Newbury Park, London.

Young, R.C. (1988), 'Is Population Ecology a Useful Paradigm for the Study of Organizations', *American Journal of Sociology*, 94: 1–24.

Index